M000265595

ISA
Istituto di storia e teoria dell'arte e dell'architettura
collana diretta da
Christoph Frank, Sonja Hildebrand, Daniela Mondini

Publishing Coordination
Tiziano Casartelli

Copy Editor
Michael Robertson

Proofreader
Christopher Davey

Graphic Concept
Andrea Lancellotti

Page Layout
Tarmac Publishing Mendrisio

This book has been peer-reviewed according to the standards
of the Swiss National Science Foundation.

The open access publication of this book has been published
with the support of the Swiss National Science Foundation.

**Schweizerischer
Nationalfonds**

ISBN (print): 978-3-85676-409-8
ISBN (pdf): 978-3-85676-424-1

DOI: https://doi.org/10.3929/ethz-b-000501065

Architectural History and Globalized Knowledge: Gottfried Semper in London

edited by
Michael Gnehm, Sonja Hildebrand

Mendrisio Academy Press / *gta Verlag*

Table of contents

Sonja Hildebrand and Michael Gnehm

Introduction

Gottfried Semper's arrival in London in September 1850 came about due to an initiative taken by a German archaeologist employed at the Instituto di corrispondenza archeologica in Rome who had a British wife and was visiting London when he happened to hear that Semper was planning to emigrate to the USA. His source for the information was an English architect, who in turn had learned of it on a recent trip to Paris.[1] The name of the archaeologist was Emil Braun, and his source was Edward Falkener; the two met during Braun's brief visit to the British capital. Braun was probably particularly alert to Falkener's news from Paris because, twenty years earlier, Semper had been a frequent presence in the same archaeological institute in which Braun had been working since 1834. Braun wrote to Semper at once, addressing the letter to be forwarded to him by Jacques Ignace Hittorff, the Cologne-born architect and archaeologist in Paris. That address was incorrect, since Semper's contact in Paris at the time was the decorator Charles Séchan, whom Semper had commissioned to decorate the Court Theatre in Dresden in the late 1830s and had befriended there. However, Hittorff knew Semper's correct contact address, and Braun's letter, forwarded in turn by Séchan, ultimately reached Semper on 18 September in Le Havre, where the fugitive from the 1848–49 revolution was planning to board the *Wilhelm Tell* for the voyage to New York the very next day. The letter only took three days to cover the entire distance.

The receipt of Braun's letter was a key event in Semper's life. If he had not received it in time and had actually continued his emigration to New York, not only would his own life have been different, but a major chapter in modern architectural history would also have taken a different course. Some of the nineteenth century's most important theoretical writings on art and architecture would be missing from it – first and foremost *Der Stil* (*Style*), but also *Wissenschaft, Industrie und Kunst* (*Science, Industry, and Art*), and most of the other texts Semper wrote after 1850. The same would also apply to the designs and projects that Semper was responsible for in London, and above all in Zurich and Vienna later on.

The significance of this key biographical event goes even further, however. It illustrates particularly well the challenges facing historiographic research on Semper: research that needs to take into account the ways in which lives and events are contingent and shaped by external circumstances; historiography in which the major subjects are characterized by processes of discussion and exchange, by the international quality of professional contacts, by the geographical expansion of spheres of action and by an environment that is politically, economically, technically, infrastructurally, and culturally dynamic.

These challenges are not unique to Semper, but in his case they apply to a particularly high degree. No other architect in the nineteenth century created buildings that continue to shape the cityscape today in so many different places which at the same time represented stages in his life. Probably no other architect immersed himself in the cultural life of so many different cities, often becoming an active part of it, in the way that Semper did. And no other nineteenth-century architect left such a significant body of work in so many fields, including architecture and design as well as research, writing, teaching, and theory. The historical significance and continuing fascination of Semper's theoretical work lies in features that are also significant for his biography: transcending (disciplinary) boundaries; a radical expansion of the subject field, combined with a theoretical reconception of the notion of architecture; often quite adventurous openness to aspects that were new, unknown, or previously unconsidered; and the courage to make these new and unknown aspects an object for reflections on art and culture.

These qualities, along with Semper's ability to process a large – and by conventional standards disparate – field of subject matter into a theory of tremendous scope, predestine him for treatment as a major figure in architectural history. The present volume emerged, along with other publications, from the research project "Architecture and the Globalization of Knowledge in the 19th Century: Gottfried Semper and the Discipline of Architectural History". The ambition of the project was to reverse to some extent a viewpoint focusing on the central figure, with contours that are then sharpened by historical contextualization. Rather than using an approach that places Semper's work at the centre in order to compare it with that of other figures in a second step, identifying processes of interchange and reception and then relating them back to Semper, the accent was shifted towards Semper's environment. Semper's work continues to be the reference point and principal subject, but his environment is given greater importance. The working hypothesis was that giving more intense and sometimes prioritized attention to his environment may significantly improve our understanding of a style of thinking that is as open as that of Semper.

The research project – funded by the Swiss National Science Foundation (SNSF) and representing a collaboration between the Institute for the History and Theory of Art and Architecture at the Università della Svizzera italiana (Sonja Hildebrand) and the Institute for the History and Theory of Architecture gta at ETH Zurich (Philip Ursprung) – was devoted to Semper's period of exile in London (1850–55). These were the years in which Semper was living in surroundings that he later described, in comparison with Zurich and Switzerland, as "grander environments" ("*grossartigere Umgebungen*").[2] London at that time was a metropolis with a population of around 2.5 million people – twice that of Paris and twenty-five times that of Dresden, the two cities where Semper had spent the past sixteen years of his life; it was the capital of a global empire, a trading hub for countless goods and cultural assets that filled the rooms and depots of shops, museums and libraries. London provided Semper with a sphere of discourse shaped by the international exchange of objects, goods and concepts, in which he developed his historically grounded architectural theory. The overarching theme of the research project was Semper's contribution to the discipline of architectural history during this period, as an architect involved in research, writing, teaching, and design. In addition to the present volume, the project also led to a series of essays,[3] two doctoral dissertations,[4] and a critical edition, with commentary, of Semper's *London Writings*.[5]

With the exception of Paris, none of the many places where Semper lived – neither Hamburg nor Dresden, Zurich nor Vienna – had as great an influence on his thought as London. It was there that the Great Exhibition, the British Museum and the British Museum Library, the Museum of Ornamental Art and the library of the Department of Practical Art (which became the Department of Science and Art in 1853), with their rich resources, were his places of work and study; it was there that he met key figures in the Design Reform movement such as Henry Cole, Richard Redgrave and Owen Jones; and it was there that he witnessed and participated in debates such as those conducted among design reformers and the members of the Royal Institute of British Architects. All of this took place at the centre of a political and economic world power in which politics, economics and culture were regarded as interconnected spheres of activity for pursuing its claim to global leadership.

Semper's years of exile in London have always been a core of Semper research. The period marks the resumption of his theoretical work, which extended beyond teaching at the Dresden Academy of Art and initial preliminary considerations for what eventually became his magnum opus, *Der Stil*. In the 1970s, Wolfgang Herrmann was the first to compile historical data concerning Semper's period in London;[6] Dieter Weidmann supplemented, clarified and corrected these in an essay written in 2014 as part of the SNSF project.[7] The London exile as a whole has been the subject of individual essays and book chapters.[8] The literature on individual aspects of Semper's London period is extensive. Authors have focused on the Great Exhibition of 1851 and Semper's theoretical-critical examination of it,[9] his relations with the Design Reform movement,[10] and on theoretical concepts (further) developed by Semper while he was in London.[11] In a dissertation submitted in 1983, Harry Francis Mallgrave conducted fundamental research on the development of Semper's theoretical work during the London years and its contextualization in the disciplinary setting.[12] The monograph on Semper that Mallgrave published in 1996 builds on this research and the approach taken in it.[13] Both of Mallgrave's works are characterized by an approach that starts from Semper's content, around which contextualizing material is then deployed.

In contrast, the SNSF research project raised the question of what sort of environment shaped Semper's design work and thinking in what ways, and which interpretations, explanations and models of order he offered – as both an observer and an active agent himself – in the context of his teaching and in his theoretical and design work. This approach is based on the assumption that the complexity of Semper's conception of architecture and the methodological and intellectual effort involved in working on it can be more adequately represented if it is also understood as a response to the vastness and complexity – which were particularly pronounced in London – of the material and intellectual discursive space in which Semper moved.

The chapters in this volume contribute to this endeavour in different ways. Murray Fraser takes the reader into the increasingly globalized London building world of the years following the mid-century. The early epitome of this was the Crystal Palace, but the formative effects of globalizing forces can also be linked to transformations taking place during the spatial growth of London that were at first glance less important, but nevertheless profound. Semper became part of this process through his design for the architectural detailing of a machine shop for the Royal Arsenal in Woolwich and his stunning proposal for a museum of applied arts in South Kensington, which envisaged a huge glazed atrium roof echoing the Crystal Palace. Philip Ursprung gathers together Karl Marx, Herman Melville, Joseph Paxton, and Semper for an imaginary conversation about the potential or – depending on the point of view – the dangers associated with developments in this increasingly industrialized architectural world. Claudio Leoni reconstructs for the first time in detail the arrangement and decoration of the Canadian Court, Semper's well-known contribution to the Great Exhibition. The architect responded to the confusion of the huge exhibition, which he and others described as challenging, with an arrangement based on the models of order of craft techniques and their materials that he was developing at the time.

In her account of the Duke of Wellington's funeral procession, Mari Hvattum describes the second mass spectacle – after the Great Exhibition – that Semper helped to stage, as newly appointed professor of metalwork in the Department of Practical Art. The funeral procession took place on 18 November 1852, moving from St. James's Park via Piccadilly and Pall Mall to St. Paul's Cathedral, and was witnessed by one and a half million people. The procession and the preparations for it were covered extensively in the popular press. An examination of the design history of the funeral car, in the light of the coverage of it in "The Illustrated London News", leads into an account of a battle over meaning in which Semper's concept of artistic representation was at odds with the expectations of a public sphere anchored in popular culture. A similar distance from popular culture can be observed in the public lectures on ceramics that Semper gave in the autumn of 1853 in the course of his teaching duties as instructor at the Department of Science and Art. Elena Chestnova examines Semper's early engagement with ceramics in the context of Design Reform, material culture as an evolving disciplinary field and the popular consumption of pottery as reflected in Victorian literature. Dieter Weidmann reconstructs the very specific communication problems that Semper had as a result of his poor command of the English language and also sheds light on the creative use of language that Semper developed in this situation.

Semper used some of the debates he witnessed in London as an opportunity for critical discussion, which then developed its own momentum. This applies not only to the problems of order that arose in the Great Exhibition and subsequently to the arrangement of objects in design exhibitions, but also to the debate conducted in the circle of the Royal Institute of British Architects about optical corrections to Greek temples, which for Semper became the starting point for his conception of a formal aesthetic in which situational conditions of perception are taken into account (Sonja Hildebrand). On other topics, such as the polychromy debate, Semper already stood for a firm position, which – as Kate Nichols points out, using the example of the Greek Court in the Crystal Palace in Sydenham – acquired a fresh profile in the context of communicating the related debates to the new mass audiences visiting the exhibition.

Issues connected with the question of national character and the ways in which it is manifested in artefacts attracted widespread interest in the London of the Great Exhibition. Beat Wyss takes up this thread in relation to Semper's theories of origins and his adaptation of methods from comparative anatomy and contrasts them with Viollet-le-Duc's narrative of the origins of architecture, which was tied to concepts of race. The evolving discipline of anthropology provided concepts and methods for this subject area, bound to everyday life, which art history at the time had only considered in a rudimentary and selective way. Caroline van Eck reads a key passage in Semper's *Der Stil* as an example of an innovative anthropology of art whose beginnings can be traced back to the eighteenth century. The transdisciplinary thinking that characterizes Semper's theoretical work provided him, in a sense, with the epistemological tools he needed to engage with the global knowledge and production of goods that he encountered in London. Alina Payne examines the role that Semper played – as a result of the epistemology that was characteristic in his work – in pioneering a scholarly engagement with global phenomena in anthropology, archaeology, empathy theory, and comparative art history.

We sincerely thank all the authors for their contributions to this volume and for the varied discussions that were involved in collaboration on it. The production of the book was organized by Tiziano Casartelli with his usual professionalism. We are particularly pleased that the collaboration between Università della Svizzera italiana and ETH Zurich within the framework of the joint research project is being continued through this book in the form of cooperation between Mendrisio Academy Press and gta Verlag. We present this book in the hope that it will not only conclude a research project, but also provide inspiration for new questions.

_1. W. Herrmann, *Gottfried Semper im Exil: Paris, London 1849–1855. Zur Entstehung des "Stil" 1840–1877*, Birkhäuser, Basel 1978, p. 30; D. Weidmann, *Through the Stable Door to Prince Albert? On Gottfried Semper's London Connections*, "Journal of Art Historiography", no. 11, December 2014, pp. 1–26 (here pp. 4–5); S. Hildebrand, *Gottfried Semper: Architekt und Revolutionär*, wbg, Darmstadt, 2020, pp. 101–2.

_2. Gottfried Semper, letter to Carolyne Sayn-Wittgenstein, 8 December 1857, gta Archives/ETH Zurich, 20-K-1857-12-08(S).

_3. See the individual references in the following notes.

_4. E. Chestnova, *History in Things: Gottfried Semper and Popularization of the Arts in London 1850–55*, PhD diss., Università della Svizzera italiana, Mendrisio 2017 (a revised version of the dissertation will be published in 2022: *Material Theories and Objects: Gottfried Semper and the Mid-Nineteenth Century*, Routledge, Abingdon 2021); C. Leoni, *Exhibition and Cognition: Gottfried Semper's Strolls in the Crystal Palace*, PhD diss., The Bartlett School of Architecture, UCL, London 2019.

_5. G. Semper, *London Writings 1850–1855*, edited by M. Gnehm, S. Hildebrand, and D. Weidmann, gta Verlag, Zurich 2021.

_6. W. Herrmann, *Semper im Exil*, see note 1.

_7. D. Weidmann, *Through the Stable Door*, see note 1.

_8. G. Reising, *Kunst, Industrie und Gesellschaft: Gottfried Semper in England*, in *Gottfried Semper und die Mitte des 19. Jahrhunderts*, Birkhäuser, Basel 1976, pp. 49–66; H.F. Mallgrave, *Gottfried Semper: Architect of the Nineteenth Century*, Yale University Press, New Haven 1996, Chapter 3; S. Hildebrand, *"… großartige Umgebungen": Gottfried Semper in London*, in W. Nerdinger and W. Oechslin (eds.), *Gottfried Semper 1803–1879: Architektur und Wissenschaft*, Prestel and gta Verlag, Munich and Zurich 2003, pp. 260–68 ; W. May, *Semper in Paris und London 1849 bis 1855*, in *Der Architekt und die Stadt: Gottfried Semper zum 200. Geburtstag*, "Dresdner Hefte", 21, no. 3, 2003, pp. 69–77; J.V.N. Soane, *Gottfried Semper und seine englischen Erfahrungen*, in H. Karge (ed.), *Gottfried Semper – Dresden und Europa: Die moderne Renaissance der Künste*, Deutscher Kunstverlag, Munich 2007, pp. 289–300; S. Hildebrand, *Gottfried Semper*, see note 1, pp. 83–131.

_9. K. Lankheit, *Gottfried Semper und die Weltausstellung, London 1851*, in *Gottfried Semper und die Mitte des 19. Jahrhunderts*, Birkhäuser, Basel 1976, pp. 23–47 ; A.M. Vogt, *Gottfried Semper und Joseph Paxton*, in *Gottfried Semper und die Mitte des 19. Jahrhunderts*, pp. 175–97; J. Nigro Covre, *Babele nel "vuoto coperto di vetro": Gottfried Semper e la Grande Esposizione di Londra del 1851*, "Ricerche di storia dell'arte", no. 16, 1982, pp. 5–20; K. Barck, *Kunst und Industrie bei Léon de Laborde und Gottfried Semper: Differente Aspekte der Reflexion eines epochengeschichtlichen Funktionswandels der Kunst*, in H. Pfeiffer, H.R. Jauß, and F. Gaillard (eds.), *Art social und art industriel: Funktionen der Kunst im Zeitalter des Industrialismus*, Fink, Munich 1987, pp. 241–68; H.F. Mallgrave, *Gottfried Semper and the Great Exhibition*, in F. Bosbach and J.R. Davis (eds.), *Die Weltausstellung von 1851 und ihre Folgen*, Saur, Munich 2002, pp. 305–14; M. Hvattum, *"A Complete and Universal Collection": Gottfried Semper and the Great Exhibition*, in M. Hvattum and C. Hermansen (eds.), *Tracing Modernity: Manifestations of the Modern in Architecture and the City*, Routledge, London 2004, pp. 124–36; H.-G. von Arburg, *Alles Fassade: "Oberfläche" in der deutschsprachigen Architektur- und Literaturästhetik 1770–1870*, Fink, Munich 2007, pp. 311–34. As part of the SNSF project: C. Leoni, *Art, Production and Market Conditions: Gottfried Semper's Historical Perspective on Commodities and the Role of Museums*, "Journal of Art Historiography", no. 11, 2014.

_10. W. Mrazek, *Gottfried Semper und die museal-wissenschaftliche Reformbewegung des 19. Jahrhunderts* in H.M. Wingler (ed.), *Gottfried Semper, Wissenschaft, Industrie und Kunst und andere Schriften über Architektur, Kunsthandwerk und Kunstunterricht*, Kupferberg, Mainz 1966, pp. 113–19; A. Varela Braga, *Une théorie universelle au milieu du XIXe siècle: La Grammar of Ornament d'Owen Jones*, Campisano, Rome 2017, pp. 189–201. As part of the SNSF project: E. Chestnova, *"Bridging Art and Science" – Semper's Teaching in London 1850–55*, "Trans", no. 24, 2014, pp. 144–51; E. Chestnova, *"Ornamental Design Is … a Kind of Practical Science": Theories of Ornament at the London School of Design and Department of Science and Art*, "Journal of Art Historiography", no. 11, 2014.

_11. W. Szambien, *Les variabels du style dans une conférence de Gottfried Semper*, "Amphion: études d'histoire des techniques", no. 1, 1987, pp. 153–59; M. Hvattum, *Gottfried Semper: Between Poetics and Practical Aesthetics*, "Zeitschrift für Kunstgeschichte", 64, 2001, pp. 537–46; J.A. Hale, *Gottfried Semper's Primitive Hut as an Act of Self-Creation*, "Architectural Research Quarterly", 9, no. 1, 2005, pp. 45–49; I. Nicka, *"The First Elements of Human Industry": Eine Abschrift von Gottfried Sempers Manuskript* Practical Art in Metals and Hard Materials *im MAK Wien*, Diploma thesis, Universität Wien 2007; A. Payne, *From Ornament to Object: Genealogies of Architectural Modernism*, Yale University Press, New Haven 2012, pp. 25–64; U. Poerschke, *Architektur als mathematische Funktion: Überlegungen zu Gottfried Semper*, in M. Eggers (ed.), *Von Ähnlichkeiten und Unterschieden: Vergleich, Analogie und Klassifikation in Wissenschaft und Literatur (18./19. Jahrhundert)*, Winter, Heidelberg 2011, pp. 121–42; U. Poerschke, *Architecture as a Mathematical Function: Reflections on Gottfried Semper*,

"Nexus Network Journal", 14, 2012, pp. 119–34, DOI 10.1007/s00004-011-0101-5; S. Hildebrand, *Towards an Expanded Concept of Form: Gottfried Semper on Ancient Projectiles,* in S. Hildebrand and E. Bergmann (eds.), *Form-Finding, Form-Shaping, Designing Architecture: Experimental, Aesthetical and Social Approaches to Form in Recent and Post-war Architecture*, Mendrisio Academy Press and Silvana Editoriale, Mendrisio and Milan, 2015, pp. 131–43; H.-G. von Arburg, *Elementares Bauen im Exil: Semper und Stifter* (Abdias), "Deutsche Vierteljahresschrift für Literaturwissenschaft und Geistesgeschichte", 90, no. 4, 2016, pp. 599–618, DOI 10.1007/s41245-016-0026-7; S. Papapetros, *Ornament as Weapon: Ballistics, Politics, and Architectural Adornment in Semper's Treatise on Ancient Projectile*s, in G. Necipoğlu and A. Payne (eds.), *Histories of Ornament: From Global to Local*, Princeton University Press, Princeton 2016, pp. 46–61; M. Hvattum, *Un historicisme hétéro-nome: L'Assyrie de Gottfried Semper*, "Revue Germanique International", no. 26, 2017, pp. 57–69. As part of the SNSF project: E. Chestnova, *"The House That Semper Built",* "Architectural Theory Review", 21, no. 1, 2017, pp. 44–61; E. Chestnova, *Substantial Differences: Semper's Stoffwechsel and Truth to Materials*, in S. Hildebrand, D. Mondini and R. Grignolo (eds.), *Architecture and Knowledge*, Mendrisio Academy Press and Silvana Editoriale, Mendrisio and Milan, 2018, pp. 112–25; S. Hildebrand, *"… verschiedene Anwendungen einer und derselben grossen Wissenschaft": Gottfried Semper und die Mathematik,* "Mathematische Semesterberichte", 65, no. 2, 2018, pp. 153–69, DOI 10.1007/s00591-018-0228-5.
_ 12. H.F. Mallgrave, *The Idea of Style: Gottfried Semper in London*, PhD diss., University of Philadelphia 1983.
_ 13. H.F. Mallgrave, *Gottfried Semper*, see note 8.

13

ENTIÈREMENT RESTAURÉ DU
PARTHÉNON D'ATHÈNES

ÉCHELLE DE 0,05 POUR MÈTRE

Murray Fraser

Gottfried Semper and the Globalizing of the London Building World in the 1850s

_ Figure 1.
Reconstruction of the
coloured entablature
of the Parthenon
in Athens, plate
from G. Semper,
*Die Anwendung
der Farben in der
Architectur und
Plastik*, 1836,
"Presented by Herr
Semper" to the RIBA
Library on 12 January
1852 (Courtesy of
RIBA Collections).

When Gottfried Semper died in Rome on 15 May 1879, the news deeply affected one of his closest acquaintances in Britain, the architect and academic Thomas Leverton Donaldson. The latter was the most Europhile of the small group that had combined in 1834 to form the Institute of British Architects (becoming the Royal Institute of British Architects, from 1837). Indeed, Donaldson for a long time held the office of "Honorary Secretary for Foreign Correspondence", a position through which he promoted his preference for continental Neoclassicism over the widespread Ruskinian influence of the Gothic Revival and later the Arts and Crafts Movement. In an issue of "RIBA Transactions", the institute's official journal, which was published later in 1879, Donaldson penned a short but touching account of Semper's life and influence: "As he was an intimate friend of mine I venture to offer a brief notice of him; it is an early tribute to one for whom I had a sincere personal regard, and whose talents I greatly admired".[1] Donaldson reminded readers that the first ever reference to Semper within the learned circles of the RIBA – and thus almost certainly the first reference to him in Britain – was in an essay of 1836 by Franz Kugler on theories of polychromy in Greek art, which in turn was a response to Semper's seminal 1834 essay *Preliminary Remarks on Polychrome Architecture and Sculpture in Antiquity*.[2] Semper had met Donaldson for the first time in London in December 1838 during a short visit to examine the latest theatres in the city while preparing his design for the Dresden Theatre.[3] The latter, completed in 1841, was also the first building by Semper to gain acclaim in Britain (it subsequently burned down, in 1869, but was rebuilt to his revised design and is known today as the Semperoper). In August 1850, while in London once again, and at a juncture when he was considering the possibility of emigrating to the United States of America, Semper had presented a copy of his publication on *Das Königliche Hoftheater zu Dresden* (1849) to the RIBA Library (Donaldson makes reference to it in his obituary),[4] and he later dedicated another copy of the same book to Donaldson, probably in 1853.[5] The Dresden Theatre, as Donaldson observed, "justly became the foundation of his European reputation".[6]

Figs. 2, 3

In his account of Semper's life, Donaldson continued: "However, in the unfortunate political disturbances, which took place in Dresden in 1849, he allowed an irrepressible and democratic feeling against kingly rule to overpower his better judgement".[7] This was a reference to the barricade that Semper had designed in his capacity as a liberal republican rebel in Dresden, which because of its strength and resistance to Prussia's royalist troops earned him the bitter enmity of the ruling classes there – an outcome that caused Semper great regret for many decades afterwards. Donaldson recounted Semper's subsequent travails in fleeing first to Paris and then "coming over to England as a place of refuge and possible employment and precarious means of subsistence".[8] During his time in London, where he resided from autumn 1850 to mid-1855, and as a result of meeting Henry Cole through the 1851 Great Exhibition, Semper was appointed to Cole's newly created Department of Practical Art in September 1852 – first as a lecturer on the decoration of metalwork, later as professor of architecture. Cole's department (which in 1853 became the Department of Science and Art) was at that point located in Marlborough House on The Mall, and part of its role was to take over the Government School of Design – allowing it supreme control over British art education.

_ Figure 2.
Title page of G. Semper, *Das Königliche Hoftheater zu Dresden*, 1849, with dedication to the Royal Institute of British Architects by Semper (Courtesy of RIBA Collections).

Donaldson's obituary also listed some of the main projects that Semper had worked upon while in London, such as the Wellington Car for the great duke's funeral procession and the dazzling design for Prince Albert for a new museum in South Kensington (of which more later). Finally, Donaldson noted the departure of Semper for Zurich in 1855, then to Vienna from 1871, and his eventual retirement to Italy just prior to his death, amid the architectural finery of the 'Eternal City':

> We must sympathise with the great artist, who returned to pass the last days of his existence among the monuments and scenes of his early emotions; leaving his ashes in the soil of a country, that nourished the art, to which he had devoted the thoughts, interests and labours of his eventful and lengthened existence.[9]

Such a heartfelt testament provokes the question of why Donaldson held Semper in so much obvious affection, and what in turn Semper could have done during his brief London sojourn that helped to make such an impact on this British admirer.[10] To begin to answer this point, it is first necessary to pan out and take in the scene that faced Gottfried Semper on his arrival in London.

16

_ Figure 3.
View of the Dresden
Theatre, plate from G.
Semper's *Das Königliche
Hoftheater zu Dresden*,
1849 (Courtesy of RIBA
Collections).

HOFTHEATER ZU DRESDEN.

17

The centre of the world

The renowned historian Eric Hobsbawm remarked long ago that due to early industrial supremacy up to around 1850, British people envisioned the rest of the world as
a "kind of planetary system circling round the economic sun of Britain".[11] Popular
opinion in Britain believed that a combination of Manchester Free Trade principles
and innate decency and fair play gave the country the fundamental and central right
to spread capitalism across the globe. Today, of course, it is easy to pick apart this kind
of delusion – the transatlantic slave trade and gunboat diplomacy in the Chinese Opium Wars spring to mind – but if one were to set aside ideology, there was a brute new
material reality being created – especially visible in London – which was unmatched
elsewhere at the time.

We cannot possibly describe what occurred in nineteenth-century London as
globalization in the sense that we understand the term today, although there were undoubtedly processes of internationalization taking place. A 1992 book edited by Celi-
na Fox, a curator from the Museum of London, traces various events and phenomena
between 1800 and 1840 to make the case that by the end of that period, London
possessed the strongest claim to being genuinely a 'world city'.[12] The contributors to
her book recount, for example, the impact of long-standing mercantile trading links,
growing imperial connections through the British Empire, fashions and tastes arriving
from continental Europe, the manifold waves of immigrants, as well as the passing observations made by curious short-term visitors. Thus, while earlier in the nineteenth
century London could not have seriously claimed to be any more of a 'world city' than

say Paris or Berlin, the runaway pace of British capitalism by the mid-nineteenth century was transforming the capital city into the strongest exemplar of internationalizing forces in that era. By the mid-century there existed a condition of proto-globalization, such that one could indeed argue that London was the only city in the world in the 1850s that to any real degree was globalized. "In the latter half of the nineteenth century", writes the novelist and London connoisseur, Peter Ackroyd, "London had become the wonder and the horror of the age, a vast new city [that] ... represented the future of the human race".[13] Numerous historians have expanded upon this theme, with a recent book on the topic claiming that the modern age began on 24 September 1851 – barely a year after Semper's arrival in the city – when a small tugboat pulled a British ship, HMS *Blazer*, down the River Thames on its way to the coastal port of Dover. There it proceeded to lay a 200-ton iron cable under twenty-five miles of sea to France, ushering in the first international telegraph service.[14] Science and industry had conquered the waves, and soon the two most rampant capitalist economies in Britain and America were tethered together by the undersea transatlantic telegraph cable, while other cables were feeding communications to and from British colonies like India.

18   This new trans-spatial technology of Britain's Industrial Revolution was of course part of the concretization of geographical patterns of finance. The capitalist theories of Adam Smith and other British political economists were predicated on the trading blocks of nation states, yet they also recognized that capitalism required a global network of spaces in which to produce and reproduce its conditions. Sitting at his desk in the British Museum Library, Karl Marx seized upon such contradictions within political economy to imagine a very different ordering of the world. And just five years after the publication of the first volume of *Das Kapital* in 1867, a startling description of proto-globalization came in a book called *London: A Pilgrimage*. It was written by a London-born playwright and journalist, William Blanchard Jerrold, who lived mostly in Paris, and was illustrated by his friend, the well-known French engraver Gustave Doré. A passage by Jerrold in his 1872 book spoke of the impact of the first underground train lines and the new sub-oceanic telegraph cables on London's links to colonial India and to America:

> men had not dreamed that they would ever pass under London from the Great Western [railway station] to the heart of the City [of London]; nor that a merchant from his counting house would be able to talk with New York and Calcutta. The New York gossip of yesterday, is ours upon our breakfast table. We can almost hear the hum of Wall Street.[15]

As mentioned before, Gottfried Semper relocated to London in mid-1850, arriving a year after Marx, and found the same booming capitalist economy that was tearing apart and expanding the city. Both of these German émigrés – who often must have sat near to each other in the Reading Room of the British Museum Library – were now able to witness for themselves the latest manifestations of the capitalist system materializing before their eyes. London at the time had around 2.5 million inhabitants, and the numbers were rising fast, making it easily the largest city thus far in human history (even the biggest in the ancient Roman Empire or China had not contained much over one million citizens). The pace of growth was scarcely believable. The 1851 census revealed that there had been 330,000 newcomers to London over

19

_ Figure 4.
Capitalism meets the city:
1867 photograph by Henry
Flather of the construction
of the Metropolitan Line
at Praed Street next
to Paddington Station,
forming part of London's
new underground railway
network (© Museum of
London).

the previous decade, meaning that one in seven of the population were fairly recent arrivals (including of course Semper and Marx).[16]

In a brilliant lecture of 1973 on *The London Building World of the Eighteen-Sixties*, subsequently turned into a short book, John Summerson pinpointed that later decade as the zenith of the Victorian expansion of London, writing that the city "was more excavated, more cut about, more rebuilt and more extended than at any time in its previous history".[17] Other historians have since concurred.[18] London was then still mostly a Georgian city in feel and layout, yet the mid-century changes were rapidly altering that. Massive new sewers were cut; urban railway lines were laid; the first-ever underground line was gouged from Paddington to Farringdon; the Victoria Embankment canalized the Thames; new streets such as Holborn Viaduct appeared across the city; and enormous buildings like Smithfield Market and St. Pancras Station were built. Summerson calculated that a total of 73,000 new buildings were erected during the 1860s, mostly terraced houses in increasingly suburban settings.[19] Semper's period in London was of course in the decade before that, but the same forces of development had already been grinding into operation then. Following the first major cholera epidemics, the late 1840s and early 1850s went through intense slum clearance projects that used the creation of new roads and shops as a means of displacing the poorest citizens of the capital – in New Oxford Street in central London, Commercial Street in Whitechapel and Victoria Street to the west. And Semper was himself directly involved in the project that best epitomized mid-Victorian building fervour, the phantasmagorical Crystal Palace erected for the 1851 Great Exhibition, for which he was asked to arrange the exhibits for the Canadian section, together with those for the Cape of Good Hope, as well as the Danish and the Swedish and Norwegian sections, and for good measure also those for Turkey and Egypt.[20]

Architectural practice and the building industry were both being uprooted by new capitalist processes. Summerson noted there were around 900,000 adult male workers in London in 1861, an estimated 91,000 of whom – 10 per cent of all workers in the city – were involved in construction. Almost all were site workers. He also pointed out the role of new professions, although this was rather hard to define, given the overlap between architects and surveyors. Nonetheless, Summerson reckoned there were 1,459 architects working in London in 1861. Most London builders at the time were one-man bands specializing in a single craft, but there were also around seventy large general contractors who employed permanent staff from all the building trades. These firms tendered competitively for contracts and were part of an increasingly legalistic and commercialized process of production, moving away from craft-based approaches. By the 1850s, for instance, the company run by George Myers employed around 2,000 men.[21] The pioneering efforts of Thomas and William Cubitt developed in the mid-nineteenth century the first thoroughly mechanized and standardized processes of building production; also ubiquitous was the large contracting firm of Samuel Morton Peto, which was responsible, among many other projects, for erecting the Houses of Parliament (1840–70). Peto was also a leading representative of the ambitious speculators and contractors who fuelled the 1840s railway boom in Britain, and he later spread his know-how to other countries such as Russia, Denmark, and Hungary.

Architects tended to come from the middle and lower middle classes, not from the gentry or proletariat, and their only means of obtaining training was in offices under the pupillage system. In a partial attempt to remedy this situation, Thomas Donaldson, who as noted had helped set up the Institute of British Architects, was appointed as Britain's first university-based professor of architecture at University College London in 1841 (the first professorial position of that title in London had been held by Thomas Sandby at the Royal Academy of Arts, back in 1780).[22] The Architectural Association was founded in 1847 by a group of dissatisfied younger architects working in larger offices, as a forum for mutual self-learning in an era in which it was hard to elevate one's skills and knowledge or to ascend the social scale. Architecture in mid-century London remained a socially static and often sterile occupation – ripe for satire by Charles Dickens in his 1844 novel, *Martin Chuzzlewit*.

The globalizing of London

Before looking at Gottfried Semper's personal experiences, it should be pointed out that London's increasingly globalized building world in the 1850s was being shaped through three primary influences: the British Empire; continental Europe; and the incipient rise of the United States of America. Taking the first influence, the British Empire involved at a fundamental level a massive flow of goods and capital within the imperial system. The inflow to Britain largely took the form of raw, unprocessed materials. As one example, Canadian timber flowed into Britain from 1809 onwards.

During the nineteenth century, it is estimated that 25 per cent of all transatlantic merchant shipping to Britain carried Canadian timber for use in hundreds of thousands of Victorian houses. The outflow from Britain to the countries of empire comprised refined, processed goods, and this also led to changes in the building industry. One common application was galvanized (i.e. zinc-coated) corrugated iron sheets, which British companies exported in the form of flat-packed prefabricated cottages, palaces, churches, etc.[23]

The 1851 Great Exhibition was a paradigm of imperialist ideology – a spectacle that was intended to show, as one historian notes, "the riches of Britain's empire in the East", and to achieve this goal it collected in space "an exhaustive display of raw materials that attested to the financial benefits of Empire".[24] The Crystal Palace reproduced on an urban scale the greenhouses built to import the plants of empire to English country houses, an activity in which its designer, Joseph Paxton – a gardener by training – led the way. Owen Jones, interior designer for the Great Exhibition, published *The Grammar of Ornament* in 1856, with its depictions of decorative patterns from the Middle East and Asia. The Great Exhibition, in its privileged Hyde Park location, thus continued a process of absorption of imperial imagery in London that was also epitomized in the early nineteenth century by the occupants of the zoological gardens in Regent's Park, and by John Nash's use of quasi-Indian motifs for one of the surrounding apartment blocks, Sussex Terrace. In this sense, the royal parks of London acted as a device by which imperial imagery and forms could be introduced right into the heart of empire.

In terms of continental Europe, many Gothic Revival architects from Britain travelled extensively on the mainland, visiting churches and delighting in reading Ruskin's masterpiece, *The Stones of Venice* (1851–53). There were direct familial links as well, as in the instances of Augustus Welby Pugin or Isambard Kingdom Brunel. Connections with Germany were especially strong, for two reasons. The most dramatic was the arrival of many German revolutionaries – including Semper – in London following the 1848–49 uprisings, as scathingly satirized by Marx and Engels in *Die grossen Männer des Exils* (The Heroes of the Exile) in 1852.[25] Secondly, there was during the nineteenth century a steady growth in trade and cultural exchanges between Germany and Britain, typified by the presence of the Prince-Consort, Albert of Saxe-Coburg and Gotha. Karl Wilhelm Siemens, a German engineer and inventor who became naturalized as British and renamed himself William Siemens, was a close friend of Semper in London.[26] Germans were in fact the largest overseas group in mid-nineteenth-century London, with an estimated 30,000 living there by 1880.[27] For these 'German Victorians', London was a specimen dish in which new ideas could be spawned and tested. Kindergartens, Christmas trees, and other German cultural habits found their place within British life. Likewise, a stream of architectural visitors, from Karl Friedrich Schinkel in 1826 through to Hermann Muthesius in the 1890s, came over to find out what was happening in new forms of building in Britain.

The third dynamic element was the United States of America, an ex-colony with numerous ethnic, economic, and cultural links with Britain. It is vital to bear in mind the growing influence of American capitalism, and above all its newly aggressive overseas trade policies. Historians estimate that Britain lost the status of having the highest

21

per capita gross national product in the world and was displaced by America by the late 1870s.[28] From 1880 to 1900, Britain's share of world manufacturing output fell from 23 per cent to 18 per cent. As if in a curious economic mirror effect, America's share of manufacturing output rose from 15 per cent to 24 per cent in the same period. Surplus profits being generated in America needed to find somewhere else to be re-invested, and Britain was the obvious target. By around 1900, numerous British commentators were thus pointing openly to an 'American invasion' of London, with US entrepreneurs now building the capital's underground railways, electric tram lines, power stations, department stores, office blocks, hotels, theme parks, cinemas, etc., and also promoting technologies such as steel-framing and electricity.[29] New trans-spatial communications networks were especially important for globalizing connections between Britain and America – such as the transatlantic cables mentioned earlier (which were also being fabricated in a Woolwich factory by Semper's friend, William Siemens, from the 1860s onwards).[30]

Yet the signs of inroads being made by the USA were already present during Semper's time in London. A tale that exemplifies the emerging globalizing tendencies arose in the early 1850s, when the American gun manufacturer Samuel Colt set up his only overseas factory, close to Vauxhall Bridge in Pimlico. There he produced military pistols with six barrels that spun round slightly after each shot – known popularly as 'revolvers'.[31] The London factory was opened because of his success in the American section of the 1851 Great Exhibition, when Colt put 500 guns on show and handed out free brandy to customers – which sounds like a deadly combination. Colt was the first-ever American to lecture to the Institution of Civil Engineers, telling them that successful mass production depended on the use of standardized, interchangeable components. Colt used this lecture, as usual, as a sales pitch for his weapons, suggesting they were just what the British Army needed. Officials clearly agreed, for the warehouse premises in Pimlico (built by Thomas Cubitt) were provided on a government lease. Colt began production in 1853, and soon two hundred workers were turning out guns using Sheffield steel on machinery brought over from the States. Queen Victoria toured the Colt Factory, and Charles Dickens was reportedly thrilled to fire off multiple shots in quick succession when he paid a visit. However, the Colt factory in Pimlico was not a lasting success and closed within two years – although not before supplying 25,000 revolvers to British troops in the Crimean War.

The primary impact that Colt had while running his London operation was, however, the turmoil that he stirred up about manufacturing methods. British arms makers were outraged, and a special Parliamentary Commission was set up in 1854 to investigate whether American mass-production systems were appropriate – in the end concluding that they were. This debate about what should be the materials and technologies of the industrial era would seem to be very close to Semper's concerns, yet although in September 1852 he wrote a report on the queen's Private Collection of Arms at Windsor Castle at the behest of the Department of Practical Art – remarking in great detail upon the close marriage of functional use and ornamental art in metals in these guns, and their clear use for understanding the history of styles – nowhere is there any recorded comment by Semper upon the cause célèbre of Colt's short-lived factory in London.[32]

When in London…

The architectural designs that Semper produced while living in London were carried out after he secured his post in the Department of Practical Art in September 1852. The received view is that Semper's design talents remained unappreciated in Britain, despite his various attempts to secure commissions. Certainly, there was to be no opera house as in Dresden and no university building as in Zurich, or museums as in Vienna. Despite support from fellow Germans such as Prince Albert, Semper did not have any deep cultural links in London, and so perhaps it is not surprising that he failed to make much headway. His son, the art historian Hans Semper, later wrote that Gottfried Semper became fed up with all of the "furniture junk" ("Möbelkram") that he had to make do with while working in London.[33] Nonetheless, there were designs for a cemetery in Woolwich, a pottery school in Stoke-upon-Trent, a hostel and a bath-cum-laundry in London, and a proposed reconstruction of a Roman amphitheatre within the second Crystal Palace in Sydenham, none of which were built – as well as a fabric shop in the rebuilt Crystal Palace, which was executed.[34] Yet despite this lack of success, there was an intriguing pattern behind the two main architectural projects on which Semper worked – which can only be really understood by viewing the spatial growth of mid-nineteenth-century London as a dramatically new geographical arrangement that was being shaped by globalizing forces. What was disappearing in this process was its model of urban development, hitherto based on two rival centres, with government in Westminster and finance in the City of London.

23

The new geography can be conceptualized as one in which east London – the poorer part, and also from the sixteenth century onwards the most internationalized, due to patterns of imperial trade and migration – became increasingly the receptacle for the material goods and peoples of the British Empire, and of the wider world beyond that, as well as increasingly the concomitant space for military defence against that outside world. Examples of this change could be seen in the new docks that were now rapidly spreading further to the east, the munitions factories springing up in the Lea Valley, and the Royal Arsenal in Woolwich. Until well into the nineteenth century, while London was always the largest port for imports in Britain, the most innovative docks were in fact to be found in industrial ports like Glasgow and Liverpool. But the centrifugal nature of the imperial system saw London grow steadily in power and dominance as its extensive eastward dock-building programme took effect from the mid-nineteenth century. "London had established itself as the world's major port by 1890, and with that, gained a position of extraordinary command over the whole British economy", writes one historian.[35]

In contrast, London's wealthier western suburbs, which began to emerge from the mid-nineteenth century onwards, can be seen as spaces for the symbolic representation of empire and other globalizing forces. This kind of growth was spearheaded through spectacles such as the 1851 Great Exhibition, the 1886 Indian and Colonial Exhibition – also in South Kensington (on the site where Imperial College now sits), the Franco-British Colonial Exhibition at White City in Hammersmith in 1908, and the Imperial Exhibition at Wembley in 1924–25. Importantly, these exhibitions were linked to the material development of suburban growth and the spreading values of domestic consumerism. As such, they featured the technologies of industrialized

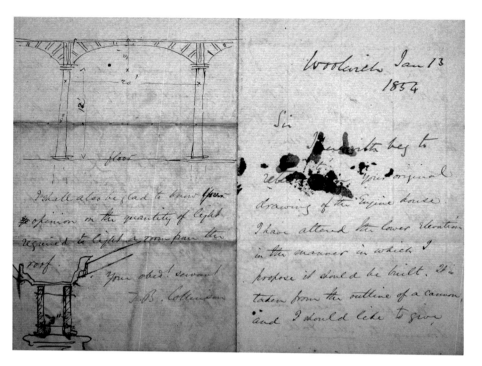

_ Figure 5.
Thomas Bernard Collinson,
first and last pages of a
four-page letter to Gottfried
Semper stipulating the
design requirements for the
new machine shop for the
Royal Laboratory, Woolwich
Arsenal, London, sent on
13 January 1854 (Courtesy
of the gta Archives/ETH
Zurich).

24

leisure from America, an aspect promoted even more strongly by the US-financed Earl's Court Exhibition Centre, which put on shows with Buffalo Bill firing off Colt revolvers and acted as the locus for Britain's first Ferris wheel. All of this was aided by the spread of the new underground railway lines, which favoured the west of the city over the poorer eastern districts (and also the northern bank of the river over the southern).

As a consequence, the two key projects that Semper designed while in London were closely linked to these globalizing forces. In connection with eastward growth, on 27 December 1853 he was invited by a Royal Engineer, Captain Thomas Bernard Collinson, to provide a detailed design for an infill structure – in Collinson's terms, "to give architectural elevations suitable for manufacturing buildings" – in the open courtyard of the Royal Laboratory at Woolwich Arsenal, the largest arms factory run by the British government.[36] The recommendation to use Semper had come from Captain Henry Charles Owen, another Royal Engineer, who had earlier worked on the 1851 Great Exhibition. The project at the Woolwich Arsenal has been examined in detail by Peter Guillery for the *Survey of London* volume covering that area, and he points out that Semper's work there was but part of a wider initiative to introduce steam-driven machinery into the Arsenal from the late 1840s – a process then hastened by the slide into the Crimean War of 1853–56.[37] It was normally the Royal Engineers who carried out the designs for any new buildings in the Arsenal, but since this project involved alterations to the Royal Laboratory, parts of which dated back to the 1690s, and because Collinson was relatively inexperienced and under considerable pressure, it was felt that external architectural help was needed.[38] As Guillery notes:

_ Figure 6.
Thomas Bernard Collinson
and Gottfried Semper,
machine shop, Royal
Laboratory, Woolwich
Arsenal, London, 1854,
as shown here in use for
ammunition production
in 1914 (Courtesy of the
Greenwich Heritage Centre).

25

Collinson's letters to Semper … indicate that Semper was given responsibility for the entire form in detail of the iron frame and roof. His designs were resolved in early 1854, just as war was declared on Russia. Ironwork was supplied by Benjamin Hick and Son of Bolton and the factory was hastily erected.[39]

This infill building was intended as the main machine shop for making ammunition. To cover over this open quadrangle in the centre of the Royal Laboratory, the design consisted of ninety octagonal-section cast-iron columns with a north-lit 'saw-tooth' roof in a space measuring 92 by 42 metres, with the columns spaced regularly at six-metre centres. Enclosed were some 500 lathes. It was estimated that their efficiency would reduce the labour costs of producing ammunition by two-thirds. The basic layout was Collinson's, and he meddled a lot in the design; the curious treatment of the exterior elevation was most likely his. It seems that Semper was primarily responsible for the detailing of the iron frame and north-lit roof, starting on his designs in January 1854 just as Britain was about to make its entrance into the Crimean War. The building was completed by mid-1854. The elegantly latticed framework was very different from Semper's usual architectural style, but served as a model for light-span glazed roofs in the Woolwich Arsenal for many decades after.[40] Semper was also asked by Collinson to supply some designs for a subsequent manufactory building, but nothing appears to have come of that request.

Figs. 5, 6

Historically, it is also notable that the innovations being introduced at the Woolwich Arsenal (and also at the Royal Small Arms Factory in Enfield in the Lea Valley) were to a large extent prompted by the impact of Colt and other American gun manufacturers in introducing mass-production techniques to cut costs. From late 1851,

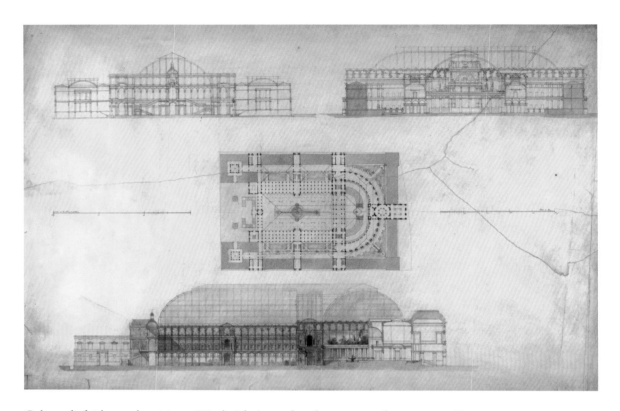

26

_ Figure 7.
Gottfried Semper, project
for a museum in South
Kensington, London,
1855 (Courtesy of the
Royal Commission for the
Exhibition of 1851).

Colt made fairly regular visits to Woolwich Arsenal to demonstrate the prowess of his weapons, leading to his contribution to the arms supply for the Crimean War, as noted earlier. Colt's jaunts to Woolwich were eagerly commented upon by the daily press, so Semper would have read about them there and probably also heard about them from other sources. Many in the British government were concerned about creating an overreliance on private companies such as Colt's for weaponry – hence the desire to modernize the Woolwich Arsenal factories, such as the one that Semper worked on. This makes it even more curious that there appears to have been no comment on such matters from Semper – even stranger for someone who was so engaged in scientific studies of ballistics and projectiles.

In relation to London's westward expansion, Semper became embroiled in Prince Albert's efforts to build upon the legacy of the 1851 Great Exhibition, by using up its 'surplus' profit of around £186,000, to create a suite of cultural and educational institutions on a site just to the south of where the Crystal Palace had stood (i.e. the area which today contains the Albert Hall, Royal College of Art, Royal College of Music, Imperial College London, Science Museum, Natural History Museum, and Victoria and Albert Museum – now widely known as 'Albertopolis'). The story is a complicated one. In what soon turned into a veritable political minefield, Prince Albert quietly solicited design proposals in late 1853 for what to do with this very large site, from three leading British architects of the day: Charles Cockerell, Thomas Donaldson, and James Pennethorne (in addition, Henry Cole also submitted a proposal in

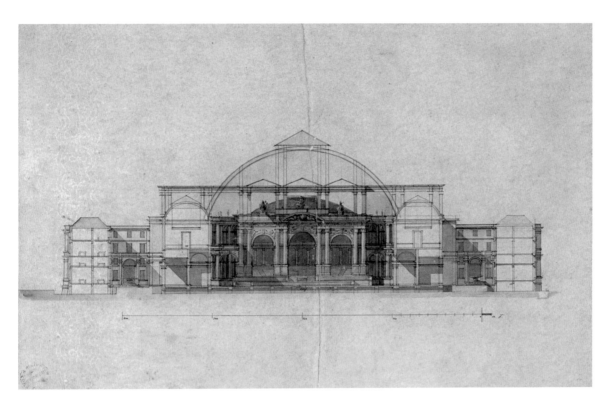

_ Figure 8.
Gottfried Semper, project
for a museum in South
Kensington, London, 1855,
section (Courtesy of the
Royal Commission for the
Exhibition of 1851).

conjunction with his assistant Richard Redgrave). All of their designs were grandiose enough in their own ways, but without any of them being remarkable architecturally, and in practice they would have been impossible to enact economically or politically. There was, for instance, at this time a huge controversy over whether or not the National Gallery would be relocated from Trafalgar Square to South Kensington.

Faced with an impasse, and in reaction to a separate dispute with the Chancellor of the Exchequer, William Gladstone, Prince Albert used his own money to commission Gottfried Semper at the end of 1854 to propose a specific design for a new museum. It was to occupy just 12 acres on the eastern side of the larger site, on which the Victoria and Albert Museum stands today and which previously held Brompton Park House. As John Physick, the V&A's official historian, recounts of the brief given to Semper:

> This, stated the prince, would probably have to be built with private money, and proposed that it might be on the lines of the Palais Royal and include shops, apartments and galleries for the collections of Marlborough House and elsewhere. At a meeting, the Prince drew a quick sketch on his blotting paper, which was extracted by Henry Cole, and is now in the Library of the Victoria and Albert Museum.[41]

By 9 June 1855, when he presented his proposal to Prince Albert, Semper had come up with a dreamlike, elegiac design that envisaged a huge T-shaped glazed atrium roof, spanning 61 metres across – with strong echoes of the rebuilt Crystal Palace in Sydenham (1852–54) – ghosted onto his more typical solid masonry style. Semper

Figs. 7, 8

_ Figure 9.
Gottfried Semper, drawing
showing a partially altered
arrangement for the
design for a museum
in South Kensington,
1855, perspective section
(Courtesy of the Royal
Commission for the
Exhibition of 1851).

28

reportedly apologized to Prince Albert for having only been able to produce some drawings of his design, but not a physical model.[42] His drawings, if somewhat tentative in feel, were stunning, and the perspective section was particularly modern in its depiction of a free-flowing public space dotted with museum-goers. Whereas his part-glazed roof in Woolwich Arsenal was prosaic in its ambitions, here the roof was entirely glazed and entirely visionary. London had seen nothing like it before. If it had actually been built, it would today be one of the truly great buildings in the city, or indeed anywhere in Britain.

There were of course a number of striking precedents on hand in London for the use of iron-and-glass roofs – not least the original Crystal Palace, and before that the Kew Palm House (Richard Turner and Decimus Burton, 1844–48), with its span of 30 metres and length of 111 metres. There were also notable precedents in counterposing masonry construction with iron-and-glass roofs in the stations and hotels at Kings Cross (Lewis and William Cubitt, 1851–52), Paddington (Isambard Kingdom Brunel and Matthew Digby Wyatt for the station, and Philip Charles Hardwick for the hotel; both 1851–54), plus subsequent high points such as St Pancras Station. Soon to be built, and in another city not that far away, was the Oxford Museum (Thomas Newenham Deane and Benjamin Woodward, 1856–60). But what Semper seems to suggest in his design for the South Kensington Museum was something else, a synthesis – indeed an innovative hybrid – of a building base that was imbued with historical meaning and executed in stone, with a clear sense of its identity as a museum-type, and then a superstructure that spoke of a new industrial culture, shaped using iron and glass, which seems to blow all sense of building types asunder. It appears to represent a mix of all his preoccupations while in the capitalist 'melting pot' of Britain – or, alternatively, a blend of Dresden and London. The design echoes, albeit expressing entirely different cultural referents, the hybridized incorporation of Brazilian 'tropical' features that Michael Gnehm detects in Semper's extraordinary (but unsuccessful) entry for the 1857 competition for a new theatre/opera house in Rio de Janeiro.[43] In the event, Semper's scheme for a museum in South Kensington was costed out by the two most celebrated general contractors of the time, William Peto and Thomas Cubitt, but was judged to be too expensive to build, and so the Board of Trade rejected the plan. Instead, London in 1857 was given the far cheaper, prefabricated 'Brompton Boilers' as the home for the new South Kensington Museum.[44] In the meantime, indeed later in 1855, Gottfried Semper had moved to Switzerland to take up a position as the professor of architecture at the recently founded polytechnic, an institution that would later become the Swiss Federal Institute of Technology in Zurich.

A legacy from Semper's London period?

In conclusion, it is worth noting Semper's contribution towards the globalizing of British architectural theory, which can be seen as the main legacy of his period in London, rather than an influence on design practice as such. The 1975 *Survey of London* volume on South Kensington posited a few possible influences from Semper on the museums that were eventually erected in Albertopolis, such as a preference for a rounded-arch Lombardic Romanesque style as an alternative to either Gothic Revival or strict Neoclassicism, the adoption of the sgraffito wall mural technique that Semper, as Francis Fowke pointed out, had used in a house that he had designed in Hamburg,[45] plus a greater attention in the Government School of Design – as the forerunner of the Victoria and Albert Museum – to the arts and crafts of ceramics and textiles.[46] Yet it remains a relatively restricted influence. In contrast, while in London, with a good deal of time on his hands and with the British Museum Library as a valuable resource, Semper was able to publish – among a substantial variety of lesser pieces – two weighty texts in the form of *The Four Elements of Architecture*, in 1851, and then *Science, Industry, and Art* in 1852.

29

The vital link for promoting the appreciation of Semperian theory in Britain was again with Thomas Donaldson, who back in the 1830s had been one of the team of art and architectural scholars who discovered that the Elgin Marbles and other Greek statues in the British Museum were originally coloured. It was this connection, indeed, that formed the basis of their friendship. In a reverential footnote in Semper's essay titled *On the Study of Polychromy, and Its Revival*, published in London in July 1851, Semper dutifully recorded that: "Among the earliest discoverers was Professor Donaldson; who, in the year 1830, fully proved that the whole surface of the marble temples of Athens was originally coloured".[47] Semper paid similar homage at the same time in the first section of *The Four Elements of Architecture*, in which he defended his position within the controversial debate about polychromy, referring to the "noted English architect and expert on antiquity, Mr T.L. Donaldson".[48] There were other overlaps between the pair. Both were professors of architecture in London (in common then also with Charles Cockerell at the Royal Academy of Arts), even if that position did not quite hold the same function it has today, since there were no architectural schools at that time. Donaldson, as noted, designed one of the proposals for the South Kensington site (as did Cockerell) that had been rejected prior to Semper's imaginative museum design.

Their mutual respect was evidenced again when Donaldson gave a lecture titled *On Polychromatic Embellishments in Greek Architecture* at the Institute of British Architects on 12 January 1852, in which he thanked Semper for information that

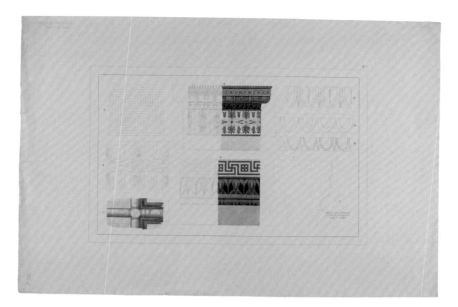

_ Figures 10–13.
Plates from G. Semper, *Die Anwendung der Farben in der Architectur und Plastik*, 1836, "Presented by Herr Semper" to the RIBA Library on 12 January 1852: details from the Temple of Hephaestus (Theseus) in Athens; Greek sarcophagi from Agrigento and pedestal from Salamis; Etruscan tomb; architectural fragments (Courtesy of RIBA Collections).

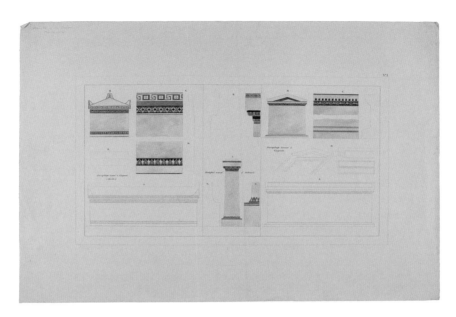

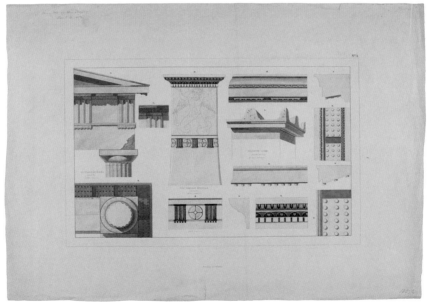

supported the argument being made, as well as for providing some drawings for the talk. In the published report of this lecture, Donaldson apparently declared that the subject of ancient Greek polychromy "was forcibly brought before the attention of learned Europe by an important series of illustrations, published in Germany, by a gentleman then present, Herr Semper, some of whose drawings were displayed upon the walls of the room".[49] Semper had indeed presented these drawings – five remarkable hand-coloured lithographs showing a part of the Parthenon, some details of the Temple of Hephaestus (Theseus) in Athens, an Etruscan tomb in Agrigento in Sicily, and a sheet of comparative polychromatic details from his publication *Die Anwendung der Farben in der Architectur und Plastik* from 1836 – to the RIBA Library on the occasion of Donaldson's lecture.[50] As the account went on to note, although Donaldson gave due praise to Jacques Ignace Hittorff, Franz Kugler, and others involved in the debate about ancient Greek polychromy, "He, however, quoted with admiration the beautiful illustrations of Semper".[51] In other words, Semper while in London in the 1850s was able to mix effortlessly with those highest-placed in the academic sphere of British architecture. The reverence in which Donaldson held Semper was profound, as could be seen from a letter that the former wrote to the latter after receiving his dedicated copy of the Hoftheater book, with Donaldson noting:

Figs. 10–13

> I have day after day been hoping to call upon you since you so kindly left the copy of yr book on the magnificent Theatre of Dresden for my acceptance[.] I esteem every thing as precious, which proceeds from yr pencil or your pen; but its value becomes doubly worth, when such a token of esteem comes from you. But there is one little word in the inscription, which I must entreat you to alter; as it seems to do away with the cordiality of friendship, which should exist between us, and places us *both* in a false position. You offer the book as a mark of *respect*[.] – Nothing could be more inappropriately expressed in *English*, for I should hope to possess your *regard*, & that would also include every other sentiment, that I could wish you to entertain for me. And I should feel ashamed from such a one as yourself to be supposed to think myself entitled to such an expression from the architect of the Theatre of Dresden.[52]

Furthermore, this chance in early 1850s London for Donaldson to commune with Semper, one of the best-known figures in the European Neoclassical scene – and one directly involved in the emergence of the new subject of architectural history, in which Germany led the field – had a genuine significance also for other aspects of British architecture. The intellectual support that Semper provided for Donaldson and others in London during his brief sojourn was a clear part of the intellectual turn in British architecture that by then was starting to dim the strength of the Gothic Revival. As is noted in files in the Public Records Office, there was even an attempt in 1857 by the Department of Science and Art – which meant in effect Henry Cole – to lure Semper back to London from Zurich.[53] Cole wrote to Semper on this matter on 4 July 1857, taking up an initiative from Semper, who had inquired (through the mediation of his friend William Siemens) about the possibility of reinstatement, given that, having now arrived in Zurich, he thought it unlikely that he could ever get the chance to work there as an architect.[54] A few years later, in 1863, Cole and his faithful associate, Richard Redgrave, went on a tour of Germany that included visiting Semper's buildings in Dresden, where they especially appreciated his picture gallery.[55] There was subsequently a weak attempt, by one Gen-

_Figure 14.
Gustave Doré, *The New Zealander* (depicting a Maori New Zealander surveying London in postapocalyptic ruin), illustration from W.B. Jerrold, *London: A Pilgrimage*, 1872.

eral Grey, to have Semper appointed as the architect for the Royal Albert Hall on the South Kensington site after its original designer, the Royal Engineer Francis Fowke, died unexpectedly in December 1865.[56] The mooting of Semper's name in this way was no doubt intended in honour of Prince Albert, who had clearly held Semper in high esteem, and who had passed away just four years earlier. However, it was generally felt that British architects would not tolerate the appointment of a foreign rival. In Lord Derby's words, when commenting upon who should be asked to rework Fowke's proposals for the Royal Albert Hall:

it would [be] … something like a slur on the whole body of British Architects, to pass them over for the construction of a really National work, in favour of a foreign Professor, who is not even resident in England, and is not known here by any of his works.[57]

Instead the completion of the Royal Albert Hall was handed to another Royal Engineer, Colonel Henry Scott.[58] Two decades later, the architect and teacher Lawrence Harvey – who had studied under Semper in Zurich from 1864–67 – gave a lecture on Semperian theory to a RIBA audience in December 1884, in a talk entitled *Semper's Theory of Evolution in Architectural Ornament*.[59] It provoked a brief flurry of interest in Semperian ideas within the architectural press in Britain that soon fizzled out, however, except in the late nineteenth-century writings of the art historian Gerard Baldwin Brown (a little-known figure today, but one of the first to call for legislation for the preservation of ancient monuments).[60]

If nineteenth-century Rationalism sought to exclude Romantic notions of subjectivity as far as possible, those who also possessed a Romantic sensibility like Semper wished to unite a sense of rationality with the full flow of the creative imagination. In the pragmatically orientated and business-minded building world of 1850s London, he was a fish out of water. London appeared to feel as if it did not really need his input – a common enough fate for exiles. Yet Semper's legacy, including not least his displays for the Great Exhibition, offers us a definite insight into the globalizing forces from Empire, continental Europe and America that were making London – not Paris or Berlin – into the capital of the nineteenth century, the place where those arriving from overseas could glimpse the future being built. London served as the main entrepôt port for ideas. However, these same capitalist convul-

33

sions also created feelings of great uncertainty, indeed pessimism, as was revealed in the astonishing engraving by Doré in the 1872 book mentioned earlier, depicting a future London in postapocalyptic ruin.[61] Or, as Marx and Engels so famously wrote in 1848 about the impact of capitalism, "all that is solid melts into air".[62] The globalizing of London's building world, of which Semper was briefly a part, was also creating those forces that made so many people in Britain cling to outmoded values of monarchy, class, and tradition, ultimately preventing the acceptance and integration of the more innovative architectural theorists from continental Europe such as Semper. In other words, Semper's London sojourn during the first half of the 1850s took place in the right city for developing his ideas, but the wrong city for promoting them with any real hope of success.

Fig. 14

Acknowledgements
A good many people helped with the writing of this chapter. In the Semper project team at USI Mendrisio and ETH Zurich, I would especially like to thank Sonja Hildebrand, Philip Ursprung, Michael Gnehm and Dieter Weidmann. Another member of the project team, Claudio Leoni, who was my doctoral student at the Bartlett School of Architecture at University College London, has been a constant source of information and support, as indeed has Claudio's co-supervisor, Peg Rawes. Two of my other Bartlett colleagues, Adrian Forty and Peter Guillery, kindly provided photographs, advice, and comments and read earlier drafts of this chapter. In connection with locating the Semper material that still survives in various London collections, I would like to express thanks to Charles Hind and Vicky Wilson of the RIBA Drawings Collection, Wendy Fish and Jonathan Ridsdale from the RIBA Library, Olivia Horsfall-Turner of the Victoria and Albert Museum, and Angela Kenny of the Royal Commission for the Exhibition of 1851 (now part of Imperial College London).

_ 1. T.L. Donaldson, *The Late Gottfried Semper of Vienna, Honorary and Corresponding Member*, "Transactions of the Royal Institute of British Architects", 1st Series, 29, 1879, pp. 233–35 (here p. 233). See also N. Pevsner, *Semper*, in N. Pevsner, *Some Architectural Writers of the Nineteenth Century*, Oxford University Press, Oxford 1972, pp. 252–68 (here p. 252).

_ 2. See F. Kugler, *On the Polychromy of Greek Architecture*, trans. W.R. Hamilton, preliminary observations by T.L. Donaldson, "Transactions of the Royal Institute of British Architects", 1st Series, 1, part 1, 1836, pp. 72–104; G. Semper, *Preliminary Remarks on Polychrome Architecture and Sculpture in Antiquity* (1834), in G. Semper, *The Four Elements of Architecture and Other Writings*, trans. H.F. Mallgrave and W. Herrmann, Cambridge University Press, Cambridge, MA 1989, pp. 45–73.

_ 3. Semper wrote to Donaldson in November 1848 about their having met "à Londres dans l'an 1839". See W. Herrmann, *Gottfried Semper: In Search of Architecture*, MIT Press, Cambridge, MA 1984, p. 280, note 293. During his theatre reconnaissance trip, however, Semper had in fact arrived in London on 14 December 1838, and stayed in the city for about a week, after which he continued on to Paris by the end of the month, travelling then onwards to Turin, Milan, Genoa, Pavia, and Venice, and being back in Dresden in early March 1839. Hence it would appear that Donaldson was slightly wrong in his recollection of the year in which he had first met Semper in London. See H. Laudel, *Erstes Hoftheater Dresden*, in W. Nerdinger and W. Oechslin (eds.), *Gottfried Semper 1803–1879: Architektur und Wissenschaft*, Prestel / gta Verlag, Munich / Zurich 2003, pp. 168–78 (here p. 173); D. Weidmann, *Through the Stable Door to Prince Albert? On Gottfried Semper's London Connections*, "Journal of Art Historiography", no. 11 (2014), pp. 1–26 (here p. 14, note 72).

_ 4. Royal Institute of British Architects, *The Report of the Council, Read at the Annual General Meeting Held 5th May, 1851*, Published at the Rooms of the Institute, 16, Grosvenor Street, London 1852, p. 26 ("Contributions to the Collection and the Library of the Institute, between the 6th of May, 1850, and the 5th of May, 1851").

_ 5. While thanking Semper for the volume, Donaldson asked Semper to change the dedication, as will be referred to again later in this chapter. For the letter concerned, see T.L. Donaldson to G. Semper, 26 May 1853 (?), gta Archives/ETH Zurich, 20-K-1853-05-26, transcription by D. Weidmann. I am greatly indebted to Dieter Weidmann for allowing me to use his transcriptions and translations of the Semper correspondence for this chapter.

_ 6. T.L. Donaldson, *Late Gottfried Semper*, see note 1, p. 233.

_ 7. *Ibid.*, p. 234.

_ 8. *Ibid.*

_ 9. *Ibid.*, p. 235.

_ 10. After Semper had moved to Zurich, Donaldson complained about Semper's silence towards him: "I think it strange, that I never hear from you. Why do you not write to me now & then? Remember our ancient friendship. And is there not a great identity of feelings between us in regard to art? You know, I & my wife went expressly to Zurich to hunt you out & your dear children, for whom we entertain really affectionate remembrance". T.L. Donaldson to G. Semper, 29 May 1867, gta Archives/ETH Zurich, 20-K-1867-05-29, transcription by D. Weidmann.

_ 11. E. Hobsbawm, *Industry and Empire: An Economic History of Britain since 1750*, Penguin, Harmondsworth 1969, p. 136.

_ 12. C. Fox (ed.), *London – World City, 1800–1840*, Yale University Press / Museum of London, New Haven / London 1992.

_ 13. P. Ackroyd, *Introduction*, in W.B. Jerrold, *London: A Pilgrimage* [1872], Anthem Press, London 2005, pp. xvii–xix (here p. xvii).

_ 14. B. Wilson, *Heyday: Britain and the Birth of the Modern World*, Weidenfeld & Nicolson, London 2016, p. xxv.

_ 15. W.B. Jerrold, *London: A Pilgrimage*, see note 13, pp. 118–19.

_ 16. A. Briggs and J. Callow, *Marx in London: An Illustrated Guide*, Lawrence and Wishart, rev. ed., London 2008, p. 16.

_ 17. J. Summerson, *The London Building World of the Eighteen-Sixties*, Walter Neurath Memorial Lectures, 5, Thames and Hudson, London 1973, p. 7.

_ 18. J. White, *Railway Town: The City, 1855–1875*, in J. White, *London in the Nineteenth Cen-*

tury: "A Human Awful Wonder of God", Cape, London 2007, pp. 37–48.

_ 19. J. Summerson, London Building World, see note 17, p. 8.

_ 20. See the chapter by Claudio Leoni in the present volume.

_ 21. J. Summerson, London Building World, see note 17, pp. 9–12.

_ 22. Thomas Sandby was appointed as the first-ever professor of architecture at the Royal Academy of Arts from 1780 to 1798. He was followed by George Dance the Younger from 1798 to 1805, who failed to give even one lecture, and so was ousted. Next came John Soane from 1806 to 1837, and on Soane's death it was William Wilkins from 1837 to 1839, who again did not deliver a single lecture. Upon Wilkins's death, he was followed by Charles Cockerell from 1839 onwards.

_ 23. C. Davies, Prefabricated Home, Reaktion Books, London 2005, pp. 47–51.

_ 24. L. Kriegel, Narrating the Subcontinent in 1851: India at the Crystal Palace, in L. Purbrick (ed.), The Great Exhibition of 1851: New Interdisciplinary Essays, Manchester University Press, Manchester 2001, pp. 146–78 (here p. 150). See also J.A. Auerbach, The Great Exhibition of 1851: A Nation on Display, Yale University Press, New Haven 1999; J.R. Davis, The Great Exhibition, Sutton, Stroud 1999; P. Young, Globalization and the Great Exhibition: The Victorian New World Order, Pallgrave Macmillan, Basingstoke 2009.

_ 25. K. Marx and F. Engels, The Heroes of the Exile (1852), in K. Marx and F. Engels, The Cologne Communist Trial, trans. R. Livingstone, Lawrence and Wishart, London 1971, pp. 135–234.

_ 26. W. Herrmann, Gottfried Semper, see note 3, pp. 78, 281, note 297; H.F. Mallgrave, Gottfried Semper: Architect of the Nineteenth Century, Yale University Press, New Haven 1996, pp. 213–14. On Siemens, see H. Kellenbenz, German Immigrants in England, in C. Holmes (ed.), Immigrants and Minorities in British Society, Allen & Unwin, London 1978, pp. 63–80 (here pp. 73–74).

_ 27. R. Ashton, Little Germany: Exile and Asylum in Victorian England, Oxford University Press, Oxford 1986; R. Ashton, Germans in Bloomsbury (2009), http://www.ucl.ac.uk/bloomsbury-project /articles/events/conference2009/ashton.pdf (accessed 28 March 2016); L. Chamberlain, German Victorians Who Helped Transform Britain, "Standpoint", September 2013, http:// standpointmag.co.uk/node/5142/full (accessed 28 March 2016); C. Lattek, Revolutionary Refugees: German Socialism in Britain, 1840–60, Routledge, London 2006.

_ 28. A. Orde, The Eclipse of Great Britain: The United States and British Imperial Decline, 1895–1956, Macmillan, Basingstoke 1996, pp. 1–4, 35–36.

_ 29. M. Fraser (with J. Kerr), Architecture and the "Special Relationship": The American Influence on Post-war British Architecture, Routledge, London

2007, pp. 39–122; W.T. Stead, The Americanization of the World, Markley, New York 1902.

_ 30. A. Saint (ed.), Survey of London, vol. 48, Woolwich, edited by P. Guillery, Yale University Press, New Haven 2012, pp. 119–25.

_ 31. P. Dicken, Global Shift – The Role of United States Transnational Corporations, in D. Slater and P.J. Taylor (eds.), The American Century: Consensus and Coercion in the Projection of American Power, Blackwell, Oxford 1999, pp. 35–50 (here p. 46).

_ 32. G. Semper, Report on the Private Collection of Arms at Windsor Castle, the Property of Her Majesty the Queen (20 September 1852), in First Report of the Department of Practical Art, Eyre and Spottiswoode for Her Majesty's Stationery Office, London 1853, pp. 364–67, edited in G. Semper, London Writings 1850–1855, edited by M. Gnehm, S. Hildebrand, and D. Weidmann, gta Verlag, Zurich 2021.

_ 33. H. Semper, Semper, Gottfried, in Schweizerisches Künstler-Lexikon, edited by C. Brun, vol. 3, Huber, Frauenfeld 1913, pp. 123–43 (here p. 128).

_ 34. W. Herrmann, Gottfried Semper, see note 3, pp. 36, 49–50, 69–71; H.F. Mallgrave, Gottfried Semper, see note 26, pp. 215–16.

_ 35. P.L. Garside, West End, East End: London, 1890–1940, in A. Sutcliffe (ed.), Metropolis 1890–1940, Mansell, London 1984, pp. 221–58 (here p. 229).

_ 36. T.B. Collinson to G. Semper, 27 December 1853, gta Archives/ETH Zurich, 20-K-1853-12-27:1, cited after P. Guillery and C. Thom, Germans, Guns and Gas in South London, "Historic England: Research News", no. 17/18, Spring 2012, pp. 14–16 (here p. 15), https://content.historicengland.org.uk /images-books/publications/research-news-17-18/ RN17_18_web.pdf/ (accessed 28 March 2016). See also W. Herrmann, Gottfried Semper, see note 3, p. 71.

_ 37. A. Saint (ed.), Survey, see note 30, pp. 164–67.

_ 38. Ibid., pp. 134–35; P. Guillery and C. Thom, German Guns and Gas, see note 36, p. 14.

_ 39. P. Guillery and C. Thom, German Guns and Gas, see note 36, p. 15.

_ 40. Ibid., pp. 14–15.

_ 41. J. Physick, Early Albertopolis: The Contribution of Gottfried Semper, in The Victorian Society Annual, The Victorian Society, London 1994, pp. 28–36 (here p. 36).

_ 42. Ibid.

_ 43. M. Gnehm, Tropical Opulence: Rio de Janeiro's Theater Competition of 1857, in C. Mattos Avolese and R. Conduru (eds.), New Worlds: Frontiers, Inclusion, Utopias, Comitê Brasileiro de História da Arte (CBHA) / Comité International de l'Histoire de l'Art and Vasto, São Paolo 2017, pp. 146–65.

_ 44. J. Physick, Early Albertopolis, see note 41, p. 36.

_ 45. F.H.W. Sheppard (ed.), Survey of London, vol. 38, The Museums Area of South Kensington and Westminster, Athlone Press, University of London, London 1975, pp. 76, 101. See F. Fowke,

A Description of the Building at South Kensington, Erected to Receive the Sheepshank Collections of Pictures, Chapman and Hall, London 1858, p. 24.
_ 46. F.H.W. Sheppard (ed.), *Survey of London*, see note 45, p. 76.
_ 47. G. Semper, *On the Study of Polychromy, and Its Revival*, "The Museum of Classical Antiquities", 1, no. 3, July 1851, pp. 228–46 (here p. 232, note), edited in G. Semper, *London Writings 1850–1855*, edited by M. Gnehm, S. Hildebrand, and D. Weidmann, gta Verlag, Zurich 2021.
_ 48. G. Semper, *The Four Elements of Architecture: A Contribution to the Comparative Study of Architecture (1851)*, in G. Semper, *Four Elements*, see note 2, p. 90.
_ 49. T.L. Donaldson, *On Polychromatic Embellishments in Greek Architecture: Being an Explanation of the System, as Illustrated in the Recent Work on the Polychromy of the Ancients, by M. Hittorff, Honorary and Corresponding Member*, Paper Read at the Ordinary General Meeting, 12 January 1852, "Transactions of the Royal Institute of British Architects", 1st Series, 3 (1850–53), pp. 1–5. There were then two general follow-up discussion sessions about Donaldson's lecture on Hittorff's theories, held at the Royal Institute of British Architects on 26 January 1852 and 9 February 1852, in which Gottfried Semper, Thomas Donaldson, Charles Cockerell, James Fergusson, Michael Faraday, Owen Jones, and others participated. See D. Van Zanten, *Architectural Polychromy: Life in Architecture*, in R. Middleton (ed.), *The Beaux-Arts and Nineteenth-Century French Architecture*, Thames and Hudson, London 1982, pp. 197–215 (here p. 211); W. Herrmann, *Gottfried Semper*, see note 3, p. 77; H.F. Mallgrave, *Introduction*, in G. Semper, *Four Elements*, see note 2, pp. 1–44 (here p. 19).
_ 50. Royal Institute of British Architects, *The Report of the Council, Read at the Annual General Meeting Held 3rd May, 1852*, London, Published at the Rooms of the Institute, 16, Grosvenor Street, 1852, p. 24 ("Contributions to the Collection and the Library of the Institute, between the 5th of May, 1851, and the 3rd of May, 1852"). This set of five hand-coloured lithographs presented by Semper still exists in the RIBA Drawings Collection, SB 140 (each of the drawings is inscribed: "Presented by Herr Semper Jany 12 1852"). I am greatly indebted to Charles Hind, Chief Curator and H.J. Heinz Curator of Drawings, RIBA British Architectural Library, for uncovering these items in their archives.
_ 51. Royal Institute of British Architects, *Report of the Council 1852*, p. 234.
_ 52. T.L. Donaldson to G. Semper, 26 May 1853 (?), gta Archives/ETH Zurich, 20-K-1853-05-26, transcription by D. Weidmann. See also the chapter by D. Weidmann in the present volume.
_ 53. F.H.W. Sheppard (ed.), *Survey of London*, see note 45, p. 76.

_ 54. W. Herrmann, *Gottfried Semper*, see note 3, pp. 80–83; H.F. Mallgrave, *Gottfried Semper*, see note 26, pp. 232–33.
_ 55. F.H.W. Sheppard (ed.), *Survey of London*, see note 45, p. 76.
_ 56. *Ibid.*, p. 183; H.F. Mallgrave, *Gottfried Semper*, see note 26, p. 312.
_ 57. Lord Derby to Colonel Grey, 17 January 1866; Archives of the Commissioners for the Exhibition of 1851, Windsor Archives, Royal Archives, Windsor Castle, XXI, 50, cited after W. Herrmann, *Gottfried Semper*, see note 3, p. 82. See also F.H.W. Sheppard (ed.), *Survey of London*, see note 45, p. 183; H.F. Mallgrave, *Gottfried Semper*, see note 26, p. 312.
_ 58. F.H.W. Sheppard (ed.), *Survey of London*, see note 45, pp. 177, 182–84.
_ 59. L. Harvey, *Semper's Theory of Evolution in Architectural Ornament*, "Transactions of the Royal Institute of British Architects", New Series, 1, 1885, pp. 29–54. See N. Pevsner, *Some Architectural Writers*, see note 1, p. 253, note 3; J.D. Berry, *The British "Semperite" Debate of 1884–1885*, in J.D. Berry, *The Legacy of Gottfried Semper: Studies in "Späthistorismus"*, PhD diss., Brown University, 1989, UMI, Ann Arbor, MI 1990, pp. 191–218; H.F. Mallgrave, *Gottfried Semper*, see note 26, p. 365.
_ 60. For example, see G.B. Brown, *Semper and the Development Theory*, "The Architect", 32, 27 December 1884, p. 414. See J.D. Berry, *Legacy of Gottfried Semper*, see note 59, pp. 196–97; H.F. Mallgrave, *Gottfried Semper*, see note 26, p. 365. On Brown, see D.J. Breeze, *Gerard Baldwin Brown (1849–1932): The Recording and Preservation of Monuments*, in "Proceedings of the Society of Antiquaries of Scotland", 131, 2001, pp. 41–55.
_ 61. Doré's wood-engraved illustration was titled *The New Zealander*, or *Macaulay's New Zealander*, in reference to a comment by the British historian and politician Thomas Macaulay in a book review of 1840, in which he imagined a future traveller from New Zealand gazing upon London in ruins. The notion of it being someone from as far away as New Zealand came in turn from a comment about a potential future civilization in New Zealand that had been made by Edward Gibbon back in the 1780s in *The History of the Decline and Fall of the Roman Empire*. In sentiment and tone, Macaulay's musing was part of a common enough trope in literature and art ever since antiquity, of a protagonist who stumbles across a former great civilization now in ruins (as in Homer, Piranesi, Diderot, Shelley and others). See D. Skilton, *Gustave Doré's London/Londres: Empire and Post-imperial Ruin*, "Word and Image", 30, 2014, pp. 225–37.
_ 62. K. Marx and F. Engels, *Manifesto of the Communist Party* [1848], trans. S. Moore, in K. Marx, *The Revolutions of 1848: Political Writings*, Volume 1, Verso, London 2010, pp. 62–98 (here p. 70).

Claudio Leoni

Staging Canada: Gottfried Semper's Contribution to the Great Exhibition of 1851

"The show from Canada is nearly in order, having been arranged by Mr Semper, the architect of the Dresden Theatre, who is called the 'Barry' of Germany".[1]

_ Figure 1.
*View of the Canadian
Court*, central part
of the illustration
from "The Illustrated
Exhibitor", no. 16,
20 September
1851 (Courtesy of
Universitätsbibliothek
Heidelberg).

The Canadian section at the Great Exhibition of 1851 aroused a great deal of attention among contemporary witnesses. Images of the Canadian Court, with a canoe hanging from the rafters of the Crystal Palace, were widely disseminated in numerous publications at the time. Up until today, the image of Gottfried Semper's design for Canada has had an almost iconic status in architectural discourse, illustrating the beginning of material culture in mid-nineteenth-century architectural theory. The Great Exhibition was of particular importance for Semper's intellectual career and consequently touches on the most central aspects in the development of his architectural theory, including his theory of style. In several publications and manuscripts, he tried to make sense of the vast array of cultural material that he encountered at the exhibition.[2] Yet despite the Great Exhibition's importance for Semper's theoretical thinking, the actual extent of Semper's designs for the exhibition is still as yet fairly unexplored.[3] My aims in this chapter are to explore Semper's arrangement and decoration of the Canadian Court and to examine the extent to which his practical work can be understood in the light of his theoretical deliberations at the time. Reconstruction drawings developed from contemporary prints and Semper's own drawings are used in an attempt to provide further points of guidance.[4]

Figs. 8–9, 11

When Semper eventually became stranded in London following his involvement in the Dresden uprising and subsequent flight from Germany, he hoped to obtain commissions in order to make a living while he was in exile and to continue his architectural career. Probably through Henry Cole, one of the organizers of the Great Exhibition of 1851, Semper received several opportunities to assist smaller countries with their displays at the Crystal Palace. While the larger nations had brought their own staff to organize and arrange their sections, smaller countries delegated the task to their diplomatic representatives, who were dependent on local support and in turn commissioned contractors and designers such as Semper.[5] The actual extent of Semper's involvement in decorating sections for various exhibitors cannot be comprehensively assessed. Semper himself mentions that he arranged the sections for Canada, Turkey, Sweden, and Denmark.[6] He also advertised his services in Germany and France, following which one German accountant and a few French businessmen contacted him.[7] However, he must have obtained a few small jobs more or less by accident. As discussed below, these include his work for the Cape of Good Hope, the exhibits from which were installed in a corner of the Canadian Court.

The arrangement of the Canadian section

In 1851, the British colonies in North America were not yet unified. At the time, Canada represented only the Province of Canada – in other words, the union of Upper and Lower Canada, which was established in 1841. Modern Canada was only established in 1867 through the Canadian Confederation.[8] At the Great Exhibition, however, Canada, New Brunswick, Nova Scotia, and Newfoundland presented a joint display.[9] Through the grouping together of all the British North American colonies, "Canadian representation expressed itself as a coherent and legitimate geographical entity".[10] Henry Houghton, the commissioner for Canada, may also have represented the other colonies, as the official catalogue does not mention another commissioner for those sections. However, the decorations were installed within a relatively short time, between mid-March and early May 1851.[11]

The sections for the British North American colonies were situated in the western wing of the Crystal Palace, which was reserved for the exhibitions from the British Empire.[12] Adjacent to the East Indies, West Indies, Medieval Court, and Sculpture Court, the British North American colonies were located between the southern

40

Figs. 2, 3

_ Figure 2.
Canada, plate from *Dickinsons' Comprehensive Pictures of The Great Exhibition of 1851*, 1854.

avenue and the nave (or main avenue). The southern avenue served for the display from Nova Scotia (P30 to P32), and the few exhibits from Newfoundland and New Brunswick were presented in the eastern passage from Nova Scotia to the West Indies Court (P/Q32). The Province of Canada was placed in the court between the southern avenue and the nave. It also occupied the three units in between the court and nave (M30 to M32). However, Canada shared the western unit with the Cape of Good Hope (M30) and the eastern unit with West African colonies (M32).

The three units between the central avenue and the Canadian Court were mainly used for the display of raw materials, primary products, and tools. The first table on the eastern side of unit M30 displayed several kinds of "ores, from Lake Huron, Lake Superior … in various stages of manufacture".[13] In unit M31, the western table presented various specimens of stone. These mineral collections had been classified and arranged accordingly by William Logan, director of the geological survey in Montreal.[14] Alongside geological specimens, there were also several kinds of timber around the tables. However, the majority of timber samples were used for the Canadian Timber Trophy in the middle of the main avenue. In the middle of the passageway were some "black walnut and other Tables".[15] The eastern table in unit M31 showed tools that settlers and trappers would need in Canada's backwoods.[16] On the adjacent table in unit M32, various fabrics and blankets were displayed, and above them were some "specimens of Carpet Manufacture, suspended".[17]

The western wall of the Canadian Court or square (N30–32/O30–32) was especially dedicated to the display of numerous samples of Canadian agricultural produce. The barrels in front of the tables contained "corn, Indian meal, barley, oats, peas, beans, flax, potatoes preserved for sea voyage … Siberian oil-seed, hemp,

41

_ Figure 3.
Plan of the Great Exhibition Building, 1851 (Courtesy of the Royal Commission for the Exhibition of 1851).

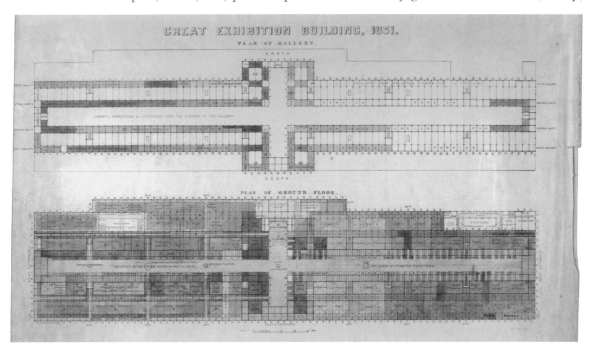

hops, and sugar from the maple tree all show the varied richness of a land, which, put to good account, might effectually relieve the distress of the older communities of the world".[18] On the table behind the barrels and in the showcases, visitors would either have looked at harvest products such as biscuits or agricultural implements such as a plough or different harnesses.

On the southern side of the square, the two display tables and cabinets presented articles that were either used for hunting or obtained from hunting. The display comprised articles such as hides and all kinds of utensils for trappers such as snowshoes and rifles. As on the western wall, barrels containing primary products were placed in front of the tables. On the northern side of the square as well, there were barrels presenting seeds and other primary products. The tables and cabinets on this side displayed articles associated with a more comfortable or urban life. Tables and cabinets on the east presented harnesses and saddles, stoves, and printing ma-

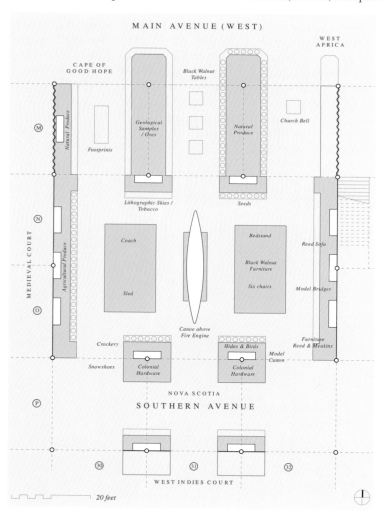

_ Figure 4.
Layout of the Canadian Court, reconstruction by the author, rendering by Philip Shelley.

chines.[19] The tables and cabinets on the west exhibited more luxurious articles such as tobacco or straw hats and even some curiosities such as the cast of "footprints of a reptilian animal" on the floor.[20]

The eastern wall of the square was mainly used for the display of furniture and articles of general domestic use, most of which had been sent by manufacturers in Montreal. There were several chairs, a sofa, and an office chair made of black walnut. There were also various musical instruments, such as a "piano, manufactured in Canadian woods, especially fitted to endure the changes induced by the vast range of temperatures in this country",[21] and two model bridges.[22]

The more voluminous objects were placed inside the square on three stands or pedestals. The pedestal on the east was devoted to furniture, like the adjacent wall, and displayed "some handsome black-walnut furniture".[23] Along the pedestal's western side were "half-a-dozen chairs, the seats and back worked in worsted and silk by the ladies of Montreal, 'for England's Queen'".[24] The pedestal on the west was devoted to sleighs and carriages, with "wrappers in which you tuck yourself and your companion" that were "of the largest and thickest bear skins".[25] The most prominent specimens of Canadian production were at the centre of the square. A "fire-engine of unusually large proportions, and remarkably elegant design and workmanship, capable of throwing two streams of water 156 feet high, or a single stream of 210 feet high" was placed on the pedestal.[26] Trials at the Serpentine Lake in London's Hyde Park had shown that the fire engine was able to propel water higher than any other in the exhibition, and it was consequently awarded a medal.[27]

The canoe that was suspended above the fire engine was the Canadian Court's central and most prominent exhibit. It was made of white birch and impressed visitors with its vast dimensions.[28] The canoe presented no especial difference from canoes we have seen a hundred times, except its size; but this canoe was actually paddled 3,000 miles of lake and river navigation, with a crew of twenty men, before being placed on board a steamer for England. It was the same description of canoe employed by the Hudson's Bay Company in their annual journeys to the vast preserves of fur-bearing animals under their command.[29]

43

_ Figure 5.
Grand Panorama of the Great Exhibition: No. V, South-West Portion of the Nave, from "The Illustrated London News", no. 539, 3 January 1852 (Courtesy of Zentralbibliothek Zürich).

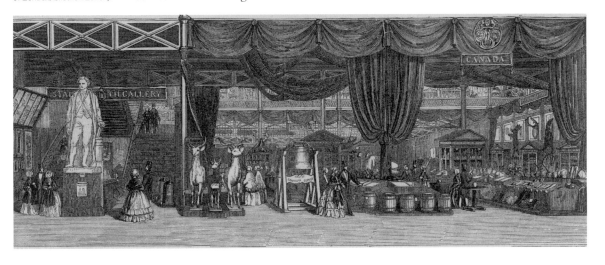

The decorations of the Canadian section

For visitors coming from the transept and walking along the south side of the main avenue, the first exhibit from Canada that would have caught the eye was a group of three stuffed deer. Placed just behind them in the first passageway to the Canadian Court, there was a church bell from Montreal "made from the copper of Lake Huron".[30] Large tables extending from the gallery spaces into the main avenue displayed raw materials and primary products. The structure of the Crystal Palace enveloping the Canadian Court was decorated with draperies of a greenish or blue-greenish colour – the hand-coloured lithographs are not consistent in the colouring. The two posts in the middle were decorated with lavish curtains, and the horizontal beams on the upper floor were covered with fabric of the same kind. In the middle of the three units, above the central passageway, there was the nameplate for Canada, as well as the emblem of the Province of Canada. After visitors had strolled through the passageway in the middle, the space opened up again as they entered into the well-lit Canadian Court, with the light coming in through the Crystal Palace's glass roof.

Fig. 5

Figs. 2, 7

Fig. 5

Fig. 6

The first item that caught the visitor's attention here would have been the huge canoe suspended above the fire engine in the middle of the square. Yet this would just have been a glimpse of the canoe, as it was hanging in the direction in which visitors would enter or leave the court. Visitors entering the court through the middle passage would thus have seen the slender prow of the canoe but not yet the impressive side view of it. The canoe was also effectively visible from both the upper galleries and especially from the adjacent staircase and landings on the east. As the eastern wall to the stairs was not fully closed, the landings would have provided a favourable view into the Canadian Court. The western wall, on the other hand, was entirely closed and thus provided a background that allowed a contextualizing staging of the canoe hanging from the rafters of the Crystal Palace. Generally, the effect of the canoe suspended in space had to be obtained by walking around it. If visitors

Figs. 2, 7
Figs. 8, 9

44

_ Figure 6.
View of the Canadian Court, from "The Illustrated Exhibitor", no. 16, 20 September 1851 (Courtesy of Universitätsbibliothek Heidelberg).

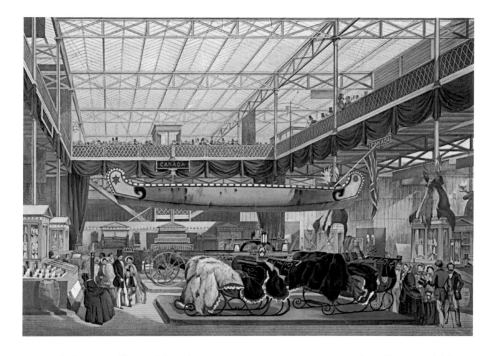

_ Figure 7.
View of the Interior of the
Canadian Division at the
Great Exhibition of 1851
(Courtesy of Library and
Archives Canada, Ottawa).

45

entered the court from either the western or eastern passage, the effect would have been different, as the side of the canoe would have become visible earlier. Several illustrations taken from the western passage give an impression of the view on entering the court. Semper himself thought about the effect that would be achieved in this way; he drew a perspective view possibly intended for a print to be made, which serves here as the source for my third reconstruction view. Unlike all the other illustrations of the Canadian Court, Semper drew this perspective view from the opposite side, from the south-eastern corner of the square. It captures more dramatically the very moment at which one enters the square, and also provides a glimpse of the western wall of the court.

    Semper planned the western wall quite carefully. A drawing of the western wall that has survived shows the degree of thought and detail that he put into the design. This drawing, a frontal view of the court, shows that the wall encroaches on the northern side (to the right of the drawing) into the next unit, which was eventually used to display products from the Cape of Good Hope, and even further into the nave.[31] The southern end of the wall (to the left of the drawing) spreads into the south avenue, where Nova Scotia was displayed. There Semper's design incorporates a passageway to the adjacent Medieval Court. The western wall in the court was divided into two areas – a lower area on the ground floor level, equipped with three glass cabinets, and an upper area with five panels for trophies (either of animals or weapons). The lower area contained three glass cabinets, the outer ones having segmentally arched gables and the one in the middle having a triangular gable. The same sheet of paper includes two other drawings – a section through the western wall (on the far right of the drawing) and a frontal view of one of the side

Figs. 2, 7

Figs. 10, 11

Fig. 12

_ Figure 8.
View of the Canadian
Court from the staircase,
reconstruction by the author,
rendering by Philip Shelley.

_ Figure 9.
View of the Canadian Court
from the upper gallery,
reconstruction by the author,
rendering by Philip Shelley.

_ Figure 10.
Gottfried Semper,
perspective view of the
Canadian Court, 1851
(Courtesy of Landesamt für
Denkmalpflege Sachsen,
Dresden).

_ Figure 11.
Reconstruction of the
Canadian Court, based
on Semper's drawing,
reconstruction by the author,
rendering by Philip Shelley.

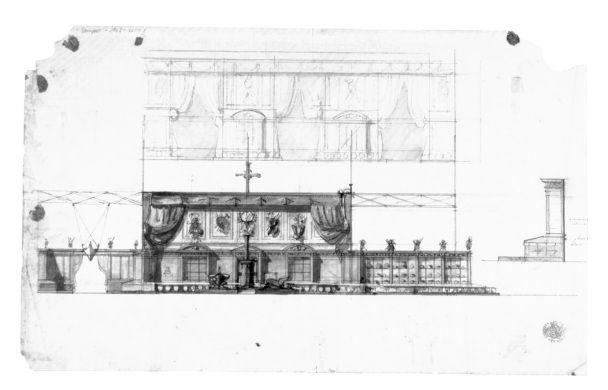

48

_ Figure 12.
Gottfried Semper, project
for the western wall of
the Canadian Court, 1851
(Courtesy of Kustodie der
Hochschule für Bildende
Künste Dresden, photo
HfBK Dresden).

walls of the Court, again with cabinets covered with segmentally arched gables (upper half of the drawing) which were not implemented at all, unlike the western wall.

There are hardly any contemporary illustrations of the western wall of the Canadian Court. The only depiction on which the wall is recognizable is a panorama taken from the nave, at the right-hand side of the view. It shows that the wall was actually executed in a similar fashion to Semper's drawing, but with all the glass cabinets uniformly covered with triangular gables. The wall covers the whole height of the square, and has gabled cabinets and spaces for trophies. The position from which the view was taken did not make it possible to include the portion of the wall belonging to the Cape of Good Hope. However, a contemporary woodcut published in December 1851 suggests that there the cabinet, or cabinets, were similar in design to those in the Canadian Court; at least, they do not have the rectangular shape in Semper's elevation drawing of the Canadian Court, as the drapery around the two buffalo heads covers an apparently bulky top. The woodcut itself proves Semper's involvement in the arrangement of the exhibition of the Cape of Good Hope. In a letter addressed to an unknown person, Semper asked to be paid for the work that he had carried out for the Cape of Good Hope together with the addressee, at the latter's request, and in particular he mentions the mounting of the buffalo heads.[32] The letter was probably addressed to the decorator William Butler Simpson, as Semper received a reply to his request from Simpson's office the same day.

There is some uncertainty about possible variants of the glass cabinets for Canada: some that were placed in the middle of the court might have had the shape of

Fig. 5

Fig. 13

_ Figure 13.
Group of Objects Selected from the Contributions of the Cape of Good Hope, from "The Illustrated Exhibitor", no. 30, 27 December 1851 (Courtesy of Universitätsbibliothek Heidelberg).

a small temple, while those set along the wall definitely had a shallow temple front. However, many of the elements Semper intended for the Canadian Court were installed. Gabled cabinets were installed at each of the posts on either side, and instead of having spaces for trophies in an upper area, the heads and antlers of deer and elk were placed at the tops of the gabled cabinets. The eastern and western walls were similarly structured in the same way, with the difference that the eastern wall had neither an upper field nor trophies above the gables. Instead, as there was no spatial division above the cabinets, it was possible to enjoy a spectacular view of the court from the adjacent staircases and landings. The lavish draperies were also installed inside the court. Greenish or blue-greenish curtains, as mentioned above, flanked each corner of the square, with their corresponding valances hanging from the upper floor. The draperies contrasted with the red fabric with which the handrail of the upper floor was covered. Initially, Semper himself had intended the draperies to be red as well, as his elaborate elevation shows. The fabric covering the tables, and the colour of the pedestals in front of them or in the middle of the square, remained in red, as indicated in the same drawing. When visitors were leaving the Canadian Court through one of the passages to the Nova Scotia section, they would encounter two other tables and gabled cabinets crowned with antlered deer heads in the southern avenue.

Fig. 2

Fig. 12

Fig. 2

49

The Canadian Timber Trophy

Fig. 14

In the entrance area of the Canadian section was another of Semper's decorations, the Canadian Timber Trophy. Placed in the middle of the main avenue and among other trophies, this gigantic heap of wood incorporated various kinds of timber and displayed the richness of the Canadian forests. Many of the pieces were simply too large to be displayed in the compartments.[33] The Royal Commission therefore suggested erecting a Timber Trophy in the main avenue. The many drawings of it by Semper that have survived indicate the care that he put into the planning. The design that was eventually implemented under the supervision of William Butler Simpson (the decorator who also supervised the arrangement for the Cape of Good Hope) consisted of a simple framework with crossed-over stiffening boards, as if for a tent.[34] The several specimens of wood were then either pushed though the frame, leaned against it, or laid on the floor around it. Eventually, the construction was crowned with a second, smaller canoe lying on a festively arranged greenish fabric – presumably the same fabric that was used for the decorations in the Canadian Court. This construction made

_Figure 14.
Canadian Timber Trophy,
from "The Illustrated
London News", no. 495,
21 June 1851 (Courtesy of
Zentralbibliothek Zürich).

50

it possible to incorporate a diverse collection of different types of wood: there were mill logs, planks, boards, and joists made of black walnut, chestnut, cherry, curled maple, hard maple, sugar maple, veneer from bird's-eye maple, birch, oak, ash, basswood or lime, rock elm, and butternut.[35] Some of "these examples were cut into such slabs as might at once show their wrought and unwrought character, one side of each being duly finished and varnished, or polished".[36] Other exhibits were processed even further. However, as the specimens were submitted by several different contributors, their sizes and processing varied considerably.

The arrangement of the trophy followed an ascending principle that illustrated several stages of wood processing. Lying on the floor were predominantly unwrought pieces of wood, or even curious objects in the process of fossilization and thus with no applied use, followed by roughly wrought pieces of timber, painted or varnished specimens, and then well-processed items such as a ship's futtock (transverse rib) made from a huge hemlock pine, and eventually the finely crafted canoe at the top.[37] (Other ways of using wood – particularly in furniture and in musical instruments made of Canadian timber – were displayed in the Canadian galleries.) In addition to samples of wood, the trophy also included a specimen from the animal world: on the western side, leaning against the lumber, was a huge lower jawbone of a sperm whale that was almost the same height as the trophy itself. Through these elements, the trophy made reference to shipbuilding and illustrated the way in which civilized peoples take advantage of technology not only to master wood but also to deploy it for further purposes such as hunting and trade. As such, the Timber Trophy was quite visionary, in view of the importance that wooden shipbuilding was to acquire for British North America in the second half of the nineteenth century.[38]

Principles of decoration and arrangement

Nine years later, when Semper was involved in establishing the plaster cast collection at the Eidgenössisches Polytechnikum (Swiss Federal Polytechnic) in Zurich, he mentioned his work in the Crystal Palace in a letter in which he stated that he had used his "principle of architecturally decorative arrangement without sacrificing purposefulness" when installing the sections in the Great Exhibition.[39] As early as 1851, Semper outlined a concept for a school of architecture in which he argued that the two professions – the architect and the decorator – had been identical in earlier times.[40] Semper hinted at the same issue in *Science, Industry, and Art* when – probably quoting his fellow countryman, Albrecht Becher – he discussed the conditions of modern architectural production. In the United States, an economically rationalized building industry was marginalizing the role of the architect, who departed from the building once the roof had been completed, at which point decorators started on the interior.[41] An architecturally decorative and functional arrangement thus means an arrangement that takes the display into account, as well as the exhibits. It tries to combine relatively different elements into a well-adjusted but encompassing arrangement.

The principles of arrangement in the Canadian compartment, as discussed above, differentiated between articles in relation to whether they needed to be processed further or could be consumed immediately. The first group included, for instance, raw materials, seeds and crops, and panels of fabric; while the latter featured, for instance, agricultural, hunting, and domestic products. The products were thus arranged in such a way as to attract the visitor's attention. Visitors considering emigrating to make a living in Canada might have regarded the agricultural products as holding out hope for an affluent future. Manufacturers who were interested in purchasing and processing materials might have been interested in high-quality raw materials. Merchants might have seen promising products to import, while consumers could inspect objects that were desirable for comfortable living.

The vertical arrangement of the tables and cabinets, on the other hand, followed a principle that was not unusual in contemporary scientific displays (e.g. in the Museum of Practical Geology in London).[42] The vertical axis of the space was used to demonstrate the gradual transformation of a material or species over time. Semper used this principle in the Canadian compartment to show the way in which a product developed out of its material – starting with the raw materials displayed in the barrels, to wrought materials such as hides, fabric, and tools, and finally to the technically more advanced products in the cabinets. The display thus vertically demonstrated the way in which products came into being through labour in the widest sense. Although labour itself was absent from the demonstration, it was still represented in the various tools on display. The remarkable aspect is that the actual consumer goods were locked away in the showcases; as such, these goods were not accessible for close examination by the visitors. Only the primary materials in the barrels and the wrought materials on the tables were physically palpable for the visitor. The display was thus conveying a message designed to spur visitors into action rather than consumption, although the promise of consumption was being presented to them at the same time.

The canoe arguably represented not only an effective visual focus for the whole arrangement, but also a centre point relating to each of the commodities surround-

51

ing it. This type of canoe could carry twenty people and was mainly used by the Hudson's Bay Company, which had held a monopoly on the fur trade with trappers and native Canadians since the seventeenth century.[43] The Hudson's Bay Company maintained several posts across Canada's vast terrain, from which goods were sent first to Montreal and subsequently to the rest of the world. The canoe thus represented the advancement of civilization, trade, and the exploitation of Canada's vast territories. As a mode of transportation, the canoe was also a symbol for the expansion of Western trade into the most remote areas of the world and the exchange of goods. Some of the animal hides and minerals on display

_Figure 15.
Birch-Bark Canoe Presented to His Royal Highness the Prince of Wales, from "The Illustrated London News", no. 1073, 9 February 1861 (Courtesy of Zentralbibliothek Zürich).

Fig. 15

may in fact have been shipped using this type of canoe for the Canadian part of their journey to the Great Exhibition. The commodities displayed in the Canadian Court were therefore related to the canoe, as their presence depended on the vessel as a means of transport, temporarily bringing all these displaced objects together so that they could be exported and eventually traded.

In Semper's definition, a commodity is generally adaptable, does not have any personal or individual characteristics (which would point to a user or producer), and is free of any defining local traits, so that it is easily adapted to any place. The quality of a commodity is thus highly generic. It is broadly adaptable in terms of usage, place, and personality.[44] As objects of trade, however, commodities depend on transportation. The canoe as a vessel represents mobility, which is crucial for the production and distribution of goods. It therefore represents a primordial form of trade. Many of the articles displayed in the Canadian Court were normally transported using this type of canoe. For their presentation, the articles were therefore dependent on such canoes in order to come together into a single space such as the Crystal Palace. As the vessel of expanding Western trade, the canoe also represented, like the Crystal Palace, the expansion of nineteenth-century capitalism, if perhaps in a more primary form. When Semper thought about an alternative taxonomy for the Crystal Palace and its objects, he questioned what "the true centre point of all relations" might be "that possesses attraction power enough to unite the heterogeneous and the unmeasured into a living, membered, and closed system".[45] Such a system would then make the "intrinsic bonds and thematic relationships of objects" visible.[46] The canoe may thus represent an "intrinsic bond" of this type that holds all the different objects together.

Several years later, Semper wrote that architecture – and thus every object that human beings make – represents "man in all his relations and connections to the world".[47] Ideas such as these already marked the beginnings of Semper's theoretical endeavours in the years of the Great Exhibition and its aftermath, however. The draft of an ideal museum that Semper outlined in 1852 links the idea of four crafts into a comprehensive system, marking architectural arrangement as the proper system – the intrinsic bond – for representing all the goods of the world.[48] Subsequently, this systematic approach eventually led to his major work, *Der Stil*. However, Semper's theoretical approach to objects was obviously also informed by his practical experience as an exhibition designer in the Crystal Palace.

_1. [H. Cole], *The Aspect of the Exhibition at the Queen's Visit, on the 15th April*, "Journal of Design and Manufactures", 5, no. 27, May 1851, pp. 57–60 (here p. 59); cf. W. Herrmann, *Gottfried Semper im Exil: Paris, London 1849–1855: Zur Entstehung des "Stil" 1840–1877*, Birkhäuser, Basel 1978, p. 62, note 220; D. Weidmann, *Through the Stable Door to Prince Albert? On Gottfried Semper's London Connections*, "Journal of Art Historiography", no. 11, 2014, pp. 1–26 (here p. 13).

_2. K. Lankheit, *Gottfried Semper und die Weltausstellung, London 1851*, in *Gottfried Semper und die Mitte des 19. Jahrhunderts*, Birkhäuser, Basel 1976, pp. 23–47; G. Reising, *Kunst, Industrie und Gesellschaft. Gottfried Semper in England*, in *Gottfried Semper und die Mitte des 19. Jahrhunderts*, pp. 49–66; W. Herrmann, *Semper im Exil*, see note 1, pp. 50–53; J. Nigro Covre, *Babele nel "vuoto coperto di vetro": Gottfried Semper e la Grande Esposizione di Londra del 1851*, "Ricerche di storia dell'arte", no. 16, 1982, pp. 5–20; H.F. Mallgrave, *Gottfried Semper: Architect of the Nineteenth Century*, Yale University Press, New Haven 1996, pp. 192–208; S. Hildebrand, *"… grossartige Umgebungen": Gottfried Semper in London*, in W. Nerdinger and W. Oechslin (eds.), *Gottfried Semper 1803–1879: Architektur und Wissenschaft*, Prestel and gta Verlag, Munich and Zurich 2003, pp. 260–68; M. Hvattum, *A Complete and Universal Collection: Gottfried Semper and the Great Exhibition*, in M. Hvattum and C. Hermansen (eds.), *Tracing Modernity: Manifestations of the Modern in Architecture and the City*, Routledge, London 2004, pp. 124–36; H.-G. von Arburg, *Alles Fassade: "Oberfläche" in der deutschsprachigen Architektur- und Literaturästhetik 1770–1870*, Fink, Munich 2007, pp. 311–34; A. Payne, *From Ornament to Object: Genealogies of Architectural Modernism*, Yale University Press, New Haven 2012, pp. 25–64.

_3. Exceptions are K. Lankheit, *Gottfried Semper und die Weltausstellung*, see note 2, pp. 34–37; J. Ziesemer, *Studien zu Gottfried Sempers dekorativen Arbeiten am Außenbau und im Interieur: Ein Beitrag zur Kunst des Historismus*, VDG, Weimar 1999, pp. 159–60; H. Laudel, *Ausstattungen auf der Weltausstellung 1851 im Crystal Palace*, in W. Nerdinger and W. Oechslin (eds.), *Gottfried Semper 1803–1879*, see note 2, pp. 275–78.

_4. I am grateful to Philip Shelley for the digital renderings.

_5. W. Herrmann, *Semper im Exil*, see note 1, pp. 50–54; H.F. Mallgrave, *Gottfried Semper*, see note 2, pp. 197–98.

_6. Gottfried Semper, draft of letter to Franz Hagenbuch, 22 August 1860, gta Archives/ETH Zurich, 20-K-1860-08-22b, p. 2: "Ich berühre nur noch dass ich auch in London, bei der grossen Industrieausstellung, 4 Abtheilungen (Canada Türkei, Schweden, Dänemark) einrichtete"; cf. W. Herrmann, *Semper im Exil*, see note 1, p. 51.

_7. For Semper's advertisements see: [F.G. Stammann], *Tagesbericht: Hamburg, den 22sten März*, "Hamburger Nachrichten: Morgen-Zeitung für Politik, Handel und Schiffahrt: Organ für hamburgische Angelegenheiten", no. 70, 22 March 1851, [p. 3]; [G. Semper], *Avis*, (1 April 1851), gta Archives/ETH Zurich, 20-DOK-1851:9; see W. Herrmann, *Semper im Exil*, see note 1, p. 50. The ensuing requests are documented in letters to Semper held in the gta Archives/ETH Zurich.

_8. S. Murray, *Canadian Participation and National Representation at the 1851 London Great Exhibition and the 1855 Paris Exposition Universelle*, "Histoire sociale/Social History", 32, no. 63, May 1999, pp. 1–22 (here p. 3).

_9. A. Short, *Canada Exhibited, 1851–1867*, "Canadian Historical Review", 48, no. 4, December 1967, pp. 353–64 (here p. 355).

_10. S. Murray, *Canadian Participation*, see note 8, p. 15.

_11. W. Herrmann, *Semper im Exil*, see note 1, pp. 50–51.

_12. *Canadian Contributions to the World's Fair*, "The Illustrated Exhibitor", no. 16, 20 September 1851, pp. 277–79; L. Bucher, *Kulturhistorische Skizzen aus der Industrieausstellung aller Völker*, Lizius, Frankfurt am Main 1851, pp. 62–65; R. Hunt, *Hunt's Hand-Book to the Official Catalogues: An Explanatory Guide to the Natural Productions and Manufactures of the Great Exhibition of the Industry of All Nations, 1851*, vol. 2, Spicer Brothers, London 1851, pp. 718–24.

_13. W.B. Jerrold, *How to See the Exhibition in Four Visits*, Bradbury and Evans, London 1851, p. 23.

_14. *Official Descriptive and Illustrated Catalogue of the Great Exhibition of the Works of Industry of all Nations, 1851*, vol. 2, Spicer Brothers, London 1851, p. 958.

_15. W.B. Jerrold, *How to See the Exhibition*, see note 13, p. 23.

_16. *Ibid.*

_17. *Ibid.*, p. 22; *The Canadian Court*, "The Crystal Palace and Its Contents: An Illustrated Cyclopædia of the Great Exhibition of 1851", no. 2, 11 October 1851, pp. 20–22 (here p. 22).

_18. *The Canadian Court*, see note 17, p. 22.

_19. J. Tallis, *Tallis's History and Description of the Crystal Palace and the Exhibition of the World's Industry in 1851*, vol. 1, Tallis, London [1851/52], p. 52.

_20. W.B. Jerrold, *How to See the Exhibition*, see note 13, p. 23.

_21. Society for Promoting Christian Knowledge, *The Industry of Nations, as Exemplified in the Great Exhibition of 1851*, vol. 1, Bentley, London 1852, p. 193.

_22. *The Canadian Court*, see note 17, p. 22.

_23. W.B. Jerrold, *How to See the Exhibition*, see note 13, p. 24.

_24. *The Canadian Court*, see note 17, p. 22.

54

_ 25. Unknown, *A Visit to the Great Exhibition by One of the Exhibitors*, Cundall and Addey, London 1851, p. 11.

_ 26. *The Canadian Court*, see note 17, p. 22.

_ 27. A. Short, *Canada Exhibited*, see note 9, p. 356.

_ 28. *Tallis's History and Description of the Crystal Palace*, see note 19, p. 52.

_ 29. *Ibid.*

_ 30. *The Canadian Court*, see note 17, p. 22.

_ 31. Hochschule für Bildende Künste Dresden, B 969. This frontal drawing has previously been attributed to the eastern wall. In view of the spatial conditions described above, and according to the visual material available, it could only have been a design for the western wall; cf. H. Laudel, *Ausstattungen auf der Weltausstellung*, see note 3, p. 276.

_ 32. Gottfried Semper, draft of letter, recipient not mentioned (presumably William Butler Simpson), gta Archives/ETH Zurich, 20-K-1851-09-04(S). I am grateful to Dieter Weidmann for this reference.

_ 33. K. Lankheit, *Gottfried Semper und die Weltausstellung*, see note 2, pp. 36–37. Lankheit assumes that Semper's trophy drawings could document an early stage of planning for the Canadian Court, in which the trophy was intended to be staged in the middle of the Canadian Court.

_ 34. For Simpson's and the Royal Commission's involvement in the Canadian Timber Trophy, see Simpson's letter to Matthew Digby Wyatt, 18 September 1851: "The Trophy … executed at the suggestion of the Committee ought, as I think, to be paid for by the Royal Commission". London, Royal Commission of the Exhibition of 1851 Archive, RC/A/1851/462.

_ 35. *The Canadian Court*, see note 17, p. 22; W.B. Jerrold, *How to See the Exhibition*, see note 13, p. 6; Society for Promoting Christian Knowledge, *Industry of Nations*, see note 21, pp. 184–85; W.A. Drew, *Glimpses and Gatherings during a Voyage and Visit to London and the Great Exhibition in the Summer of 1851*, Homan and Manley, Augusta 1852, p. 340; *Tallis's History and Description of the Crystal Palace*, see note 19, pp. 45–46.

_ 36. *Tallis's History and Description of the Crystal Palace*, see note 19, p. 45.

_ 37. *The Canadian Court*, see note 17, p. 22.

_ 38. In the second half of the century, Nova Scotia became a leading manufacturer of wooden sailing ships and was also home to large shipbuilding companies; E.W. Sager and G. Panting, *Maritime Capital: The Shipping Industry in Atlantic Canada, 1820–1914*, McGill-Queen's University Press, Montreal and Kingston 1990.

_ 39. Gottfried Semper, draft of letter to Franz Hagenbuch, see note 6, pp. 2–3: "Ich berühre nur noch dass ich auch in London, bei der grossen Industrieausstellung … mein Prinzip der architektonisch dekorativen Anordnung verfolgte ohne Detriment der Zwecklichkeit". Cf. W. Herrmann, *Semper im Exil*, see note 1, p. 51.

_ 40. Gottfried Semper, draft of letter to Rudolph Schramm, 25 February 1851, gta Archives/ETH Zurich, 20-K-1851-02-25(S):2.

_ 41. G. Semper, *Science, Industry, and Art: Proposals for the Development of a National Taste in Art at the Closing of the London Industrial Exhibition (1852)*, in G. Semper, *The Four Elements of Architecture and Other Writings*, trans. H.F. Mallgrave and W. Herrmann, Cambridge University Press, Cambridge, MA 1989, pp. 130–67 (here pp. 139–41); for the possible identification of Albrecht Becher as Semper's source for this passage, cf. D. Weidmann, *Through the Stable Door*, see note 1, p. 3.

_ 42. S. Forgan, *Bricks and Bones: Architecture and Science in Victorian Britain*, in P. Galison and E. Thompson (eds.), *Architecture and Science*, MIT University Press, Cambridge, MA 1999, pp. 181–208.

_ 43. E.E. Rich, *The History of the Hudson's Bay Company, 1670–1870*, vol. 2, Publications of the Hudson's Bay Record Society, London 1959.

_ 44. G. Semper, *Science, Industry, and Art*, see note 41, p. 141.

_ 45. Gottfried Semper, [*Notes on the Great Exhibition of 1851*] (1851), gta Archives/ETH Zurich, 20-Ms-94, fol. 2r (translation by the author); the German text is edited in G. Semper, *London Writings 1850–1855*, edited by M. Gnehm, S. Hildebrand, and D. Weidmann, gta Verlag, Zurich 2021.

_ 46. G. Semper, *Science, Industry, and Art*, see note 41, p. 132.

_ 47. G. Semper, *On Architectural Styles (1869)*, in G. Semper, *The Four Elements of Architecture*, see note 41, pp. 264–84 (here p. 269).

_ 48. G. Semper, *The Ideal Museum: Practical Art in Metals and Hard Materials*, edited by P. Noever, Schlebrügge, Vienna 2007, p. 57.

55

Philip Ursprung

Traces of Labour: An Imaginary Roundtable with Marx, Melville, Paxton, and Semper in the Crystal Palace in 1851

_Figure 1.
Crystal Palace, London,
photo by Benjamin
Brecknell Turner, 1852
(© Victoria and Albert
Museum, London)

At a banquet held in preparation for the Great Exhibition, Prince Albert of Saxe-Coburg and Gotha, the driving force behind the project, declared: "The *great principle of division of labour*, which may be called the moving power of civilization, is being extended to all branches of science, industry, and art".[1] Prince Albert's diagnosis has not lost any of its accuracy. The continuing extension of this principle of the division of labour has not ended. On the contrary, it reigns today more firmly than ever in science, industry, and art. It reigns also in the field of higher education – for instance, in the European Higher Education Area, which has been called 'Bologna' since the declaration inaugurating it was signed in that city in 1999.

The research project on Gottfried Semper conducted with Sonja Hildebrand is no exception. It was generously funded by the Swiss National Science Foundation, and its planned lifespan was three years. Its structure was based on the division of labour in time and space, with research taking place in Mendrisio, Zurich, and London. Unlike the other members of the group, I am not an expert on Semper and did not conduct any archival research. But, of course, our meetings and the process of research have drawn me more and more into the subject matter. My own contribution involved accompanying the project, giving feedback, and helping to formulate questions.

I would therefore like to propose here a new set of questions and speculations. I will base my contribution on an imaginary scenario in which Semper met up with Joseph Paxton, Herman Melville, and Karl Marx to hold a roundtable discussion under one of the elm trees in the Crystal Palace in October 1851, after the exhibition was over. Of course, this is a projection from my own present-day standpoint. Knowledge in 1851 was not produced and mediated in the guise of roundtables held in exhibition spaces. Quite probably the interlocutors would not have been able to 'discuss' in our present sense. Knowledge was mediated in the guise of manifestos – the *Manifesto of the Communist Party* by Marx and Engels, for instance, had been published in 1848 – in lectures by individuals, and in books and articles, although we know that Semper opted to speak in exhibition spaces. The tone would probably have been more polemical and dogmatic than today, in an age when interlocutors tend to react subtly to each other, aiming for consensus rather than controversy.

Let us assume that the four met under the elm tree just to talk, without an audience, alone in the huge, cold, nearly empty space, interrupted perhaps by some noises from porters carrying crates. Marx, in his early thirties, Semper, in his late forties, and Paxton, exactly the same age as Semper, were actually in London during the period of the exhibition. Melville, a year younger than Marx, had just bought a farm in Massachusetts. He had been in London in 1849, but did not return until 1857 – when he did in fact visit the Crystal Palace, but after its move to Sydenham. His book *The Whale* appeared in London on 18 October 1851, in three volumes. On 14 November 1851, it was published in New York in one volume under the title *Moby-Dick*. So, it is plausible that he could have come to London in connection with the promotion of his book in October 1851.

I suggest that Semper might have opened the discussion with a frontal attack on Paxton: "My dear Joseph, I have great respect for the efficacy of your work and for your meeting the deadlines. But Crystal Palace is not architecture – it is a glass-covered vacuum!" What would Paxton have responded? Was Semper being provocative because he had not received the commission for the interior decoration, which Paxton gave to Owen Jones? They could have started a conversation about greenhouses – after all, it was not only Paxton who had considerable experience with them; Semper had also built one at the villa of Conrad Hinrich Donner, a Hamburg merchant, in the mid-1830s. And in an essay on the Jardin d'Hiver in Paris published in 1849, Semper had dismissed its greenhouse architecture as being constructed in the "roughest and most primitive way" and in a "bare railway style".[2]

But the mid-nineteenth century was an age of controversy. Paxton therefore probably defended himself with a counter-attack:

"But Gottfried, what is your problem with a vacuum? Are you suffering from *horror vacui*, are you afraid of emptiness? Is this the reason why you cover every detail of your buildings over and over with ornamentation, works of art, reliefs? You should take care not to lose touch with your own time. One day you will see that it is precisely your fear of the vacuum that will marginalize you in the history of architecture".

This might have irritated Semper, because it touched a nerve. Was he, Semper, at all capable of producing a space of neutrality, a space that would be a backdrop, a stage *for* something else and not something that was staging *itself*, one might add? Was this the reason why he would not succeed in building an opera house for his friend Richard Wagner?

Melville (placing the three new volumes of *The Whale* on the table): "My dear Professor, it is precisely the vacuum that interests me. You know, I feel a great deal of sympathy for this building. In fact, Mr. Paxton and I are in some sense doing the same thing, only in a different medium. After years of travelling around the world on whaleboats, I was finally able to write my masterpiece within a very brief time".

Paxton: "Well said, my young friend. You wrote it almost faster than I built the exhibition hall – although I had much more help, an entire army of workers, many of them experienced in building railroads. But I agree with your viewpoint. Weren't our earlier works, your writing as well as my own greenhouse architecture, just fragments and preparations for something gigantic to come?"

Semper: "Fragments, yes. That is exactly the problem. Because they are not a *whole*. I hate to tell you, my young friend, but your book is really very long. I've started reading it, but I haven't finished yet. I counted 135 chapters. My English is still poor, but I am making a lot of progress with reading, and I have the impression that not much happens in your book. It is all about attempts to define the whale, to understand its anatomy, its metabolism, its movements. The book deals with the formlessness, the immensity of the whale and the ocean".

Melville: "I apologize for its length, Professor – my publisher and my father-in-law are also rather worried that it won't sell. But I am confident. The Crystal Palace contained more than 100,000 objects and was seen by several million visitors. Our age is an age of big numbers. It is about the encounter with the non-human, the sublime that eludes our capacity to grasp it". (Interestingly, Melville was to dislike the palace when he finally saw it in 1857. In his diary, he noted "overdone" and "smaller would look larger" and considered it a "vast toy – no substance".[3])

Paxton might now point to the glass ceiling. During the summer months, it had been covered with cloth in order to prevent too much heat developing. Now in October the temperature was lower, but the mysterious milky light that had fascinated so many observers still prevailed.

Paxton: "Never has so much space been surrounded by so little mass!" (He could not know that 150 years later the structure of Richard Rogers's Millennium Dome in London would weigh less than the air contained within the building.)

Melville: "A miracle, indeed. That's exactly what I was interested in when I was describing the contours of the whale. Looking for the outer limits of the whale, Ishmael, the main character in my book, describes the 'blubber' that envelops the whale in many layers. He identifies 'an infinitely thin, transparent substance', 'as flexible and soft as satin' that can be scraped off the dead body of a whale. Yet this mysterious substance also resists definition – Ishmael calls it 'the skin of the skin'".[4]

Semper: "I agree that membranes are key components of architecture, but they are meant to define space, not to become invisible. The 'skin of the skin' of your whale, my young friend, is in fact comparable to the glass sheet above our heads. The correspondent of 'The Times' was well aware of this phenomenon when he wrote on the occasion of the inauguration on 1 May 1851 that it was 'something more than sense could scan or imagination attain'".[5]

Paxton: "But that was meant as a compliment, Gottfried. My building had a good press. The 'Art Journal Catalogue' published another compliment by an author who stated that 'the effect of the interior of the building resembles that of the open air. It is perhaps the only building in the world in which *atmosphere* is perceptible'".[6]

Semper: "I hate to disappoint you, but I don't think that is a compliment".

This could have been the prompt Karl Marx was waiting for.

Marx: "I agree with my fellow German. To dissolve the clouds of ideology is the aim of my writing. Please allow me to quote from the *Communist Manifesto*, which I wrote with Friedrich Engels in 1848: 'Constant revolutionising of production, uninterrupted disturbance of all social conditions, everlasting uncertainty and agitation distinguish the bourgeois epoch from all earlier ones. All fixed, fast-frozen relations, with their train of ancient and venerable prejudices and opinions, are swept away, all new-formed ones become antiquated before they can ossify. All that is solid melts into air, all that is holy is profaned, and man is at last compelled to face with sober senses, his real conditions of life, and his relations with his kind'".[7]

Melville: "Bravo".

Marx: "The dynamics of capitalism tend to blur the phenomena, but the role of philosophy is to unveil the hidden truth and to help people to acquire sober senses".

Paxton: "I realize you didn't like the exhibition, and I'm grateful that you didn't smash the glass panes".

Marx: "I am not against your building".

Paxton: "But you are not *for* it either. I kept the article you wrote in the 'Neue Rheinische Zeitung'. Allow me to quote from it: 'For this exhibition they have summoned all their vassals from France to China to a great examination, in which they are to demonstrate how they have been using their time; and even the omnipotent tsar of Russia feels obliged to order his subjects to appear in large numbers at this great examination. This great world congress of products and producers ... is a striking proof of the concentrated power with which modern large-scale industry is everywhere demolishing national barriers and increasingly blurring local peculiarities of production, society and national character among all peoples. By putting on show the massed resources of modern industry in a small, concentrated space, just at a time when modern bourgeois society is being undermined from all sides, it is also displaying materials which have been produced, and are still being produced day after day in these turbulent times, for the construction of a new society. With this exhibition, the bourgeoisie of the world has erected in the modern Rome its Pantheon, where, with self-satisfied pride, it exhibits the gods which it has made for itself. ... The bourgeoisie is celebrating this, its greatest festival, at a moment when the collapse of its social order in all its splendour is imminent, a collapse which will demonstrate more forcefully than ever how the forces which it has created have outgrown its control. In a future exhibition the bourgeoisie will perhaps no longer figure as the owners of these productive forces but only as their ciceroni'".[8]

Melville and Semper: "Bravo!"

Semper: "That's exactly what I mean. You know, *mein lieber* Karl, back in Dresden, during the revolution in May 1849, I designed the barricades and then had to flee".

Marx: "Aha!"

Semper: "We are probably in the midst of a crisis".[9]

Marx: "*Certainly*, not *probably*..."

Semper: "Well, I am not sure if our societies are actually in a phase of collapse, or if the crisis is ephemeral. As an architect I have to be optimistic, although I can perceive the political and social trend towards disintegration. Nevertheless, I believe that those artists, especially in the applied arts, who are subject to the rules of industry become mere servants and lose their creative freedom. That is the situation of contemporary applied art, which despite its high technical level – in cutting stone, casting metal, cutting glass, etc. – is merely a pale echo of earlier times".

Paxton: "You are not an optimist; in reality you are a pessimist".

Semper: "And you are not an architect; you are a businessman".

Paxton: "We must not dissociate architecture from business".

Semper: "But design should be autonomous. I will be publishing a report soon; the draft is already finished – let me see if I can find it". (He shuffles some papers around.) "Here is a sentence that I am particularly proud of: 'The process that our industries and the whole of art will inevitably follow is clear: Everything will be designed for and tailored to the marketplace'".[10]

Paxton: "What's wrong with the market?"

Marx (peering up at the branches of the elm tree): "I could tell you, but we would need a lot more time…"

Semper: "The market is running smoothly, but art is not. If machines take over the production of artefacts, the connection with human labour becomes lost. Joseph, I recall that you tried to hide the traces of labour. I wanted to come and watch how the workers were erecting the palace, but there was nothing to see. The first decision you took was to put a wooden fence around the construction site".

Paxton: "Well observed, Gottfried. But we used the wooden beams for the floor, so it disappeared".

Marx: "You are hiding the obscene nature of your building, with its roots in exploitation and primitive accumulation".

Melville: "You know what, Professor, you remind me of my character Captain Ahab. The same nostalgia for the past, the same pessimism, the same tragic attitude, always ruminating over the unbearable fate that modernity had torn apart the system he had believed in. The future, trust me, belongs to *entrepreneurs* such as our friend Paxton. If you remain tied to the past, you will be torn into an abyss of oblivion like my tragic hero".

Here we leave the participants in our imaginary conversation. It leaves many questions open. Was the Great Exhibition the cause of what happened later in the history of architecture; did it prefigure the course of architectural history; or was it instead a snapshot summing up a trend that had already started earlier? What if the Great Exhibition had never happened – would the history of art and architecture have taken a different path? What if it had been held in Paris rather than in London? What if Semper had been the architect, not Paxton? How would the work of Semper, of Paxton, and of Marx have developed without it? These are all speculations, but the ephemeral nature of the exhibition as such encourages one to speculate on what *might* have been. In any case, we can state that with this event and its enormous impact on visual culture, the issue of representation moved to the centre stage in architecture, economy, science, and culture in general. For a brief moment, the whole scale of society, economy, art, and science was made visible simultaneously at a single level of representation, in one space. Such a concurrence of factors had never arisen before, and it was never again repeated.

All four participants in the imaginary dialogue were at the peak of their careers. And they all were dealing with the challenges that industrialization and the division of labour were bringing to society, the arts, language, and mentalities. The strong influence that their work had on their contemporaries, as well as on later generations, is linked to the way in which all four of them contained contradictions and were marked by deep ambivalences. To some extent, it would even be possible to let them change roles in the imaginary dialogue. Semper's own writings and work are characteristic of this ambivalence and internal contradiction.

The conversation has been preserved for eternity in a photograph – or, to be more precise, a calotype. It shows the elm tree. The interlocutors were apparently moving

Fig. 1

61

about and are therefore invisible due to the long exposure time needed to capture pictures in the mid-nineteenth century. There is something melancholic in the image, which is also echoed in Semper's own account in *Wissenschaft, Industrie und Kunst* (*Science, Industry, and Art*), dated 24 November 1851: "Scarcely four weeks have passed since the close of the Exhibition, some wares still stand unpacked in the deserted halls of the Hyde Park building, and already public attention has turned away from this "world-renowned event" ["Welterscheinung"] toward other, perhaps more gripping events close at hand. None of the enthusiastic newspaper correspondents who on the opening day of the 'world market' proclaimed the inauguration of a new era any longer voice their opinion on the subject. Yet the stimulation the event has left behind still ferments in the pensive minds and aspiring hearts of thousands. The far-reaching consequences of this impulse cannot be measured". – And: "Likewise, a kind of Babel will be induced by the building of 1851, to which people of the world brought their products. This apparent confusion, however, is nothing more than the clear manifestation of certain anomalies within existing social conditions, whose causes and effects up to now could not be seen by the world so generally and so distinctly".[11]

_1. *Speech Given by Prince Albert at a Banquet at the Mansion House Held on 21 March 1849*, in T. Martin, *The Life of His Royal Highness the Prince Consort*, vol. 2, Appleton, New York 1877, pp. 203–6 (here p. 205, italics in original).

_2. G. Semper, *Ueber Wintergärten* (1849), in G. Semper, *Kleine Schriften*, edited by M. and H. Semper, Spemann, Berlin 1884; facsimile reprint: Mäander Kunstverlag, Mittenwald 1979, pp. 484–90 (here p. 484, my translation).

_3. "April 29th 30th–May 1st – Thursday, Friday & Saturday. – … Chrystal Palace – digest of universe. Alhambra – House of Pansi – Temple of –. &c &c &c. – Comparison with the pyramid. – Overdone. If smaller would look larger. The Great Eastern. Pyramid. – Vast toy. No substance. Such an appropriation of space as is made by a rail fence. Durable materials, but perishable structure. Can't exist 100 years hence. – Beautiful view from terraces of Chrystal Palace". J. Leyda (ed.), *The Melville Log: A Documentary Life of Herman Melville, 1819–1891*, vol. 2, Gordian Press, New York 1969, p. 576. Thanks to Michael Gnehm for this reference.

_4. H. Melville, *Moby-Dick; or, The Whale*, ed. by H. Beaver, Penguin Books, Harmondsworth 1972, Chapter 68: "The Blanket", pp. 411–14 (here pp. 411–12).

_5. Cited after J. McKean, *Joseph Paxton, Crystal Palace, London 1851*, in J. McKean, S. Durant, and S. Parissien, *Lost Masterpieces*, Phaidon, London 1999, unpaginated (here p. [32]).

_6. Cited after J. McKean, *Joseph Paxton*, see note 5, p. [32] (italics in original). The twenty-year-old Richard Lucae, later known as architect of the Frankfurt Opera and a colleague of Semper, would state that – unlike a train station, which "in the strict sense of art was not yet a completed space", the magic of the Crystal Palace lay in the fact that "we are in an artificial environment that *was no longer a space*". He observed that if "we could pour air like a liquid", it would give the impression of standing in a "piece of cut-out atmosphere". R. Lucae, *Ueber die Macht des Raumes in der Baukunst*, "Zeitschrift für Bauwesen", 19, 1869, cols. 293–306 (here col. 303, my translation and italics).

_7. K. Marx and F. Engels, *Manifesto of the Communist Party* (1848), trans. S. Moore, in K. Marx, *The Revolutions of 1848: Political Writings*, vol. 1, Verso, London 2010, pp. 62–98 (here pp. 70–71).

_8. K. Marx and F. Engels, *Reviews from the "Neue Rheinische Zeitung Revue": Review: May–October 1850*, trans. P. Jackson, in K. Marx, *The Revolutions of 1848*, see note 7, pp. 285–318 (here pp. 294–95).

_9. G. Semper, *Der Stil in den technischen und tektonischen Künsten, oder Praktische Ästhetik*, vol. 1, 2nd ed., Bruckmann, Munich 1878, p. vii.

_10. G. Semper, *Science, Industry, and Art: Proposals for the Development of a National Taste in Art at the Closing of the London Industrial Exhibition (1852)*, in G. Semper, *The Four Elements of Architecture and Other Writings*, trans. H.F. Mallgrave and W. Herrmann, Cambridge University Press, Cambridge, MA 1989, pp. 130–67 (here p. 141).

_11. *Ibid.*, p. 130.

63

THE STRAND.—THE PROCESSION PASSING SOMERSET HOUSE.—THE SCOTS GREYS.—(SEE PAGE 475 OF SUPPLEMENT.)

London: Printed and Published at the Office, 198, Strand, in the Parish of St. Clement Danes, in the County of Middlesex, by WILLIAM LITTLE, 198, Strand, aforesaid. SATURDAY, NOVEMBER 27, 1852.

Mari Hvattum

"A Triumph in Ink": Gottfried Semper, "The Illustrated London News", and the Duke of Wellington's Funeral Car

_ Figure 1.
The Duke of
Wellington's funeral
procession passing
Somerset House,
illustration from "The
Illustrated London
News", no. 593, 27
November 1852 (©
Illustrated London
News Ltd. / Mary
Evans).

In a prescient passage from *In welchem Style sollen wir bauen* (1828), Heinrich Hübsch pondered the possibilities of a contemporary architectural style: "The buildings of the new style will no longer have an historical and conventional character, so that emotional response is impossible without prior instruction in archaeology: they will have a truly natural character, and the layman will feel what the educated artist feels".[1] Only by ridding architecture of its inherited store of forms and appealing directly to the layman's emotions could architecture once again become meaningful, Hübsch suggested. Gottfried Semper begged to differ. The historical styles, which for Hübsch were mere conventions, constituted for Semper meaningful links between the past and the present. Yet Semper did not escape Hübsch's dilemma altogether. In this chapter, I will investigate a brief but significant episode that propelled Semper into a battle over meaning, convention, and human emotions. It took place not within the confines of scholarly discourse but in the midst of popular culture and on the pages of the popular press. It was, in fact, one of the biggest media events of the nineteenth century, involving Semper himself, his London circle, and – to an overwhelming degree – the press. It was the Duke of Wellington's funeral.

Death of the Duke of Wellington

When he passed away on 14 September 1852, Arthur Wellesley, the first Duke of Wellington, was an unsurpassed national hero. Born in Ireland of minor nobility, Wellington long pursued a rather undistinguished military career. His rise to fame started in India around 1800, continued during the Napoleonic wars when he became the foremost British commander, and culminated with the defeat of Napoleon at Waterloo in June 1815. After retiring from the army, Wellington enjoyed a long career as a Tory politician. He was twice prime minister and an advisor to and confidant of the queen. By the 1840s, Wellington had become a superstar in the modern sense – a hero whose status depends on his or her augmented presence in the mass media. His star was particu-

THE ILLUSTRATED LONDON NEWS

No. 231—Vol. IX.]   FOR THE WEEK ENDING SATURDAY, OCTOBER 3, 1846.   [Sixpence.

COLOSSAL STATUE OF THE DUKE OF WELLINGTON—BY M. C. WYATT, Esq.

Fig. 2

_ Figure 2.
The Wellington monument from 1846, erected on top of the Wellington Arch at Hyde Park Corner, illustration from "The Illustrated London News", no. 231, 3 October 1846 (© Illustrated London News Ltd. / Mary Evans).

larly high in the Tory-friendly illustrated press, which displayed an almost obsessive interest in Wellington himself and the innumerable Wellington monuments erected up and down the British Isles. The great equestrian statue erected at Hyde Park Corner in 1846 is a case in point. Cast in bronze from French canons confiscated at Waterloo, the giant monument was presented in several issues of "The Illustrated London News", showing its casting, construction, and mounting in meticulous detail. By the time of his death, then, the "Iron Duke", the "Hero of Waterloo", or – as "The Times" called him – "the perfect ideal of the Englishman",[2] had long been subject to a cult. And his funeral, "The Illustrated London News" promised its readers, would be "a public funeral, such as was never before seen or imagined in any other country".[3]

Preparations started immediately, both at court and in the press. Prince Albert himself took charge of planning the event, which was to comprise a lying-in-state at Walmer Castle; transferral of the body to Chelsea Hospital in London; and a grand funeral procession from St. James's Park to St. Paul's Cathedral. "The Illustrated London News" for its part prepared the audience for the spectacle by showing historical funeral processions – everything from the hearse of Sir Philip Sidney in 1586 to Lord Nelson's spectacular burial in January 1806 – but even more importantly by printing page upon page about Wellington and his achievements in weekly "Wellington Supplements". Running for the entire autumn of 1852, the supplements amounted to hundreds of pages of text and images. The series was an enormous success, allowing "The Illustrated London News" to increase its weekly print run from 130,000 to 150,000 copies.[4]

Despite the urgency of the occasion, things moved somewhat slowly at first. Only in mid-October 1852 was the Lord Chamberlain authorized by the queen to commission designs for a funeral car. "It is H. M. desire", it was stated, "that the funeral car should be made from drawings, which should do justice to the immense services of the illustrious individual and at the same time do credit to the taste of the artists of England".[5] The Lord Chamberlain first contacted Owen Jones and Digby Wyatt, but as both were abroad at the time, he approached Henry Cole at the

Government School of Design in South Kensington. Cole delegated the task to his art superintendent, Richard Redgrave, but also asked Semper – recently appointed tutor in the metal department – to prepare drawings for a funeral car.

As has often been noted, Semper's and Redgrave's accounts of the event differ quite a bit. Redgrave claimed that Semper's sketches were rejected by Prince Albert and that Semper ended up simply executing Redgrave's design. "[T]hough Semper carried it out, the full design was mine", he later noted in his diary.[6] Semper for his part indicated on several occasions that the car was designed in large parts by himself, recalling with somewhat ambiguous pride that he once "had the opportunity to execute a ... work for the funeral of our century's second greatest military commander".[7] The contradictory claims have caused debate among Semper scholars. In one of the few scholarly articles written on the funeral car, Leopold Ettlinger ascribes the total design to Semper on the grounds that "his sensitive character would have hardly allowed him to supervise a work designed by another artist".[8] Wolfgang Herrmann credits Semper with rather less bargaining power. A poor refugee with few connections and no steady position, Semper had to do what he was told, according to Herrmann, and in this case Redgrave had obviously been in charge.[9] Nineteenth-century accounts seem to support Herrmann. According to Henry Cole (an account repeated everywhere in the contemporary press), Redgrave made the overall design, while Semper was in charge of the construction and ornamentation of the lower part, i.e. the metal-clad carriage and the dais below the bier.[10] That does not mean that Semper merely executed Redgrave's design, however. Judging from the drawings as well as from the car itself, Semper was instrumental in shaping the overall result, but the process took place in close collaboration with others, both designers and manufacturers. Wellington's funeral car is perhaps best seen as the product of a debate – a debate between Redgrave, Cole, and Semper, but also of a wider argument played out in the public press. It was a discussion on how best to honour a national hero, but even more a deliberation over reality, history, and the limits of representation in the modern world.

67

Wellington's funeral car

According to the *Official Account of the Funeral Car of the Duke of Wellington*, printed in "The Illustrated London News" and several other papers, the main idea of the funeral car had been to "obtain soldier-like simplicity, with grandeur, solemnity, and reality. Whatever there is – coffin, bier, trophies, and metal carriage, are all real, and everything in the nature of sham has been eschewed".[11] "The Illustrated London News"'s full-page print allows us to scrutinize this 'reality'. On top, we see the mahogany coffin covered in crimson velvet, with Wellington's hat and sword.[12] The coffin rests on a wooden bier, with the gilded bearers' handles projecting from it. The bier is draped with black velvet embroidered with the duke's crest and baton. Silver lace fringing completes the drapery, across which runs the text "Blessed are the dead who die in the Lord". Like the rest of the textile arrangement, the drapery was designed by Octavius Hudson and made by students from the Female School of Ornamental Art.[13]

Fig. 3

The bier rests on a wooden platform or dais, decorated with gilded laurel wreaths inside of which are inscribed the names of the duke's victories. On each corner of the dais are depictions of Roman standards with laurel wreaths and emblems. Real trophies such as guns, spears, helmets, flags, and drums of Indian and French origin are placed around the platform, which in its turn rests on the actual carriage: 21 feet 4½ inches long and 10 feet 3½ inches wide, built in wood and cased in cast bronze, carried on six giant wheels.[14] The lavishly ornate bronze casing displays exotic foliage, ribbons, and swords, with lion heads placed around the guilloche-patterned rim and with a Roman helmet set above each wheel.[15] Between the wheels are framed sections containing figures of Fame and Victory holding laurel branches in their hands. The wheel bosses are made of massive bronze decorated with dolphins, foliage, and lion heads on the axle ends. At the very front of the car is a bronze bumper in the shape of the duke's coat of arms, framed by real spears, guns, and flags.[16]

While the official description emphasized the representational apparatus, the car was also an ambitious piece of technology, with intricate systems for turning, braking, and shock absorption. The bier was a vehicle in its own right, equipped, we are told, with four large wheels for manoeuvring inside St. Paul's. The dais was designed to rotate, apparently to facilitate the removal of the bier and coffin upon its arrival at the cathedral. The rotation circle can still be seen on top of the carriage.[17] The mechanism seems not to have worked to plan, for "The Illustrated London News" reported how the "assembled multitude watched, with curious interest, the exertions of the undertaker's assistants, which appeared to be of some little difficulty and intricacy, in the arrangement of machinery and draperies".[18] The whole funeral car weighed some eleven tons and was pulled by twelve black brewery horses draped in black velvet.[19] It was designed and constructed in only three

_ Figure 3.
The Duke of Wellington's funeral car, illustration from "The Illustrated London News", no. 591, 20 November 1852 (© Illustrated London News Ltd. / Mary Evans).

weeks, involving students and staff at South Kensington and numerous manufactories up and down the country.

There was also a canopy over the coffin – a florid affair in silver, silk, and Indian embroidery, carried by four halberds. It must have been an elaborate construction, for according to a contemporary description it was designed to be "lowered by Machinery in passing through Temple Bar".[20] In "The Illustrated London News" print, however, the canopy was left out. "The canopy has been omitted in our representation, by the wish of Professor Semper", it was announced somewhat bluntly in the middle of the official description.[21] Why did Semper meddle with the presentation of the car in the popular press? Did he want to make his own part of the design more visible, or was there something else at stake? I will turn to that in a moment, but first we need to follow the car on its one and only journey: the grand funeral procession that took place on Thursday, 18 November 1852.

Wellington's funeral procession

Whatever brought Semper to order the canopy to be removed – when the funeral car was revealed to the public in St. James's Park in the early morning of 18 November, the canopy was in place. "The Illustrated London News" described the moment:

69

> The twelve horses attached to the funeral car were now urged to a simultaneous effort, and the car was drawn from under the tent. Its ponderous weight is seen in the traces left by the wheels. But the horses walked away easily with their magnificent load. The Colonels carrying the bannerols now surrounded the car, and their gaily-painted flags, the rich bronze of the funeral car, the guilt bier, the trophies of modern arms, the canopy of silver and silk tissue, and the splendid crimson and gold of the coffin, relieved, by the brilliancy of their colours, the funeral black of the rich silk velvet pall, which is, moreover, powdered with silver heraldic collars. With such pomp and stateliness the mortal remains of the hero left the scene consecrated by his labours no less than by his victories.[22]

Fig. 1   The procession was very long, made up mainly of military battalions. From "The Illustrated London News"'s printed overview of the procession – a remarkable list reading like a plan drawing – we know that the funeral car came almost last, followed some metres further back by Wellington's horse, with the duke's boots dangling from the empty saddle.

From the Horse Guard in St. James's Park, the procession went up past Buckingham Palace to Hyde Park Corner and through the Wellington Arch with the gigantic equestrian statue of the duke towering above. For a moment, the procession faced Apsley House – Wellington's London residence – before turning down Piccadilly, St. James's Street, Pall Mall, and the Strand, through Temple Bar, and across Ludgate Hill, before finally ending up at St. Paul's Cathedral. One and a half million people watched the procession, making it the largest spectacle in nineteenth-century Britain – bigger than any single event at the Great Exhibition.[23]

"The Illustrated London News" covered every metre of the event. In a minute-by-minute account, it described the mood, the music, and the crowds; the suspense when the unwieldy vehicle became stuck in the mud; the relief when it was pulled loose. The report was interspersed with tales from the duke's historical victo-

_ Figure 4.
The Duke of Wellington's funeral procession along the Strand, illustration from "The Illustrated London News", no. 594 ("Wellington Supplement"), 27 November 1852. Notice the "Illustrated London News" inscribed on the left façade (© Illustrated London News Ltd. / Mary Evans).

ries and with lavish full-page and double-page prints of the procession as it moved through the city. The scenes were depicted from a raised viewpoint, displaying both the procession and the urban streetscape to maximum advantage. Widening the streets and applying considerable artistic licence to tidy up London's urban grit, "The Illustrated London News"'s anonymous artists gave the English capital a thorough pictorial makeover.

Wellington's funeral was a carefully choreographed journey from the medieval Walmer Castle, via Charles Robert Cockerell's lavish design for the lying-in-state at Chelsea Hospital, the procession's slow movement through the Wellington Arch to Christopher Wren's Temple Bar – the traditional ceremonial entrance into the City – and finally to St. Paul's Cathedral. Describing and depicting this journey in painstaking detail, "The Illustrated London News" recast London as an imperial capital. As the editors enthused: "England's metropolis – vast, populous, mighty London – empress of modern cities – the huge living wonder of the nineteenth century – never before presented a scene so amazing to men of other lands or even to her own sons".[24] "The Illustrated London News" was itself part of this "living wonder". The careful observer can make out the magazine's name across one of the façades in The Strand, a building that was indeed "The Illustrated London News" headquarters. The insertion was more than an in-house joke. It was the new media – not just as observer, but as participant – that was charged with transforming the chaotic nineteenth-century city into a state of urban order. An event such as Wellington's funeral was a way of doing that. On the pages of the illustrated press, as Peter Sinnema has argued, the duke's funeral became a vehicle for re-narrating that city, re-enacting and consolidating the nation's glory and victory.[25]

Fig. 4

Harnessing history

Back to the question: Why did Semper insist on omitting the canopy in "The Illustrated London News"? Did he simply not like it, or were there more fundamental reasons for his editorial intervention? To answer this question, it is necessary to return to the *Official Account*'s insistence on the funeral car's 'reality': "Whatever there is – coffin, bier, trophies and metal carriage, are all real, and everything in the nature of sham has been eschewed".[26] The point was elaborated by Henry Cole in a public lecture given on 24 November, only a few days after the funeral. The idea behind the car, Cole insisted, had been to avoid fake upholstery and make the duke's coffin "the principal object".[27] This took more than simply crafting the car from real materials, for as Cole saw it, "Truth in effect must arise from the perfect reality of all the attendant circumstances".[28] To be really real, the car had not only to display the duke's coffin but to place it in a context in which the duke's achievements could be appreciated. It had to create the conditions in which the duke could be seen *in truth*, as it were. That was the car's mission, and this being the mid-nineteenth century, it was a mission to be fulfilled by means of history.

For what was the true context of the Duke of Wellington? Nineteenth-century England, to be sure, but just as much it was imperial Rome. Wellington was, after all, the conqueror of Europe's last, self-proclaimed emperor and had, as it were, written himself into an imperial context. Combining political and military leadership in an unprecedented way, Wellington seemed not only like the ideal Englishman but also the ideal Roman. "He was the Catullus of our Senate, after having been our Caesar in the field", wrote "The Times", calling Wellington by the Roman title *Parens Patriae*.[29] "The Illustrated London News" followed along the same line, casting the duke in an elaborate Roman setting. In the Wellington supplements, the duke was shown with an exaggerated Roman profile, his head encircled by a laurel wreath and surrounded by the spoils of war.

If Wellington were England's Caesar, then his funeral had to be a Roman event. Furthermore, it had to be not just a mourning of his death but a celebration of his victories. "[A]ll the decorations were emblematical of triumph, as well as of mourning", noted "The Illustrated London News" on the funeral decoration of the Temple Bar.[30] The same can be said for the procession itself, containing all the ingredients of a Roman triumph: the trumpeters, the brandishing of enemy arms, the ritual passage through triumphal arches (the Wellington Arch and Temple Bar), the

_ Figure 5.
Masthead to the "Wellington Supplement" of "The Illustrated London News", no. 580, 18 September 1852 (© Illustrated London News Ltd. / Mary Evans).

_ Figure 6.
The Duke of Wellington's
funeral procession passing
the Wellington Arch and
Apsley House, illustration
from "The Illustrated London
News", no. 594 ("Wellington
Supplement"), 27 November
1852 (© Illustrated London
News Ltd. / Mary Evans).

lavish carriage.[31] "The Illustrated London News" used the analogy for what it was worth, not only through images but through texts as well. The lyrical descriptions of the funeral procession ring heavy with classical precedents, adopting the rhythm and timbre of John Dryden's 1683 translation of Plutarch's *Life of Aemilius Paulus*, perhaps the most famous description of a Roman triumph ever written.[32]

The choice of Imperial Rome as an historical reference was a considered one. It resonated, as Sinnema points out, with a general British admiration for Roman culture and a widespread knowledge of classical art and literature among the middle and upper classes.[33] In the autumn of 1852 this symbolism took on a new urgency, however, for Wellington's funeral took place within weeks of the coronation of Emperor Napoleon III in France. Louis-Napoléon had been president since the fall of the July Monarchy in 1848, but failing to be elected for a second term, he staged a *coup d'état* on 2 December 1851, the anniversary of the coronation of Emperor Napoleon I. While England was planning Wellington's funeral in the autumn of 1852, Louis-Napoléon made a triumphal tour of France, rallying for a second empire. "Nous avons partout enfin des ruines à relever, de faux dieux à abattre, des vérités à faire triompher. Voilà comment je comprendrais l'Empire, si l'Empire doit se rétablir", he proclaimed in Bordeaux on 9 October 1852.[34] To the French, this may have seemed like a promise (he was elected emperor by an overwhelming majority on 21–22 November 1852), but to the British it sounded very much like a threat. "The Illustrated London News" described the restoration of Bonapartism as "a reversal of the great work which made the Duke of Wellington so famous" and commented glumly on the "accidental coincidence" that the funeral of Napoleon's eradicator should take place at the same time as the coronation of Napoleon's succes-

Fig. 6

sor.[35] The elaborate romanization of Wellington was part of this political impasse. After all, what could counter the threat of a new French emperor more effectively than to conjure up, symbolically, an emperor of one's own?

By means of imperial paraphernalia, Plutarch pastiches, and general references to Roman triumphs, London – on the pages of the illustrated press – was transformed into a second Rome. The city was even made to look like Rome. "The Illustrated London News"'s panoramas emulated famous prints of Rome, as in the way the raised view of the funeral procession turning down Piccadilly from under the Wellington Arch evokes views of the Roman Forum seen from the Capitoline Hill.[36] With the Wellington monument framing and heightening the urban scene below, Piccadilly was transformed into London's Via Sacra.

It was to this historically and politically saturated reality that Henry Cole was appealing when he insisted that the funeral car be "real". Rather than simply mourning a dead hero, England wanted to celebrate its heroic victories – a purpose for which the Roman triumph was expressly designed. Cole's proud announcement leaves no doubt as to how the commission was understood: "We were asked by the Lord Chamberlain to suggest a design for a triumphal car".[37]

Semper's triumphal car

Fig. 7

The task facing Semper and Redgrave in late October 1852, then, was to create not simply a funeral hearse but a Roman triumphal car. They approached the commission in very different ways. Redgrave's earliest sketch shows a simple car with a low bier covered with a textile canopy structured by two crossing halberds. There is nothing triumphal about it; rather, it fits into a long tradition of canopied funeral cars known from antiquity, through the Middle Ages, and well into modern times.[38] Redgrave's

_ Figure 7.
Richard Redgrave, first proposal for the Duke of Wellington's funeral car, October 1852 (© Victoria and Albert Museum, London).

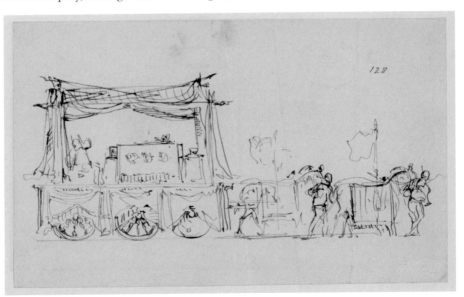

second sketch (presumably the one shown to Prince Albert) is somewhat more festive; the six-wheeled carriage covered with arms clearly induces triumphal associations. The textile canopy held by four upright halberds breaks the spell, however. A distinctly unclassical weapon, the halberd is associated primarily with late medieval Switzerland.[39] It can be seen in depictions of festive processions in the Middle Ages and the Renaissance – for instance Maximilian I's famous (and fictitious) triumphal procession.[40] In a Roman triumph, however, the halberd would never have been seen – it simply did not exist.

Semper's own proposals were loyal to Cole's demand for a triumphal car. In a series of sketches made before the momentous meeting with Prince Albert, we can follow Semper's efforts to merge the type of the triumphal car with the requirements of a contemporary funerary arrangement.[41] His earliest sketch shows a four-wheeled metal-cased carriage with candelabras in each corner. The dais, bier, and coffin are covered with a canopy whose rigid roof is supported not with halberds but with six slender posts. With laurel wreaths attached at the capitals and human figures holding each post at the base, the scene evokes the standard-bearers from Roman triumphal depictions. Similar references are at play in another of Semper's sketches, showing a textile canopy carried by spears adorned by laurel wreaths. In yet another proposal, the canopy was replaced by drapery loosely arranged over the coffin, with the duke's spear, sword, and hat placed on top. The proposal that Semper himself seems to have favoured – or at least it was selected for presentation in the posthumously published *Die Bauten, Entwürfe und Skizzen* (1881) – was a project with no canopy whatsoever. The lower part is very similar to what was actually executed: a bronze-clad carriage and a gilded dais, adorned with trophies. Instead of halberds, however, Semper surrounded the bier with four candelabras. Presumably intended

Fig. 8

Fig. 9

Fig. 10

Fig. 11

Fig. 12

74

_ Figure 8.
Richard Redgrave, proposal for the Duke of Wellington's funeral car, October 1852, in private ownership (© Bonhams).

_ Figure 9.
Gottfried Semper, proposal for the Duke of Wellington's funeral car, October 1852 (Courtesy of the Museum für Kunst und Gewerbe Hamburg).

_ Figure 10.
Gottfried Semper, proposal for the Duke of Wellington's funeral car, October 1852. Below right is written in pencil "Redgrave design", presumably making this Semper's elaboration of Redgrave's initial sketch (© Victoria and Albert Museum, London).

76

to hold torches, the candelabras would preclude any kind of canopy,[42] presenting instead a composition that united triumphal and funerary traditions.

Where did Semper find his precedents for merging the triumph and the funeral? In *Der Stil* he mentions Alexander the Great's funeral car – a primary example, as Ettlinger notes, of this particular combination.[43] Semper's low-set carriage, with its massive wheels and lion-headed axle ends, certainly recalls Alexander's car as it had been reproduced by Quatremère de Quincy, for example.[44] Yet classical sources describe Alexander's funeral car as a moving building: an interior that concealed, rather than displayed, its precious charge.[45] Semper, on the other hand, was trying to make the duke's coffin "the principal object", as Cole put it. The Roman tradition was the obvious place to turn for examples of this.[46] As the classicist Mary Beard shows, the combination of triumph and funeral was not uncommon in Roman culture.[47] Augustus's famous grand funeral in 14 CE is an example of this, as is the ceremony for Augustus's stepson Drusus, whose body, as Seneca writes, "reached Rome in a procession which resembled a triumph".[48]

Semper knew this tradition well, both from classical literature and from his own stay in Rome. He might also have known Johann Christian Ginzrot's *Die Wagen und Fahrwerke der Griechen und Römer und anderer alten Völker*, published in 1817, in which the classical triumphal tradition was thoroughly documented.[49] In the London of 1852, however, the most obvious – and magnificent – example of a Roman triumph was even closer at hand. Andrea Mantegna's *Triumphs of Caesar* had hung at Hampton Court since the early seventeenth century. In 1838, Queen Victoria had opened

_ Figure 11.
Gottfried Semper, proposal for the Duke of Wellington's funeral car, October 1852 (Courtesy of the gta Archives/ETH Zurich).

_ Figure 12.
Gottfried Semper, proposal for the Duke of Wellington's funeral car, October 1852, plate from G. Semper, *Die Bauten, Entwürfe und Skizzen*, 1881 (Courtesy of the gta Archives/ETH Zurich).

BESTATTUNGSWAGEN DES HERZOG VON WELLINGTON.

LONDON 1852

Fig. 13

Fig. 14

Hampton Court to the public, free of charge, and the *Triumphs* were well known to the London populace.[50] The fact that Mantegna paid tribute to Caesar's victory over the Gauls must have made it a particularly suitable tribute to a man who had defeated a French emperor.[51]

Semper's design for Wellington's funeral car does indeed seem to echo Mantegna. The low-set hull against the massive wheels resembles that of Mantegna's Caesar, a similarity heightened by the ornamental axle ends and the lavishly adorned wheel bosses. While the hull of Caesar's carriage (at least in the painting's present state) is without adornment, another carriage in Mantegna's procession appears to be made of cast or embossed bronze with plant ornaments, not unlike Semper's bronze foliage. Caesar's carriage, moreover – like most other Roman triumphal cars – has no canopy. Instead, the emperor is shielded with palm branches and a laurel wreath, both signifying victory. Wellington's car had similar attributes, for not only was it decorated with victory emblems in bronze and textiles, but also with real laurel, cypress, and branches of date palm, laid out on top of the coffin and bier. "The Illustrated London News" vividly relates the difficulty in procuring palm branches in London in mid-November: "It may be interesting to note that in obtaining this palm – the true date-palm that grows about Jerusalem – there was much difficulty, and it was only through the kindness of Sir William Hooker that a supply was obtained from the only available source – the gardens at Kew".[52] Piecing together funerary and triumphal iconography from the classical tradition, Semper aligned with Cole and "The Illustrated London News" in making Wellington's funeral a classical triumph, reinterpreted for

the modern age. Tying a contemporary event to a larger historical continuum by means of style, Semper sought – as he always did – motifs that carried echoes of the past while at the same time being capable of facilitating the needs of the present. This may be at least part of the reason why the canopy had to be removed. To Semper, Redgrave's halberds must have seemed out of place and out of time, anachronisms detracting from the reality of the funeral car.

_ Figure 13.
Andrea Mantegna, *The Triumphs of Caesar*, section 9, *Caesar on His Chariot* (Royal Collection Trust/ © Her Majesty Queen Elizabeth II 2016).

_ Figure 14.
Wellington's funeral car in the crowds, illustration from "The Illustrated London News", no. 594, 27 November 1852 (© Illustrated London News Ltd. / Mary Evans).

78

WELLINGTON'S FUNERAL CAR.

Crisis of representation

The story could have ended there. If it had, Semper would have come out the hero. Drawing on his in-depth knowledge of classical art, Semper sought an historically correct triumphal car, far superior to Redgrave's clumsy hybrid. That is at least how Ettlinger presents the case.[53] The story has another twist, however, hinging on the car's reception. For despite the efforts involved in its execution and the fervour of its public dissemination, Wellington's funeral car was pretty much a fiasco. Charles Dickens, for one, deemed it unsurpassed in "ugliness, horrible combinations of colour, hideous motion, and general failure".[54] Similar verdicts were rife. A friend of Wellington described it as too "frightful" for words, while Charles Greville – whose mother was reputed to have been the mistress of the duke himself – reviled it as "tawdry, cumbrous, and vulgar".[55] Even Henry Cole had to conclude that despite high aspirations, the venture had failed. In the public lecture of 24 November 1852, printed in part in "The Illustrated London News" a few days later, a dejected Cole stated:

> Although the car was essentially a reality in its materials, it was, perhaps, less a reality viewed on true aesthetic principles than a simple bier borne by soldiers would have been, and less impressive than the Duke's horse with the dangling empty boots. Truth in effect must arise from the perfect reality of all the attendant circumstances. Triumphal cars belong to a past age – the artilleryman's gun-carriage, or the soldiers themselves, carry their comrade to the grave in these days.[56]

79

Cole's self-critical rumination questions not only the funeral car but nineteenth-century beliefs in historical representation. While the aim of the whole enterprise had been to achieve reality, reality itself had somehow slipped away in the attempt. Truth, it seemed, had been obscured by the representational apparatus meant to ensure it. But why? The designers had, after all, applied a well-tested formula for such occasions, namely using a stylistic apparatus to link a contemporary event to an historical tradition, in this case the tradition of imperial Rome. Enormous efforts had been made to get it right, not only by commissioning the foremost designers in the country but also through the formidable production apparatus that had been set in motion. Cole recounts how the bronze foundry workers "had not had their clothes off their backs" for days and weeks and how the helmets and the lion heads on the lower car had to be remodelled several times to get the desired result.[57] After the application of so much talent, skill, and effort, why had it failed?

Cole's answer was as simple as it was radical: modern reality is beyond conventional representation. Echoing Hübsch's lament a quarter of a century earlier, Cole concluded that truth in the modern world could no longer be captured by means of a stylistic apparatus. Artistic truth arises from "the perfect reality of all the attendant circumstances", said Cole, intimating that when the attendant circumstances changed, the representational strategies manifesting them must change as well. Wellington's funeral took place on the cusp of such a change. The modern hero could no longer be absorbed into a conventional historicizing narrative but required different means of representation – a task that seemed better fulfilled by the duke's horse with the boots dangling from an empty saddle than by the funeral car. Both Cole himself and the press emphasized the sense of 'reality' emanating from

Fig. 15

THE DUKE'S HORSE, LED BY HIS GROOM.—(SEE PAGE 479.)

_ Figure 15.
The duke's horse in
the funeral procession,
illustration from "The
Illustrated London News",
no. 594, 27 November 1852
(© Illustrated London News
Ltd. / Mary Evans).

the image of the horse. Stripped of all representational pomp, the animal seemed to sum up the event in one natural, moving, and above all real image. "The Illustrated London News" described its effect on the crowds: "The suggestive picture formed by this mute mourner excited great sympathy along the line of route, and caused tears to spring unbidden from a thousand eyes, which had looked upon the long and princely train of mourning-coaches unmoved".[58] For Cole, as for Hübsch, modernity implied the collapse of conventional representation. It had instead to embrace the "influence of reality in all its complexity", as Hübsch put it, and seek "a truly natural character" comprehensible to the layman with no prior knowledge of historical codes.[59] To this sensibility, the ponderous monumentality of the funeral car was no longer relevant or comprehensible. A horse with dangling boots would do.

Semper never commented on the critique of the funeral car directly. In fact, judging from his remarks in *Der Stil*, he did not even acknowledge it as a failure.[60] Yet the representational collapse noted by Cole could nonetheless be said to have deep repercussions in Semper's thinking. A simple but all-encompassing question sums up his reflections on this issue: what makes artistic form meaningful? His answer is well known. For Semper, art appropriates ancient types and motifs, reworking them according to contemporary circumstance. Only by means of such timely reworking can art become "our own flesh and blood" – a meaningful, recognizable, and real phenomenon.[61] In some historical periods, however, the gradual transformation of ancient motifs into time-specific materials and techniques is interrupted. In such times, a more radical disintegration of old motifs is needed for art yet again to be meaningful. This is the point of the cosmic analogy appearing in a manuscript dating from Semper's first Zurich period, which ultimately entered the "Prolegomena" to *Der Stil*.[62] Art is in a state of transformation, Semper stated, and old form has to disintegrate before anything new can emerge.[63] That does not mean that history is to be rejected, however. As Semper made clear in his critique of contemporary "materialists", attempts to strip away conventional representation tend to lead to confusion, not to "natural" expression.[64] Semper believed neither in direct imitation nor blanket rejection of historical style. Rather, he believed in working the motifs of history so intensely that they became transformed into a relevant style for the present. His designs for Wellington show his struggle to do exactly that.

The necessity to disintegrate conventional representation lies at the heart of the dispute over the Duke of Wellington's funeral car and, in particular the discrepancy between Cole and Semper regarding the vehicle's ambiguous 'reality'. In his November lecture, Cole dismissed the conventional representation of the car in favour of the natural symbol of the horse. In this, he was aligned with Hübsch's dream of "natural character" – an artistic expression that was immediately comprehensible to everybody. For Semper, it was not quite as simple. Art, he famously pointed out, relies on masking, on "the destruction of reality, of the material", if it is to emerge as a meaningful symbol.[65] Semper's solution was not to strip the car down to its material reality but to mask it, using an historically meaningful garb. In other words: he responded to Cole's demand for reality not by eliminating the mask but by executing it with greater historical consistency than Redgrave had done. To no avail. The symbolic apparatus evoked by Semper – though historically coherent – left the "thousand eyes" of the crowd unmoved.

81

A triumph in ink

Was it an inkling of this impending failure that made Semper intervene in "The Illustrated London News"'s presentation of the funeral car? Was he trying to ensure – so far as he was able – that the funeral car presented to "The Illustrated London News"'s million or so readers would be more real than the real thing? If so, his intervention could be seen as a testimony to the way in which new printed media was beginning to shape the possibilities of representation in mid-nineteenth-century Europe.

Wellington's death – like his life – was the ultimate media event. The one and a half million people who watched the funeral car passing on its way to St. Paul's had been prepared for the spectacle by newspapers and illustrated magazines. The reality to which Henry Cole appealed, then, was not first and foremost a reality of material facts but a mediated reality, constructed and disseminated on the pages of the public press. The funeral car was part of that precarious construction. Establishing an historical context and lineage for the duke's achievements, the car was part of an effort to make sense of a turbulent contemporary world. When it failed, it was perhaps because the new, mediated reality required new means of representation, means that – as Hübsch had predicted many years before – shunned conventional symbols, appealing instead directly to the spectator's emotions. The car was a failure not, as later critics have claimed, because it was a stylistic hybrid but because a conventional stylistic apparatus in itself was becoming problematic in a world of individualized, mediated reception. Conceived and experienced in the popular press, Wellington's funeral car was – much like historicism itself – made and unmade in print. Even as a failure, then, it was indeed a "triumph in ink".[66]

_1. H. Hübsch, *In What Style Should We Build?*, in *In What Style Should We Build? The German Debate on Architectural Style*, introduction and trans. W. Herrmann, Getty Center for the History of Art and the Humanities, Santa Monica, CA 1992, pp. 63–101 (here p. 99).

_2. "The Times", 18 September 1852, p. 3, cited after H. Garlick, *The Final Curtain: State Funerals and the Theatre of Power*, Rodopi, Amsterdam 1999, pp. 93, 106.

_3. "The Illustrated London News", 21, no. 579, 18 September 1852, p. 214. See also H. Garlick, *Final Curtain*, see note 2, pp. 106–7.

_4. See C. Hibbert, *The Illustrated London News: Social History of Victorian Britain*, Angus & Robertson, London 1976, p. 13.

_5. The Lord Chamberlain to Owen Jones, 19 October 1852, cited after L. Ettlinger, *The Duke of Wellington's Funeral Car*, "Journal of the Warburg and Courtauld Institutes", 3, no. 3–4, April–July 1940, pp. 254–59 (here p. 256).

_6. R. Redgrave, *A Memoir, Compiled from his Diary by His Daughter, Miss F.M. Redgrave*, Cassell, London 1891, p. 100. Redgrave wrote that both his own and Semper's sketches were presented to Prince Albert by Henry Cole during a meeting at Windsor Castle in late October 1852: "Cole told the Prince that he thought the finest thing would have been, to have carried the Duke up from Walmer by soldiers, making several days' march of it; but he then showed first Semper's two sketches. The Prince looked at them, talked of those he had already seen (Banting's), and listened attentively to our idea of making the car a solid, substantial thing, rather than a piece of upholstery. I then unrolled my little sketch, and the Prince at once said, 'This is the thing!'" (*ibid.*, p. 101). Further on in his memoirs, Redgrave elaborated – somewhat patronizingly – on Semper's role: "This *mêlée* of interests makes the completion of the car in the time a perfect wonder. To render it at all possible it was necessary to prepare the work so that it might be placed in the hands of several metal founders at the same time ... Now it was that Semper's great talent came into action; he was incessantly employed, night and day, until the completion of the car, and he ought to have every credit for the details and the carrying out" (*ibid.*, p. 102). See also H. Garlick, *Final Curtain*, see note 2, p. 120; L. Ettlinger, *Duke of Wellington's Funeral Car*, see note 5, p. 256.

_7. G. Semper, *Style in the Technical and Tectonic Arts; or, Practical Aesthetics*, introduction by H.F. Mallgrave, trans. H.F. Mallgrave and M. Robinson, Getty Research Institute, Los Angeles 2004, p. 448, note 207; see also *ibid.*, note 215. Semper boasted about the "opportunity [that] presented itself, when I was entrusted with the execution of the metal works of the funeral car of the late Duke of Wellington. Two modellers, Mr. Whittaker and Mr. Wills, executed in common with myself and after my working-drawings, the models of the ornamental posts of the car, and were afterwards employed in inspecting the operations of moulding and chasing the bronze casts. A third student of Somerset House, was afterwards employed in chasing some parts of the ornaments of the car, which for want of time would not be finished before the funeral took place. One of the students so employed, has, in consequence of his share at this work, since been appointed as modeler in one of the great industrial establishments at Sheffield". G. Semper, *Report of Professor Semper on the Class for Practical Construction, Architecture, and Plastic Decoration*, in *First Report of the Department of Science and Art*, Eyre and Spottiswoode for Her Majesty's Stationery Office, London 1854, pp. 210–11, edited in *G. Semper, London Writings 1850–1855*, edited by M. Gnehm, S. Hildebrand, and D. Weidmann, gta Verlag, Zurich 2021.

_8. L. Ettlinger, *Duke of Wellington's Funeral Car*, see note 5, p. 257, note 4.

_9. W. Herrmann, *In Exile: Semper in Paris and London, 1849–1855*, in W. Herrmann, *Gottfried Semper: In Search of Architecture*, MIT Press, Cambridge, MA 1984, pp. 9–83 (here pp. 67–69).

_10. H. Cole, *Lecture Delivered on Wednesday Evening* [of 24 November 1852], "The Illustrated London News", 21, no. 593, 27 November 1852, p. 463: "The general design of the car was chiefly suggested by Mr. Redgrave; but the successful realisation of the structure, with its ornamental details, was due to the ability of Professor Semper". This passage in the context of the whole lecture in H. Cole, *An Introductory Lecture on the Facilities Afforded by the Department of Practical Art, to All the Classes of the Community for Obtaining Education in Art, 24 Nov. 1852*, in *Addresses of the Superintendents of the Department of Practical Art, Delivered at Marlborough House*, Chapman and Hall, London 1853, pp. 3–38 (here p. 31). Cited also in W. Herrmann, *In Exile*, see note 9, p. 68.

_11. *Official Account of the Funeral Car of the Duke of Wellington*, "The Illustrated London News", 21, no. 591, 20 November 1852, p. 439.

_12. For an illustration of the coffin alone, see *The Duke's Coffin*, "The Illustrated London News", 21, no. 591, 20 November 1852, p. 456.

_13. *Official Account of the Funeral Car*, see note 11, p. 439; H. Cole, *Introductory Lecture*, see note 10, pp. 30–31.

_14. The measurements vary with different sources. Here I rely on *Description. The Funeral Car: Field Marshal the Late Duke of Wellington, R.S.*, 1852, Stratfield Saye Archives, Research Collection 6.1.6, *Description of 1st Duke of Wellington Funeral Carriage*. The car as a whole measured, according to "The Illustrated London News", 27 feet long, 10 feet broad, and 17 feet high. *The Grand State Funeral of Arthur Duke of Wellington*, "Wellington Supplement to the Illustrated

London News", 21, no. 594, 27 November 1852, pp. 470–86 (here p. 475).

_15. B. von Orelli-Messerli, *Gottfried Semper (1803–1879): Die Entwürfe zur dekorativen Kunst*, Imhof, Petersberg 2010, p. 214, writes that the carriage is clad in sheet iron (*Eisenplatten*). As both the car itself and the primary sources testify, this is not correct: all of the decorative metalwork was made of cast bronze.

_16. The car can still be seen at Stratfield Saye, the Duke of Wellington's estate in Hampshire. Many thanks to Jane Branfield and Derrick Goddard for their assistance during my visit to Stratfield Saye in October 2015.

_17. "The Dais was constructed to turn on a centre Axis so that on its arrival at St. Paul's, the Bier which stood on it might be moved into the Cathedral". *Description: The Funeral Car*, see note 14.

_18. *The Duke of Wellington's Funeral – The Procession and Funeral Obsequies*, "The Illustrated London News", 21, no. 591, 20 November 1852, pp. 431–35 (here p. 434).

_19. The weight estimates vary considerably, ranging from six to eighteen tons. Richard Redgrave, for instance, wrote in his diary that the car weighed "between six and seven tons" (R. Redgrave, *Memoir*, see note 6, p. 105), while the plaque accompanying the car at its present Stratfield Saye exhibit describes it as "weighing eighteen tons". Here I use the estimate in *Grand State Funeral of Arthur Duke of Wellington*, see note 14, p. 475.

_20. *Description: The Funeral Car*, see note 14.

_21. *Official Account of the Funeral Car*, see note 11, p. 439. The fact that Semper had the authority to intervene in this way is interesting and prompts further investigation into Semper's contacts in "The Illustrated London News".

_22. *Grand State Funeral of Arthur Duke of Wellington*, see note 14, p. 474.

_23. For a detailed account of the planning and organization of Wellington's funeral procession, see P.W. Sinnema, *The Wake of Wellington: Englishness in 1852*, Ohio University Press, Athens 2006, and H. Garlick, *Final Curtain*, see note 2.

_24. *Grand State Funeral of Arthur Duke of Wellington*, see note 14, p. 473.

_25. P.W. Sinnema, *Death and National Glory*, in P.W. Sinnema, *Dynamics of the Pictured Page: Representing the Nation in the Illustrated London News*, Ashgate, Aldershot 1998, pp. 180–203.

_26. *Official Account of the Funeral Car*, see note 11, p. 439.

_27. H. Cole, *Lecture Delivered on Wednesday Evening*, see note 10, also in H. Cole, *Introductory Lecture*, see note 10, p. 30.

_28. *Ibid.*, p. 31.

_29. "The Times", 15 September 1852, p. 4, cited after P.W. Sinnema, *Dynamics of the Pictured Page*, see note 25, p. 183 (written as "*Parens Patrie*").

_30. *Temble-Bar* [sic], *Decorated for the Duke's Funeral*, "The Illustrated London News", 21, no. 591, 20 November 1852, p. 430.

_31. On the Roman triumphal tradition, see M. Beard, *The Roman Triumph*, Belknap Press of Harvard University Press, Cambridge, MA 2007.

_32. Plutarch, *Life of Aemilius Paulus* (ca. 75 CE), with the Dryden translation published in numerous versions; see, for example, *Plutarch's Lives: The Translation Called Dryden's*, ed. by A.H. Clough, vol. 2, Little, Brown, and Company, Boston 1859, pp. 155–97 (esp. pp. 188–92).

_33. P.W. Sinnema, *Dynamics of the Pictured Page*, see note 25, pp. 183–86.

_34. Louis-Napoléon's speech of 9 October 1852 in Bordeaux, published for example in "L'Illustration", 20, no. 503, 16 October 1852, pp. 241–42 (here p. 242).

_35. *Wellington's Work: Has It Been Neutralised by the Revival of Bonapartism?*, "The Illustrated London News", 21, no. 589, 13 November 1852, pp. 393–94 (here p. 393).

_36. I am indebted to my colleague, Professor Victor Plahte Tschudi, for this observation.

_37. H. Cole, *Lecture Delivered on Wednesday Evening*, see note 10, also in H. Cole, *Introductory Lecture*, see note 10, p. 29.

_38. See J.C. Ginzrot, *Der Leichenwagen*, in J.C. Ginzrot, *Die Wagen und Fahrwerke der Griechen und Römer und anderer alten Völker*, vol. 2, Cotta, Stuttgart 1817, pp. 91–118.

_39. See J. Waldman, *Hafted Weapons in Medieval and Renaissance Europe: The Evolution of Staff Weapons between 1200 and 1650*, Brill, Leiden 2005 (esp. pp. 17–32, chapter on "Halberds"). See also E.A. Gessler, *Das Aufkommen der Halbarte von ihrer Frühzeit bis zum Ende des 14. Jahrhunderts*, in *Aus Geschichte und Kunst: Zweiunddreissig Aufsätze: Robert Durrer zur Vollendung seines sechzigsten Lebensjahres dargeboten*, Hans von Matt, Stans 1928, pp. 127–46.

_40. See, for example, H. Burgkmair, *Triumph of the Emperor Maximilian I* (commissioned 1512, made ca. 1516–19), Victoria and Albert Museum, London, Museum no. 2904: 106. See also the woodcut by Wolf Huber for the Triumphal Arch of Maximilian (1512–15), in private ownership, printed in J. Waldman, *Hafted Weapons*, see note 39, p. 65, fig. 61. A version of the latter image, but attributed to Wolf Traut, can be seen at Albertina, Vienna, object no. DG1935/979/16. For a thorough overview of the depiction of halberds in medieval and Renaissance art, see *ibid.*, pp. 33–62 (chapter on "Extant Examples of Halberds").

_41. Semper's drawings for the funeral car are presented in B. von Orelli-Messerli, *Gottfried Semper*, see note 15, pp. 210–35. The date of Cole and Redgrave's meeting with Prince Albert has been subject to some confusion. Redgrave writes in his memoirs that the department was commissioned on Thursday 22 October 1852, and that the meeting with Prince Albert took place on Satur-

83

day 24 October; R. Redgrave, *Memoir*, see note 6, pp. 100–102. However, 22 October 1852 was a Friday, not a Thursday, throwing some doubt on the exact date of the meeting. Given Redgrave's emphasis on the weekdays (that the commission was received on a Thursday and that the meeting took place on a Saturday), it seems likely that the days are correct but that Redgrave misremembered the dates. This is also Ettlinger's assumption, when he writes that the department was approached on 21 October and that the meeting took place on 23 October – i.e. Thursday and Saturday, respectively; L. Ettlinger, *Duke of Wellington's Funeral Car*, see note 5.

_42. I am indebted to Michael Gnehm for this observation.

_43. G. Semper, *Style*, see note 7, pp. 299–300, with notes 204–7. L. Ettlinger, *The Duke of Wellington's Funeral Car*, see note 5, pp. 254–55, 257, 258–59.

_44. A.-C. Quatremère de Quincy, *Monuments et ouvrages d'art antiques restitués*, Renouard, Paris 1829. Semper refers to this work in *Style*, see note 7, p. 448, note 204. See also L. Ettlinger, *Duke of Wellington's Funeral Car*, see note 5, p. 258.

_45. The Greek historian Diodorus Siculus describes Alexander's funeral car as a chariot covered with "a vault of gold, eight cubits wide and twelve long, covered with overlapping scales set with precious stones. Beneath the roof all along the work was a rectangular cornice of gold, from which projected heads of goat-stags in high relief". Diodorus of Sicily, *The Library of History*, vol. 9, trans. R.M. Geer, Heinemann, London 1947, p. 89 (Book XVIII, chapter 26). In addition to Diodorus and Quatremère de Quincy, Semper also refers to A. Hirt, *Geschichte der Baukunst* (1821–27) in connection with Alexander's burial; G. Semper, *Style*, see note 7, p. 448, note 204.

_46. Semper touches on the triumphal tradition several times in *Der Stil* and refers frequently to the Jewish first-century CE historian Flavius Josephus, who was one of the authoritative chroniclers of the triumphal ceremony. See, for example, *Style*, see note 7, pp. 288–90.

_47. For the fusion of funeral and triumph, see M. Beard, *Roman Triumph*, see note 31, esp. pp. 280–86 (chapter on "The Triumph of Death").

_48. Lucius Annaeus Seneca, *To Marcia: On Consolation*, in Seneca the Younger, *Minor Dialogs: Together with the Dialog "On Clemency"*, trans. A. Stewart, Bell, London 1900, pp. 162–203 (here p. 166). See also M. Beard, *Roman Triumph*, see note 31, p. 286.

_49. J.C. Ginzrot, *Wagen und Fahrwerke*, see note 38, p. 100 and plate 52A. Some of Semper's sketches resemble those found in Ginzrot – for instance, in the way the stepped figure of the car, dais, bier, and coffin resemble the ziggurat shape of a Roman funeral pyre. See gta Archives/ETH Zurich, 20-108-4.

_50. Mantegna's *Triumphs* are included for ex-

ample in Edward Jesse's popular 1842 guidebook to Hampton Court Palace. Jesse describes the *Triumphs* as hanging in the "Mantegna Gallery" and insists that "they demand and will repay attention". E. Jesse, *A Summer's Day at Hampton Court; Being a Descriptive Road-Book to the Palace, and a Guide to Its Picture Gallery and Gardens*, John Murray, London 1842, p. 102. The *Triumphs* are also mentioned in John Grundy's popular guidebook, published in numerous editions from the 1830s onwards. See, for example, J. Grundy, *The Stranger's Guide to Hampton Court Palace and Gardens*, Bell, London 1850, p. 52.

_51. See also P.W. Sinnema, *Wake of Wellington*, see note 23, pp. 75–76.

_52. *Grand State Funeral of Arthur Duke of Wellington*, see note 14, p. 475.

_53. L. Ettlinger, *Duke of Wellington's Funeral Car*, see note 5, p. 257: "Instead of a badly balanced structure Semper gave a superb severe car".

_54. C. Dickens to Miss Burdett Coutts, 19 November 1852 (the day after the funeral), cited after C. Dickens, *Selected Journalism 1850–1870*, ed. by D. Pascoe, Penguin, London 1997, p. 632, note 10. See also C. Dickens, *Trading in Death*, "Household Words", 27 November 1852, in C. Dickens, *Selected Journalism*, pp. 438–47.

_55. Lady de Ros, quoted in E. Longford, *Wellington*, vol. 2, Harper & Row, New York 1969, p. 403; C.C.F. Greville, *The Greville Memoirs (Third and Concluding Part): A Journal of the Reign of Queen Victoria from 1852 to 1860*, ed. by H. Reeve, Appleton, New York 1887, p. 6. Greville's description is interesting, as he goes quite some way to blame Semper for the fiasco: "November 21st. – I saw the Duke's funeral from Devonshire House. Rather a fine sight, and all well done, except the car, which was tawdry, cumbrous, and vulgar. It was contrived by a German artist attached to the School of Design, and under Prince Albert's direction – no proof of his good taste". C.C.F. Greville, *Memoirs*, pp. 6–7. See also H. Garlick, *Final Curtain*, see note 2, p. 120; P.W. Sinnema, *Wake of Wellington*, see note 23, p. 77.

_56. H. Cole, *Lecture Delivered on Wednesday Evening*, see note 10, also in H. Cole, *An Introductory Lecture*, see note 10, p. 31.

_57. *Ibid.*, p. 30.

_58. *Grand State Funeral of Arthur Duke of Wellington*, see note 14, p. 474.

_59. H. Hübsch, *In What Style Should We Build?*, see note 1, p. 99.

_60. G. Semper, *Style*, see note 7, p. 448, note 207, and p. 888, where the design for the funeral car's front bumper is shown with the caption "not built according to design owing to lack of time".

_61. G. Semper, *Science, Industry, and Art: Proposals for the Development of a National Taste in Art at the Closing of the London Industrial Exhibition (1852)*, in G. Semper, *The Four Elements and Other Writings*, trans. H.F. Mallgrave and W. Herr-

84

mann, Cambridge University Press, Cambridge, MA 1989, pp. 130–67 (here p. 144). See also M. Hvattum, *Gottfried Semper and the Problem of Historicism*, Cambridge University Press, Cambridge, MA 2004, p. 159.

_62. G. Semper, *A Critical Analysis and Prognosis of Present-Day Artistic Production* (ca. 1856/59), in W. Herrmann, *Gottfried Semper*, see note 9, pp. 245–60 (here p. 245); G. Semper, *Style*, see note 7, p. 71.

_63. G. Semper, *Critical Analysis*, see note 62, p. 253. This passage reiterates the one in Semper's *Science, Industry, and Art*, cited above, see note 61.

_64. G. Semper, *Critical Analysis*, see note 62, p. 255. Semper repeats the same critique in the "Prolegomena" to *Der Stil*; see G. Semper, *Style*, see note 7, pp. 77–78.

_65. G. Semper, *Style*, see note 7, pp. 438–39, note 85.

_66. I borrow this expression from M. Beard, *Roman Triumph*, see note 31, p. 330.

HANDBUCH
DER
ENGLISCHEN SPRACHE
UND LITERATUR,
oder

Auswahl interessanter chronologisch geordneter Stücke

aus den Klassischen Englischen Prosaisten u. Dichtern

Nebst Nachrichten von den Verfassern

und ihren Werken.

von H. Nolte und L. Ideler.

Ex ungue leonem.

Erster Theil.

Die Prosaisten,

von Bakon bis zum Schluss des 18ten Jahrhunderts.

Sechste, verbesserte und vermehrte Auflage.

Berlin, 1844,

in der Nauckschen Buchhandlung.

Dieter Weidmann

Gottfried Semper's "Broken English"

_ Figure 1.
J.W.H. Nolte and C.L.
Ideler, *Handbuch der
Englischen Sprache
und Literatur*, vol. 1,
6th edition, Nauck,
Berlin 1844, title
page (Courtesy
of Bayerische
Staatsbibliothek
München, L.g.sept.
45 s-1).

Against his original intentions, Gottfried Semper moved from Paris to London in 1850 for a period of nearly five years. While he was there, he had to speak and write in a language with which he was never to become wholly familiar. The manuscripts of the lectures he held at the Department of Science and Art in 1853 and 1854 show, however, that he was able to inventively compensate for his linguistic shortcomings and developed a kind of pidgin in which he mixed English not only with his mother tongue but also with other languages.

Linguistic backgrounds

From the age of three, Gottfried Semper grew up in the city of Altona, which at the time was ruled by Denmark but belonged to the German-speaking area.[1] From autumn 1819 to spring 1823, he learned Latin and ancient Greek at the Johanneum, Hamburg's oldest grammar school, earning the qualification "magnam literarum cupiditatem" from the school's headmaster.[2] Following a preparatory semester at the Akademisches Gymnasium in Hamburg, Semper began studies in mathematics and history at the University of Göttingen in October 1823.[3] In August 1824, he inquired through his former teacher, Carl Friedrich Hipp, whether he might be able to move to the Ecole Polytechnique in Paris.[4] Hipp informed him that the college did not accept any foreigners.[5] In December 1824, Semper wrote to his father: "I want … to go to Paris to spend six months partly to learn French thoroughly and partly to benefit from the academic teaching there".[6] Returning to the subject of the Ecole Polytechnique five months later, he asked his father again: "Could you … somehow get me reliable information about whether it would be possible for me to be accepted at the polytechnic institute in Paris – after a previous examination, of course? Some time ago you mentioned ancient national rights that I might be entitled to as a descendant of a French family; can you give me some *definite* information about that?"[7] As it turned out that his father had merely imagined that such nationality rights might exist – based on the fact that his wife was descended from French Huguenots – Semper abandoned his initial plan.[8] All the same, he moved to Paris, in his own words a "dung-heap and whore-house", in December 1826 to study architecture.[9] He was to remain in the French capital for a total of two years, interrupted by a two-year stay in Altona and Germany.[10]

In June 1830, Semper informed his mother that he was planning to travel "via Lyons through the south of France to Genoa and from there further into Italy".[11] When Paris became the scene of a brief revolution in the following month, his parents tried in vain to persuade him to travel to London, where several of their relatives and friends were staying.[12] His father encouraged him in particular "to take a look at the tunnel"[13] – meaning the Thames Tunnel, the construction of which had started in 1825. However, Semper replied in August 1830: "I shall not be going to England *under any circumstances*[.] … Even if London had ever so many cousins and relatives of all sorts thrice removed – and the same applies to business friends and tunnels – it wouldn't tempt me to go there, because I don't have any reason to go there and I can't bear the smell of coal smoke".[14] In September 1830, Semper started on a three-year study trip which would take him to the south of France, Italy, Sicily, and Greece.[15] In September 1834, he was appointed professor of architecture at the Academy of Art in Dresden.[16] Up to the time of his flight from Germany in June 1849 because of his involvement in the Dresden uprising,[17] he only crossed the German border three times, with the exception of a few trips to Altona: from December 1838 to February 1839, he travelled to view new theatre buildings in Belgium, southern England, France, and northern Italy;[18] in August and September 1844, he attended the third assembly of German architects and engineers in Prague;[19] and in September 1846, he returned to northern Italy to gather inspiration for the design of the Royal Picture Gallery in Dresden.[20]

Following his visit to London – which out of consideration for his companion on the journey, Wolf Adolph August von Lüttichau, the director of the Dresden Court Theatre, was limited to the short period from 14 to 20, 21, or 22 December 1838[21] – Semper reported to his brother Johann Carl: "Paris still seems like a nest of vipers when you arrive from London, but at least you can breathe clean air, speak a human language and manage to stay for four months without going bankrupt".[22] About ten years later, he would have to become accustomed to the inhuman English language becoming his everyday tongue. Only five days after his flight from Dresden, on 14 May 1849, he decided to emigrate to North America.[23] Out of concern for his family, however, he established himself provisionally in Paris,[24] where in June 1849 he declared: "Still, the language in America and in France will continue to be an obstacle to advancement".[25] In July 1849, he claimed: "I have a command of the pen in German and I know French and Italian. A little English as well, and also Latin and Greek".[26] Three months later, he put this more precisely: "I understand English, but do not speak it; however, the will and diligence to overcome this deficiency will not be lacking".[27]

How had Semper acquired his knowledge of English? His posthumous papers contain one fragment each of two manuscripts in which – if Wolfgang Herrmann's speculation is accurate – he recorded his "Dresden reference books" for customs purposes in 1852.[28] The longer fragment lists one book that suggests he had indeed attempted to learn English: Johann Christian Fick's *Praktische englische Sprachlehre für Deutsche beyderley Geschlechts*, the first edition of which had been published in 1793 and the twenty-second edition in 1846.[29] He had probably purchased the book in 1838 to prepare for his first journey to London.[30] The same fragment also suggests that he had hardly practised English in Dresden through reading literary or scientific texts, as it only contains a few English titles: M.A. Alderson's *An Essay on the Nature and Application of Steam*, Thomas Leverton Donaldson's *A Collection of the Most Approved Examples of Doorways*, and several issues of the "Transactions of the Royal Institute of British Architects".[31] In addition, it lists three volumes by British authors in German translation: the appendix volume by Charles Robert Cockerell and others to *The Antiquities of Athens* by James Stuart and Nicholas Revett, and a two-volume selection of plays by Ben Jonson and others.[32]

First steps towards learning English

Since Semper, while staying in Paris, never definitively abandoned his plan to emigrate to North America,[33] one can assume that he was trying to improve his knowledge of English already in his French exile. There is a lack of evidence that he read some relevant textbooks,[34] but he obviously consulted specialist journals and books in English for the first part of his work on "Comparative Architecture", which he drafted in Paris.[35] However, several of the books that he referred to in "Comparative Architecture" were available in German or French translation.[36]

After fifteen unsuccessful months in Paris, Semper decided to move to New York to join the office of the architect Karl Gildemeister, who was originally from Bremen.[37] On the eve of his planned departure on 19 September 1850, he received – through the assistance of Jacques Ignace Hittorff and Charles Séchan – a letter from Emil Braun, the secretary of the Instituto di corrispondenza archeologica in Rome.[38] Braun declared: "As an admirer of your fine talent and your splendid works, I would like to do everything possible to keep you here with us. I believe I am in a position to offer or at least to show you a field for your artistic activity that promises to be no less prestigious than the one you have left".[39] This uncertain prospect was enough to dissuade Semper from leaving, and after receiving a second letter, in which Braun outlined the field mentioned, he moved to London on 28 September 1850.[40]

The first surviving draft of an English letter written by Semper in London is addressed to Moses Montefiore, the president of the Committee of Deputies of British Jews. It reads: "Sir! I take leave to enclose the introductory note of Dr. Smith and shall feel highly honoured by your appointing whenever convenient a day for waiting upon you in person. I have the honour to sign myself Sir your obedient servant Gottfried Semper".[41] Since the draft does not contain any corrections, one can assume that Semper intended to send it in that form, but after receiving advice from a native speaker he ultimately replaced it with a letter that would be more easily understandable. Draft letters written to the secretaries of the Royal Institute of British Architects and to Edwin Chadwick indicate that during his initial weeks in England he did not write all of his letters alone: both drafts show the handwriting of Edward Falkener.[42]

Shortly after arriving in London, Semper began making efforts to improve his English by taking lessons from a certain R. Barton, who lived nearby.[43] This private tutor may have been Robert Barton, who in 1844, on the occasion of an exhibition of a model of Venice in the Egyptian Hall in Piccadilly, had translated Andrea Giordano's *Venezia nello autunno dell'anno 1838* into English and provided it with addenda.[44] Barton was probably also the translator of two books by the ballet dancer and choreographer Carlo Blasis, who had occasionally lived and worked in London.[45] Apart from these lessons, Semper followed the principle of learning by doing, although he took every opportunity to avoid using English. Between the autumn of 1850 and the summer of 1851, for example, he drafted three academic articles in French, intending to have them translated into English by Rachel Chadwick, the wife of his mentor, Edwin Chadwick, and probably by Edward Falkener, in whose office he initially had a study;[46] and in that same summer he was still communicating in French with Falkener and in German with Joanna Hilary Bonham Carter.[47] In an advertisement in which he offered his assistance to French industrialists in setting up their stalls at the Great Exhibition in London six months after his arrival in England, he claimed however to be able to speak and write French, English, German, Italian, modern Greek, ancient Greek, and Latin.[48]

90

A "natural way" to spoken English

When Semper accepted a professorship in the Department of Practical Art in September 1852, he also agreed to give occasional public lectures.[49] He did not have to hold any during the first term, but there was one in the second term, on 20 May 1853, and there were several in the third term.[50] The manuscript of his first public lecture starts with the following words: "Ladies and Gentlemen. A Foreigner must naturally feel very timid and embarrassed in addressing to You a paper written in broken English".[51] During revision, Semper crossed out the word "broken". Was this intended to suggest that he no longer thought his English was broken, or that he was assuming his audience would consider it broken anyway? In any case, he explained that his anxiety and embarrassment were also due to the subject matter.[52] He had indeed taken up a difficult topic. On the basis of Georges Cuvier's exhibition of fossilized and recent skeletons of animals in Paris, he attempted to persuade the audience of the advantages of comparison between older and newer works of art:

> A method, analogous to that which Baron Cuvier followed applied to art, and especially to architecture would at least contribute towards getting a clear insight over its whole province and perhaps also it would form the base of a doctrine of *Style*, and of a Sort of topic or Method, how to invent, which may guide us, to find out the natural way of invention which would be more than could be allowed to the great Naturalist to do for his sublime science.[53]

The audience probably found this sentence challenging, and not merely because of its length. The suggestion that Cuvier's comparative osteology might be transferred to the field of art in order to develop "a Sort of topic or Method, how to invent" was all the more difficult to understand in that the English word "topic" in the singular does not mean what Semper was trying to say, namely *topics*, a rhetorical theory on the inventive use of arguments and phrases.[54] Later in the lecture, Semper declared: "Every work of art is a *result*, or, using a Mathematical Term, it is a *Function* of an indefi[ni]te number of quantities or powers, which are the variable coefficients of the embodiment of it".[55] To illustrate this statement, he presented it – probably on the blackboard – as a mathematical equation: "$U = \Phi\, x, y, z, t, v, w$".[56] In the next sentence, linking the term "Style" to the equation made things even more difficult for the listeners.[57] Despite these complexities, his superior, Henry Cole – one of the two secretaries of the Department of Science and Art – considered that the lecture was "suggestive".[58]

In his second public lecture, given on 11 November 1853, Semper returned to the equation to discuss it in greater detail.[59] Anticipating the objection that he was mixing or confusing artistic and mathematical problems, he now observed that he was using the equation only "as a crutch for leaning on it in explaining the subject".[60] A sentence crossed out in the manuscript shows that it was ultimately because of his inadequate knowledge of English that he had decided to use the equation as a crutch: "I only wanted this general shedula as a crutch for leaning on it in explaining a subject which otherwise it would be difficult for me to explain as shortly and clearly in a liguage which I know but little".[61]

Two speculative questions regarding his spoken English arise here. In his manuscripts, Semper occasionally replaced the letter *c* in English words with a *k*. (Under the obvious influence of French, he did the opposite only in the word "Greec".[62]) Did he combine this use of *k* – in "kall", "skotch", and "Musik",[63] for example – with a correspondingly hard pronunciation? The second question involves words that were written completely wrong, such as "lath", "past", "angels", "rifles", "staffs", and "Jokes", which should have been *lathe, paste, angles, riffles, stuffs,* and *Yokes*.[64] Did Semper pronounce these words as they were written, or as what they meant? He was in luck when he confused one word with another that had the same pronunciation, such as *tail* with "tale" or *piece* with "peace" (in the combination "pennypeace").[65]

In one of his manuscripts, Semper described the lecture series given in the winter term of 1854–55 as "the curse [meaning *course*] of my lectures".[66] This might be forgiven as a Freudian slip, to use a twentieth-century term. With the exception of Cole's assessment mentioned above, no contemporary opinions of the lectures he gave in English are known. Almost thirty years after Semper's departure from London, an anonymous Briton wrote: "poor Semper revelled in speculations. He expressed himself in English with difficulty, and we fear that when he did so he was considered a bore".[67] However, Semper indicated on 24 January 1856, in one of the opening sentences of the first public lecture he gave in Zurich, that in his London lectures he had been struggling not only with the English language but also with language as such: "I would … request my honoured listeners to bear in mind that they are being addressed by an artist who is able to present matters in his own way, but who does not command an ability to present them in spoken form".[68] When Georg Herwegh reviewed the lecture, he implicitly agreed with Semper here, noting:

> We must admit that it does indeed appear superfluous for the fine artist to show any particular oral skills; it may also be that greater eloquence can be heard in St. Peter's or in the Fraumünster Church, just as we believe that Michelangelo can scarcely have been able to give a speech as good as those of any member of the German parliament. And while we are speaking of Michelangelo, we may in conclusion mention the comparison he once made between two contemporaries, which in the present case seems to be fully applicable: "*l'uno dice delle parole, l'altro dice delle cose*" – the one is speaking words, the other is speaking things.[69]

Translation as a way to written English

A manuscript sheet, kept in Zurich, with two columns written on the front and back, may serve as a link to Semper's written English.[70] The first column, in German, is headed "Historischer Ueberblick der Englischen Sprache. Grund ihrer Unregelmäs-sigkeit[.] Ihr Reichthum verglichen mit der Franzosischen Sprache". The second column, in English, is headed "Historical View of English language. Account of his irregularity[.] Its copiousness, compared with the frensh[.]" The sheet may have been written as an exercise that Semper was given by his private tutor, Barton, shortly after his arrival in London.[71] The facts that both columns – despite all the corrections they contain – show some grammatical errors and that the German column is two sentences longer than the English one prove that Semper was copying neither the German nor the English column but instead was translating an unnamed English source into German and afterwards retranslating his own German translation into English. What source was he using? He would not have been able to consult Johann Christian Fick's *Praktische englische Sprachlehre für Deutsche beyderley Geschlechts* even if his copy had not at that time been located in a customs warehouse in New York, along with most of his other books,[72] since the historical overview it contains is in German. Matthäus Weishaupt's *Historischer Ueberblick der Entwickelung der englischen Sprache*, the title of which is similar to the first part of the heading on the German column, can be excluded for the same reason.[73] Besides, it is divided into five sections, supplemented with etymological and grammatical addenda. The traces finally lead to the first volume of the *Handbuch der Englischen Sprache und Literatur*, edited by Johann Wilhelm Heinrich Nolte and Christian Ludwig Ideler – probably in the sixth edition.[74] The work reprints an extract from one lecture of a series the Scottish philologist and theologian Hugh Blair started giving at the University of Edinburgh in 1759 but did not publish until 1783, under the heading "Historical view of the English Language; its irregularities accounted for; its copiousness, compared with the French Language".[75] The lecture also found its way into other books, such as *The Classical Reader* by Francis William Pitt Greenwood and George Barrell Emerson, at least ten editions of which were printed between 1826 and 1847, and Ottomar Behnsch's *English Made Easy*, published in five editions between 1840 and 1849;[76] but no other book, including Blair's own *Lectures on Rhetoric and Belles Lettres*, contains a heading similar to that given by Semper.[77]

What did Semper note on the sheet? He wrote that the original language of Britain had been Celtic, which probably had come to Britain with the first settlers from Gaul. Starting in 450 CE, the Britons – and with them the Celtic language – had been pushed back into Wales, Scotland, and Ireland by the invading Saxons. After that, the language spoken in the southern part of the largest British island had been Saxon, from which English had developed, with a few additions from Danish, until the Norman invasion. By using French as the language of the royal court, the Normans had caused substantial changes in the indigenous language.

The brief overview breaks off here, but a few points may be added to it. Starting in 449 CE, what is now England was invaded not only by the Saxons but also by the Jutes and Angles – after whom the southern part of the largest British island is now named – from the parts of the continent's Atlantic coast that now belong to Den-

Figs. 2, 3

mark, Germany, and the Netherlands. These three Germanic tribes only adopted a few linguistic elements from the Celtic Britons. The Vikings settled in parts of the island between the late eighth and the early eleventh century, bringing with them two closely related languages, Danish and Norse. Following the Norman invasion in 1066, French also gradually entered the language of the common people in England. Alongside it, Latin was used in the church and in academia. In the fourteenth century, a form of English that was enriched to a greater extent with French and to a lesser extent with Latin began to predominate as the language of the royal court, the law courts, and politics. Towards the end of the seventeenth century, it reached the phase of development that is now known as Modern English, associated with increased adoption of non-European words.[78] In 1844, in a booklet entitled *Ueber das Verhältniss der deutschen und romanischen Elemente in der englischen Sprache*, in which the word "deutsch" (German) is incorrectly used for *Germanic*, Ottomar Behnsch held that English grammar largely consisted of German elements alone and that the English vocabulary had been expanded usually with French words to describe new terms from the sphere of "the salon, the refined world, science, academia and art".[79]

Semper's use of English could be summed up, with a certain amount of exaggeration, by saying that he to some extent reiterated the decisive phase of development of the language itself between 1066 and the fourteenth century, at the same time adding German elements on top of the Saxon-Anglian-Jutish-Danish-Norse base. On the sheet mentioned above, Semper wrote about Celtic:

> Dieses also war die Sprache der ersten Britten, der ersten Bewohner unserer Insel so viel uns bekannt ist; und blieb es bis zur Ankunft der Sachsen in England, im Jahre unseres Herren 450. welche, nachdem sie die Britten besiegt hatten, sich nicht mit ihnen vermischten, sondern sie von ihren Wohnungen vertrieb und sie mit ihrer Sprache in die Berge von Wallis jagte.[80]

Semper had apparently already lost the thread here, since he ought to have written *vertrieben* and *jagten* (the third-person plural forms of the verbs) instead of "vertrieb" and "jagte" (the singular forms). His own English retranslation of the sentence reads:

> This, then, was the language of the first Britons, the primitive inhabitants of this island as we know, and continued so till the arrival of the Saxons in England in the jear of our lord 450, who, having conquered the Britons did not intermix with them, but expelled them from their habitations and drow them with their tongue into the mountains of Wales.[81]

Following his source, Semper only deviated from German sentence structure on one point: he translated the subclause "nachdem sie die Britten besiegt hatten" with the participial construction "having conquered the Britons". As he forgot the comma after "England", so that the phrase "in the jear of our lord 450" was not marked as a parenthesis, the divergence is fatal – the Britons are now not being conquered and driven out by the Saxons but rather by "our lord".[82] Semper distorted the meaning of the German sentence even more by translating the ambiguous expression "mit ihrer Sprache" as "with their tongue".[83] His English sentence suggests that "our lord" used the language or even the physical tongue of the Britons to drive them into the Welsh mountains. The fact that the English column, with the exception of the sentence in question, barely diverges from the source can be explained by Semper's good memory, which possibly

93

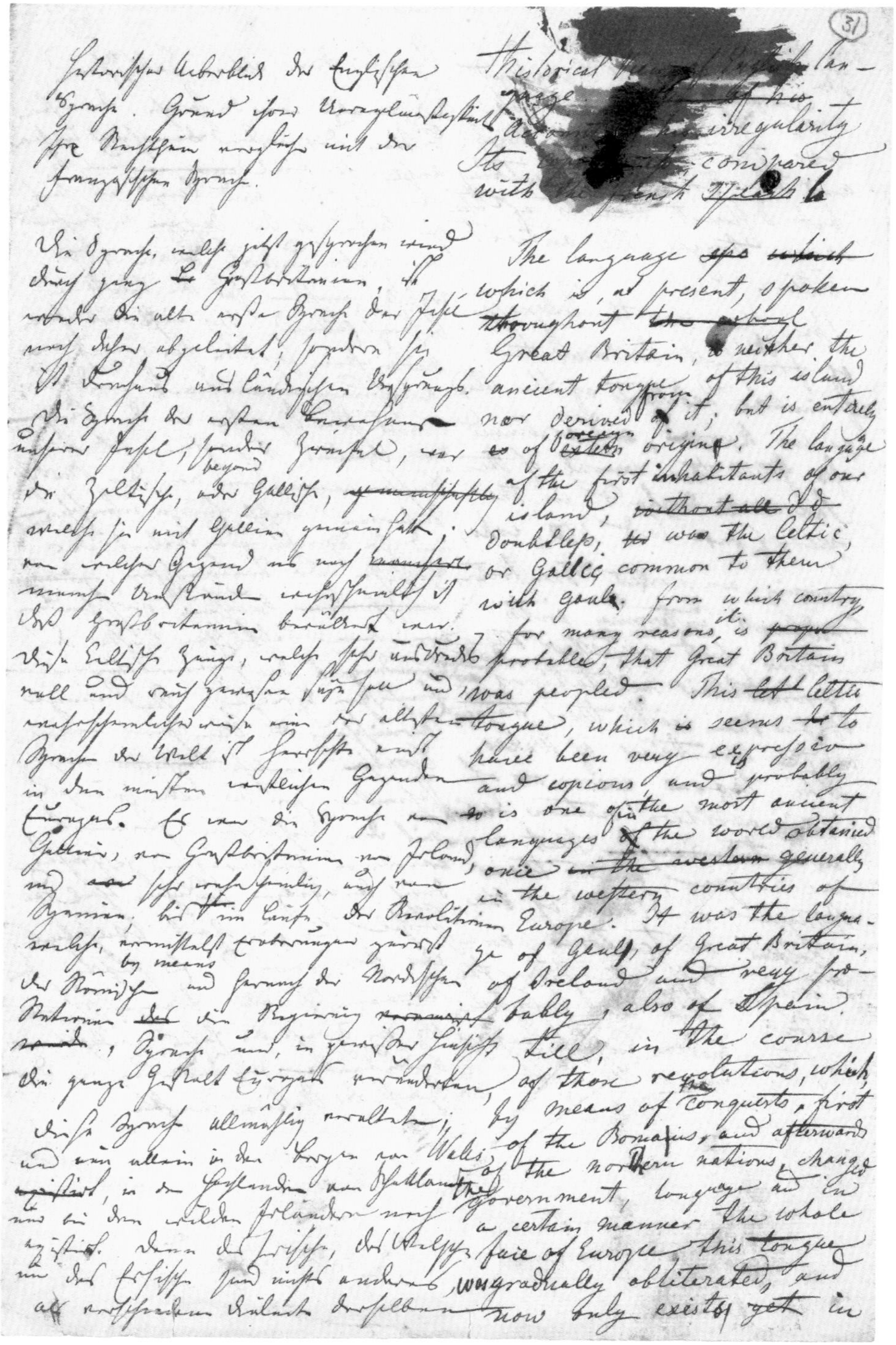

94

_Figure 2.
Gottfried Semper,
*Historical View of
English Language*,
undated manuscript
(probably 1850), gta,
20-Ms-149, fol. 22r
(Courtesy of the gta
Archives/ETH Zurich).

_ Figure 3.
Gottfried Semper,
*Historical View of
English Language*,
undated manuscript
(probably 1850), gta,
20-Ms-149, fol. 22v
(Courtesy of the gta
Archives/ETH Zurich).

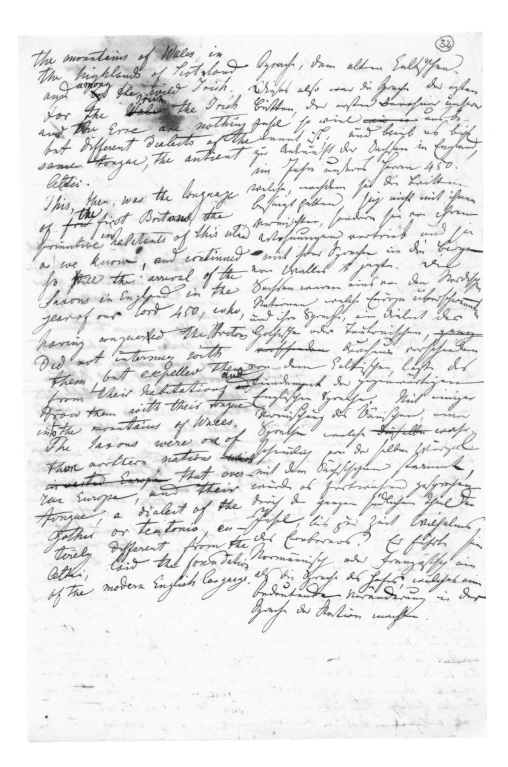

95

also had the effect that German spelling only affected two words, "expressiv" and "jear", and that the intrusive French vowels in "origine", "Romains", and "existes" were corrected in addition to the French word "habitants".

Harry Francis Mallgrave has noted "Semper's at times rather Germanic turn of phrase and choice of words".[84] In contrast to Ottomar Behnsch, Mallgrave might correctly have replaced the word "Germanic" with *German* here. Two sentences written in the spring of 1853 for his first public lecture may serve as examples of the difficulty Semper had in freeing himself from German syntax. In the first, he was referring to the origin of Assyrian and Egyptian monuments in the applied arts: "But what see we at the ruins of Niniveh and Theben?"[85] (*Aber was sehen wir an den Ruinen von Niniveh und Theben?*) In the second sentence, Semper was attempting to explain the aerodynamic behaviour of an ancient Greek slingshot projectile: "If such a leaden bird is fliing in the air, it is surronded by an Envelop of atmospheric air, which before it is condensed and behind it is rarefied"[86] (*Wenn ein solcher bleierner Vogel in der Luft fliegt, wird er von einer Hülle atmosphärischer Luft umgeben, die vor ihm verdichtet wird und hinter ihm verdünnt wird*).[87] The relative clause "which is being condensed before it and rarefied behind it" or even "which is condensing before it and rarefying behind it" would have been correct and more easily understandable. Semper's Germanic choice of words can hardly be confirmed if it means that in certain contexts he used inappropriate German-inspired synonyms instead of words an English speaker would have used.[88] By contrast, his Germanic choice is easy to detect in words borrowed or derived from German. For example, Semper translated the German construction *einerseits … anderseits* (on the one hand … on the other hand) three times as "onesides … othersides".[89] Sometimes he adopted proper names and other words from German without any change – such as "Niniveh", "Theben", "Tempel", and "Tabernakel".[90] In a few words, such as "joung" and "nacked",[91] German spelling only shimmers through. Even "misformation" betrays German influence, namely from the word *Missbildung*.[92]

However, Semper drew more strongly on French vocabulary than on German. The surviving lecture manuscripts show that even after three or four years in London, he was often approximating English words that were derived from French to their French originals, or even using the corresponding French words instead: he changed *founders* into "foundators", *subtleties* into "subtilities", *exerting* into "exercing", *elongated* into "allongated", *favoured* into "favorised", *ornamented* into "ornemented", *marvellously* into "merveillously"; and he replaced *Mosque* with "Mosquée", *Trophies* with "Trophees", *example* with "exemple", *masons* with "maçons", *review* with "revue", *event* with "evenement", and *representatives* with "representants".[93] On rare occasions, he anglicized French words that have not been adopted into English, turning *dépassé* into "depassed" (exceeded or surpassed) and *versé* into "versed" (poured).[94] If neither German nor French provided any help, or if he did not have the time or desire to consult a dictionary, he invented his own English words – sometimes mixing two English words together or mingling an English word with an Italian or Latin one, sometimes adopting sounds from a corresponding English word that he only remembered vaguely. If he mixed *language* and *lingua* into "linguage", he was still understandable to English speakers.[95] By contrast, words such as "barches", "fricture", "sutt", and "didges" were only comprehensible in context. The first meant *barks*, possibly mixing the word with *birches*.[96] The second combined the English words *fracture* and *friction*, both adopted from French, but what was meant was *friction*.[97] The third, meaning *soot*, was probably fusing this word with *smut*.[98] The meaning of the fourth word alternated between *ditches* and *dikes*, although "didges" in the second meaning was probably also borrowing from the word *ridges*.[99]

"Inadequate knowledge of the language"?

As a whole, these examples show that Semper developed "a Sort of Method how to invent" for his own English.[100] When using it, however, he sometimes failed to achieve the goal that he was to describe a few years later as the most important aspect of word formation: "being understood".[101] He himself admitted in 1853 that he knew English "but little".[102] Later that same year he received a letter that must have seemed like a confirmation of his self-assessment. Thomas Leverton Donaldson, one of his best English friends, accused him of having used an inappropriate word in the dedication of his book *Das Königliche Hoftheater zu Dresden*. Donaldson wrote to him: "there is one little word in the inscription, which I must entreat you to alter; as it seems to do away with the cordiality of friendship, which should exist between us, and places us *both* in a false position. You offer the book as a mark of *respect*[.] – Nothing could be more inappropriately expressed in *English*, for I should hope to possess your *regard*, & that would also include every other sentiment, that I could wish you to entertain for me".[103] In the autumn of 1854, when Semper was drafting a letter to inform Henry Cole that he had been offered a professorship at the Polytechnic in Zurich, he confessed: "I can hardly deny that many things argue in favour of accepting the offer, and among them, the consideration of the difficulties my work as a professor and architect is facing, due to inadequate knowledge of the language and of English conditions, takes the first place".[104] He ultimately accepted the offer and departed from London on 26 or 27 June 1855 to move to Zurich, stopping in Paris on the way.[105] As he could not easily adjust to his new surroundings there, he negotiated with Cole two years later regarding the possibility of returning to London. He drafted the letters to Cole in German and then had them translated by the Anglicist Hermann Behn-Eschenburg into "quite elegant English".[106]

The catalogue *Practical Art in Metals and Hard Materials; Its Technology, History and Styles*, which Semper compiled for Cole between April and August 1852, betrays "Semper's scanty knowledge of English" in the view of Isabella Nicka and Kathrin Pokorny-Nagel.[107] Wolfgang Herrmann and Harry Francis Mallgrave have considered that the manuscripts of the lectures he gave in 1853 and 1854 are evidence of "his peculiar and often faulty English" and "his awkward, sometimes failing, knowledge of English".[108] It is true that Semper not always sufficiently anglicized the Germanic and Romance elements, that he made many syntactical and orthographic errors, and that he hardly ever used any typically English idiomatic expressions. Despite this, the language skills that he did acquire within a relatively short time should not be underestimated, and one can hardly resist the comment that his own word formations and borrowings from other languages give his English its own special charm.

[English translation Michael Robertson]

97

Appendix

Extract from Hugh Blair's ninth lecture on rhetoric and belles-lettres, cited after J.W.H. Nolte and C.L. Ideler, *Handbuch der Englischen Sprache und Literatur*, vol. 1, 6th ed., Nauck, Berlin 1844, pp. 437–41 (here pp. 437–38):

Historical view of the English Language; its irregularities accounted for; its copiousness, compared with the French Language.

The language which is, at present, spoken throughout Great Britain, is neither the ancient primitive speech of the island, nor derived from it; but is altogether of foreign origin. The language of the first inhabitants of our island, beyond doubt, was the Celtic, or Gallic, common to them with Gaul; from which country, it appears, by many circumstances, that Great Britain was peopled. This Celtic tongue, which is said to be very expressive and copious, and is, probably, one of the most ancient languages in the world, obtained once in most of the western regions of Europe. It was the language of Gaul, of Great Britain, of Ireland, and, very probably, of Spain also; till, in the course of those revolutions, which, by means of the conquests, first, of the Romans, and afterwards, of the northern nations, changed the government, speech, and, in a manner, the whole face of Europe, this tongue was gradually obliterated; and now subsists only in the mountains of Wales, in the Highlands of Scotland, and among the wild Irish. For the Irish, the Welch, and the Erse, are no other than different dialects of the same tongue, the ancient Celtic.

This, then, was the language of the primitive Britons, the first inhabitants, that we know of, in our island; and continued so till the arrival of the Saxons in England, in the year of our Lord 450; who, having conquered the Britons, did not intermix with them, but expelled them from their habitations, and drove them, together with their language, into the mountains of Wales. The Saxons were one of those northern nations that overran Europe; and their tongue, a dialect of the Gothic or Teutonic, altogether distinct from the Celtic, laid the foundation of the present English tongue. With some intermixture of Danish, a language, probably, from the same root with the Saxon, it continued to be spoken throughout the southern part of the island, till the time of William the Conqueror. He introduced his Norman or French as the language of the court, which made a considerable change in the speech of the nation; and the English, which was spoken afterwards, and continues to be spoken now, is a mixture of the ancient Saxon, and this Norman French, together with such new and foreign words as commerce and learning have, in progress of time, gradually introduced.

Gottfried Semper's translation into German of the above extract from Hugh Blair's ninth lecture on rhetoric and belles-lettres, undated (probably 1850), gta Archives/ ETH Zurich, 20-Ms-149, fol. 22r–v:

Historischer Ueberblick der Englischen Sprache. Grund ihrer Unregelmässigkeit Ihr Reichthum verglichen mit der Franzosischen Sprache.

Die Sprache, welche jetzt gesprochen wird durch ganz Grossbritanien, ist weder die alte erste Sprache der Insel noch daher abgeleitet; sondern sie ist durchaus ausländischen Ursprungs. Die Sprache der ersten Bewohner unserer Insel, sonder Zweifel, war die Zeltische, oder Gallische, welche sie mit Gallien gemein hatte; von welcher Gegend es nach manchen Umständen wahrscheinlich ist dass Grossbritannien bevölkert war. Diese Celtische Zunge, welche sehr ausdrucksvoll und reich gewesen seyn soll und, wahrscheinlicherweise eine der ältesten Sprachen der Welt ist herrschte einst in den meisten westlichen Gegenden Europas. Es war die Sprache von Gallien, von Grossbritanien von Irland, und sehr wahrscheinlich, auch von Spanien; bis im Laufe der Revolutionen welche, vermittelst Eroberungen zuerst der Römischen und hernach der Nordischen Nationen die Regierung, Sprache und, in gewisser Hinsicht die ganze Gestalt Europas veränderten, diese Sprache allmählich veraltete; und nun allein in den Bergen von Walis, in den Hochlanden von Schottland und bei den wilden Irländern noch existirt. Denn das Irische, das Welsche und das Ersische sind nichts anderes, als verschiedene Dialecte derselben Sprache, dem alten Celtischen.

Dieses also war die Sprache der ersten Britten, der ersten Bewohner unserer Insel so viel uns bekannt ist; und blieb es bis zur Ankunft der Sachsen in England, im Jahre unseres Herren 450. welche, nachdem sie die Britten besiegt hatten, sich nicht mit ihnen vermischten, sondern sie von ihren Wohnungen vertrieb und sie mit ihrer Sprache in die Berge von Wallis jagte. Die Sachsen waren eins von den Nordischen Nationen welche Europa überschwemmten und ihre Sprache, ein Dialect des Gothischen oder Teutonischen, durchaus verschieden von dem Celtischen, legte das Fundament der gegenwärtigen Englischen Sprache. Mit einiger Vermischung des Dänischen, einer Sprache welche wahrscheinlich von der selben Wurzel mit dem Sächsischen stammt, wurde es fortwährend gesprochen durch den ganzen südlichen Theil der Insel, bis zur Zeit Wilhelms des Eroberers. Er führte sein Normännisch oder Französisch ein als die Sprache des Hofes, welches eine bedeutende Veränderung in der Sprache der Nation machte.

Gottfried Semper's retranslation into English of his German translation of the above extract from Hugh Blair's ninth lecture on rhetoric and belles-lettres, undated (probably 1850), gta Archives/ETH Zurich, 20-Ms-149, fol. 22r–v:

Historical View of English language. Account of his irregularity Its copiousness, compared with the frensh

The language which is, at present, spoken throughout Great Britain, is neither the ancient tongue of this island nor derived from it; but is entirely of foreign origin. The language of the first inhabitants of our island, doubtless, was the Celtic, or Gallic, common to them with Gaul, from which country, for many reasons, it is probable, that Great Britain was peopled. This Celtic tongue, which seems to have been very expressiv and copious, and is probably is one of the most ancient languages in the world, obtained once generally in the western countries of Europe. It was the language of Gaul, of Great Britain, of Ireland and very probably, also of Spain. till, in the course of those revolutions, which, by means of the conquests, first of the Romans, and afterwards of the northern nations, changed the government, language and in a certain manner the whole face of Europe, this tongue was gradually obliterated, and now only exists in the mountains of Wales, in the highlands of Scotland and among the wild Irish. For the Irish, the Irish and the Erse are nothing but different dialects of the same tongue, the antient Celtic.

This, then, was the language of the first Britons, the primitive inhabitants of this island as we know, and continued so till the arrival of the Saxons in England in the jear of our lord 450, who, having conquered the Britons did not intermix with them, but expelled them from their habitations and drow them with their tongue into the mountains of Wales. The Saxons were one of those northern nations that overrun Europe, and their tongue, a dialect of the Gothic or teutonic, entirely different from the Celtic, laid the foundation of the modern English language.

_1. Semper's parents moved from Hamburg to Altona in 1806. H. Hipp, *Der Hamburger Gottfried Semper*, in H. Karge (ed.), *Gottfried Semper – Dresden und Europa: Die moderne Renaissance der Künste*, Deutscher Kunstverlag, Munich 2007, pp. 77–100 (here pp. 78–80).

_2. Johannes Gurlitt, certificate for Gottfried Semper, 30 March 1823, gta Archives/ETH Zurich, 20-DOK-1823:1.

_3. Carl Friedrich August Hartmann, certificate for Gottfried Semper, 10 October 1823, gta Archives/ETH Zurich, 20-DOK-1823:3; Christoph Wilhelm Mitscherlich and Gabriel Riedel, certificate for Gottfried Semper, 30 March 1825, gta Archives/ETH Zurich, 20-DOK-1825:1.

_4. Gottfried Semper, letter to Johanna Maria Semper (née Paap) and Gottfried Emanuel Semper, 5 August 1824, gta Archives/ETH Zurich, 20-K-1824-08-05(S).

_5. Carl Friedrich Hipp, letter to Gottfried Semper, 10 August 1824, gta Archives/ETH Zurich, 20-K-1824-08-10:1.

_6. Gottfried Semper, letter to Gottfried Emanuel Semper, undated (probably 24 December 1824), gta Archives/ETH Zurich, 20-K-1824-12-24(S). Cf. Gottfried Emanuel Semper, letter to Gottfried Semper, 12 February 1825, gta Archives/ETH Zurich, 20-K-1825-02-12.

_7. Gottfried Semper, letter to Gottfried Emanuel Semper, 29 April 1825, gta Archives/ETH Zurich, 20-K-1825-04-29(S):1.

_8. Semper had already written to his father on 14 March 1825: "Your ideas about Paris and … my rights as a French national seem to be quite far-fetched and unreliable. Because firstly, it's not Napoleon on the throne any more, but a *Bourbon*, and secondly my French descent would probably be of little assistance because it comes from the maternal side". His father's response to the questions raised on 29 April has not survived, but on 25 July, Semper's sister informed him: "Our inquiries about the Polytechnic College have unfortunately not been very encouraging, as Mother and Father have probably already told you". Gottfried Semper, letter to Gottfried Emanuel Semper, 14 March 1825, gta Archives/ETH Zurich, 20-K-1825-03-14(S); Elise Semper, letter to Gottfried Semper, 25 July 1825, gta Archives/ETH Zurich, 20-K-1825-07-25.

_9. Gottfried Semper, letter to August Wilhelm Döbner, 5 August 1827 (copy), gta Archives/ETH Zurich, 20-K-1827-08-05(S).

_10. Semper lived in Paris from December 1826 to October 1827 and from August 1829 to September 1830. He worked as a harbour engineering trainee in Bremerhaven for some months in 1828.

_11. Gottfried Semper, letter to Johanna Maria Semper, 20 June 1830, gta Archives/ETH Zurich, 20-K-1830-06-20(S). Cf. Gottfried Semper, letter to Wilhelm Semper, 19 March 1830, gta Archives/ETH Zurich, 20-K-1830-03-19(S).

_12. Gottfried Emanuel Semper, letter to Gottfried Semper, 6 August 1830, gta Archives/ETH Zurich, 20-K-1830-08-06:1; Johanna Maria Semper, letter to Gottfried Semper, undated (probably 6 August 1830), gta Archives/ETH Zurich, 20-K-1830-08-06:1.

_13. Gottfried Emanuel Semper, letter to Gottfried Semper, 6 August 1830, gta Archives/ETH Zurich, 20-K-1830-08-06:1.

_14. Gottfried Semper, letter to Gottfried Emanuel Semper, 26 August 1830, gta Archives/ETH Zurich, 20-K-1830-08-26(S).

_15. G. Moeller, *"Grau teurer Freund ist alle Theorie und grün des Lebens goldner Baum": Sempers Studienreise durch Italien, Sizilien und Griechenland 1830–1834*, in W. Nerdinger and W. Oechslin (eds.), *Gottfried Semper 1803–1879: Architektur und Wissenschaft*, Prestel and gta Verlag, Munich and Zurich 2003, pp. 105–8.

_16. Gottfried Semper, letter to Johanna Maria Semper, 30 September 1834, gta Archives/ETH Zurich, 20-K-1834-09-30(S).

_17. Gottfried Semper, letter to Bertha Semper (née Thimmig), 10 June 1849, gta Archives/ETH Zurich, 20-K-1849-06-10(S):1; Gottfried Semper, letter to Johann Carl Semper, 10 June 1849, gta Archives/ETH Zurich, 20-K-1849-06-10(S):2. "Germany" here refers to the German states, which were not yet united.

_18. Gottfried Semper, letters to Bertha Semper, 18 December 1838 and 14 January 1838 (i.e. 1839), gta Archives/ETH Zurich, 20-K-1838-12-18(S) and 20-K-1839-01-14(S); Gottfried Semper, letter to Johann Carl Semper, 3 April 1839, gta Archives/ETH Zurich, 20-K-1839-04-03(S).

_19. Anonymous author, *Verzeichniss der Theilnehmer an der dritten Versammlung der deutschen Architekten und Ingenieure zu Prag, am 29., 30., 31. August und 1. September 1844*, "Allgemeine Bauzeitung", 9, 1844, pp. 248–50 (here p. 250).

_20. The exact route taken on the journey is not known. While staying in Weilheim in Bavaria, Semper supposed that he would travel to Verona, Mantua, Vicenza, and Venice and only stay there for "four to six days at the most". Gottfried Semper, letter to Bertha Semper, 21 September 1846, gta Archives/ETH Zurich, 20-K-1846-09-21(S).

_21. Semper gave varying information about the length of his stay. In a draft letter of January 1839, he complained: "The obstinacy of Mr. v. L. [i.e. von Lüttichau] prevented me from staying longer than 8 days in London". In a letter of April 1839, however, he wrote: "I was in London only for six or seven days". Gottfried Semper, draft letter to Otto von Wolframsdorf, 2 January 1839, gta Archives/ETH Zurich, 20-K-1839-01-02(S); Gottfried Semper, letter to Johann Carl Semper, 3 April 1839, gta Archives/ETH Zurich, 20-K-1839-04-03(S).

_22. Gottfried Semper, letter to Johann Carl Semper (see note 21).

100

_23. Gottfried Semper, letter to Johann Carl Semper, 15 (i.e. 14) May 1848 (i.e. 1849), gta Archives/ETH Zurich, 20-K-1849-05-14(S). Cf. Gottfried Semper, letter to Bertha Semper, 17 May 1849, gta Archives/ETH Zurich, 20-K-1849-05-17(S).

_24. In June 1849, Semper reported to his wife, Bertha: "As you explicitly requested, I travelled to Paris in order to await the course of events here, again following your advice". Four months later, he stated in a draft letter to a benefactor in Dresden: "I will gladly abandon the decision to emigrate to America, although in Europe the curse of the refugee will always follow me, no matter where I go. – If I were alone in the world, nothing would hold me back from this step, but my wife has shown that she is strongly opposed to it, and with such a large family it is, without any definite prospects, too risky a venture. I therefore scarcely need to assure you that I would regard it as a great and unexpected stroke of luck if the noble and kindred Britons were to show me hospitality and offer me a place among them". Gottfried Semper, letter to Bertha Semper, 21 June 1849, gta Archives/ETH Zurich, 20-K-1849-06-21(S); Gottfried Semper, draft letter to Friedrich Krause, 19 October 1849, gta Archives/ETH Zurich, 20-K-1849-10-19(S).

_25. Gottfried Semper, letter to Bertha Semper, 21 June 1849, gta Archives/ETH Zurich, 20-K-1849-06-21(S).

_26. Gottfried Semper, draft letter to August Jochmus, undated (probably 16 July 1849), gta Archives/ETH Zurich, 20-K-1849-07-16(S).

_27. Gottfried Semper, draft letter to Friedrich Krause, 19 October 1849, gta Archives/ETH Zurich, 20-K-1849-10-19(S).

_28. W. Herrmann, *Gottfried Semper: Theoretischer Nachlass an der ETH Zürich. Katalog und Kommentare*, Birkhäuser, Basel 1981, p. 114.

_29. Gottfried Semper, fragmentary list of books, undated (probably 1852), gta Archives/ETH Zurich, 20-Ms-148, fol. 4r, edited in G. Semper, *London Writings 1850–1855*, edited by M. Gnehm, S. Hildebrand, and D. Weidmann, gta Verlag, Zurich 2021.

_30. If this assumption is accurate, Semper probably owned the 19th edition, which had been published in 1837.

_31. Gottfried Semper, fragmentary list of books (see note 29), fol. 3r. Cf. *ibid.*, fol. 5r. Donaldson had published two books, one on ancient portals and one on modern ones. Semper did not note which of the books he owned, but in the shorter fragment of the manuscript he only mentioned one. In the library catalogue of the Deutsches Technikmuseum in Berlin, Alderson's forenames are recorded as "Matt Atkinson". However, I have not been able to confirm them by inquiry or research. Cf. H.H. Flexner, *The London Mechanics' Institution: Social and Cultural Foundations 1823–1830*, PhD diss., University College London, 2014, pp. 332–33, https://archive.org/details/londonmechanicsinstitution (accessed 15 January 2020).

_32. Gottfried Semper, fragmentary list of books (see note 29), fols. 1r, 4r.

_33. It was not until August 1852 that Semper definitively decided to stay in Europe. Gottfried Semper, fragmentary letters to Bertha Semper, undated (August 1852) and 17 August 1852, gta Archives/ETH Zurich, 20-K-1852-08(S) and 20-K-1852-08-17(S).

_34. There is evidence, however, that Semper's eldest daughter and eldest son, Elisabeth and Manfred, started to learn English around this time. Manfred Semper, letter to Gottfried Semper, 27 August 1850, gta Archives/ETH Zurich, 20A-K-1850-08-27(M); Friedrich Krause, letter to Gottfried Semper, 10 March 1851, gta Archives/ETH Zurich, 20-K-1851-03-10.

_35. S. Luttmann, *Gottfried Sempers "Vergleichende Baulehre": Eine quellenkritische Rekonstruktion*, unpublished PhD diss., ETH Zurich, 2008, pp. 216–17, 310–11, 391–92, 394, 413, 490, 495–97, 500, 503, 505–6, 510, 514–16, 539–40, 547, 555. The imprecise details given by Semper suggest the following journals and books: "The Journal of the Royal Asiatic Society of Great Britain and Ireland", "The Journal of the Asiatic Society of Bengal", the transactions of the same society, which were published under the title *Asiatick Researches*, James Fergusson's *Illustrations of the Rock-Cut Temples of India* (with a volume of plates), G.A. Hoskins's *Travels in Ethiopia*, E.K. Kingsborough's *Antiquities of Mexico* (with four volumes of plates), Rám Ráz's *Essay on the Architecture of the Hindus*, C.J. Rich's *Second Memoir on Babylon*, H. Salt's *Essay on Dr. Young's and M. Champollion's Phonetic System of Hieroglyphics*, T. Skinner's *Excursions in India*, G. Turnour's *The Maháwanso in Roman Characters*, J.G. Wilkinson's *Manners and Customs of the Ancient Egyptians* (with a volume of plates), and H.H. Wilson's *Select Specimens of the Theatre of the Hindus*. Semper also referred to two works that only contain plates with legends: T. and W. Daniell's *Oriental Scenery* and A.H. Layard's *The Monuments of Nineveh*.

_36. S. Luttmann, *Gottfried Sempers "Vergleichende Baulehre"*, see note 35, pp. 282, 286, 381, 389, 391–94, 396–98, 404, 406–7, 412–14, 419, 423, 447, 449, 481–82, 487, 496, 504, 507–8, 510, 576, 585, 588–90, 592, 594. The imprecise details given by Semper suggest the following books: A. Burnes's *Travels into Bokhara and Cabool*, W. Chambers's *Designs of Chinese Buildings, Furniture, Dresses, Machines, and Utensils* (with a section of plates), R. Heber's *Narrative of a Journey through the Upper Provinces of India*, T. Hope's *An Historical Essay on Architecture* (with a volume of plates), A.H. Layard's *Nineveh and Its Remains* (with a section of plates), J. Morier's *Journeys through Persia, Armenia, and Asia Minor, to Constantinople*, R.K. Porter's *Travels in Georgia, Persia, Armenia, Ancient Babylonia, &c. &c.*, C.J.

Rich's *Memoir on the Ruins of Babylon*, T. Skinner's *Adventures during a Journey Overland to India*, and G. Valentia's *Voyages and Travels to India, Ceylon, the Red Sea, Abyssinia, and Egypt*.

_37. Karl Gildemeister, letters to Gottfried Semper, 2 July and 16 December 1850, gta Archives/ETH Zurich, 20-K-1850-07-02 and 20-K-1850-12-16.

_38. Emil Braun, letter to Gottfried Semper, 16 September 1850, gta Archives/ETH Zurich, 20-K-1850-09-16:1; Charles Séchan, letter to Gottfried Semper, 17 September 1850, gta Archives/ETH Zurich, 20-K-1850-09-17:2. In an earlier essay, I have incorrectly assumed that Semper described Braun as his "former benefactor and colleague in the Society of Antiquities in Rome". The phrase actually refers to Christian Carl Josias Bunsen. D. Weidmann, *Through the Stable Door to Prince Albert? On Gottfried Semper's London Connections*, "Journal of Art Historiography", no. 11, December 2014, pp. 1–26 (here p. 4). Cf. Gottfried Semper, letter to Johann Carl Semper, 30 September and 1 October 1850, gta Archives/ETH Zurich, 20-K-1850-10-01(S); W. Herrmann, *Gottfried Semper: In Search of Architecture*, MIT Press, Cambridge, MA 1984, p. 32.

_39. Emil Braun, letter to G. Semper, 16 September 1850, gta Archives/ETH Zurich, 20-K-1850-09-16:1.

_40. Emil Braun, letter to Gottfried Semper, 22 September 1850, gta Archives/ETH Zurich, 20-K-1850-09-22; Gottfried Semper, letter to Johann Carl Semper, 30 September and 1 October 1850, gta Archives/ETH Zurich, 20-K-1850-10-01(S).

_41. Gottfried Semper, draft letter to Moses Montefiore, 9 November 1850, gta Archives/ETH Zurich, 20-K-1850-11-09(S). By "Dr. Smith", Semper may have meant the London merchant and parliamentarian John Abel Smith, to whom he may have been recommended by Carl Kaskel, a Dresden banker and Swedish–Norwegian consul. Cf. Bertha Semper, letters to Gottfried Semper, 2, 6, and 7 June and 27 November 1850, gta Archives/ETH Zurich, 20-K-1850-06-07 and 20-K-1850-11-27.

_42. Gottfried Semper, draft letter to Charles Charnock Nelson and Joseph John Scoles, undated (November 1850), gta Archives/ETH Zurich, 20-K-1850-11(S):1; Gottfried Semper, draft letter to Edwin Chadwick, undated (probably 13 November 1850), gta Archives/ETH Zurich, 20-K-1850-11-13(S).

_43. On 14 January 1851, Barton informed Semper: "Depuis quelques semaines, j'ai été un peu indisposé ainsi je me flatte que vous m'excuserez si je ne suis pas venu chez vous[.] – Je vous prie cependant de me faire savoir s'il vous sera commode de reprendre les leçons d'Anglais, ou si vous preferez de les suspendre pour le moment[.]" Barton lived at "n° 9 Grafton Sᵗ Fitzroy Square", a maximum of 500 metres away from Semper, who was staying at 27 University Street, near Gower Street. Grafton Street is today called Grafton Way. R. Barton, letter to Gottfried Semper, 14 January 1851, gta Archives/ETH Zurich, 20-K-1851-01-14:3.

_44. A. Giordano, *Venice Described, from the Original Italian: Adapted to Assist as a Guide to the Model of Venice, Now Exhibiting at the Egyptian Hall, Piccadilly*, trans. R. Barton, M'Gowan, London 1844. Cf. A. Giordano, *Venezia nello autunno dell'anno 1838*, 1st ed. not traceable; 2nd ed., de Lacombe, Paris 1841. Barton's forename is added in handwriting on the cover of the copy of *Venice Described* held in the British Library, with an old shelfmark (1300.a.28). The model of Venice was exhibited for an unknown period starting in September 1843. Anonymous author, *Our Weekly Gossip*, "The Athenaeum: Journal of English and Foreign Literature, Science, and the Fine Arts", pt. 189, no. 828, 9 September 1843, pp. 820–21.

_45. C. Blasis, *The Code of Terpsichore: A Practical and Historical Treatise, on the Ballet, Dancing, and Pantomime*, trans. R. Barton, 1st ed., Bulcock, London 1828; 2nd ed. with different title, Bull, London 1830; 3rd ed. with different title, Bull, London 1831; C. Blasis, *Notes upon Dancing, Historical and Practical*, trans. R. Barton, Delaporte, London 1847.

_46. Gottfried Semper, *Die vier Elemente der Baukunst*, manuscript, undated (1850), gta Archives/ETH Zurich, 20-Ms-78; Gottfried Semper, *On Tapestry & the Origin of Polychronic Decoration*, manuscript, undated (1851), gta Archives/ETH Zurich, 20-Ms-79; Gottfried Semper, *Sur l'origine de l'architecture polychrome*, manuscript, 2 August 1851, gta Archives/ETH Zurich, 20-Ms-82. The first manuscript was partly translated; the second and third were not translated.

_47. Edward Falkener, letter to Gottfried Semper, 7 June 1851, gta Archives/ETH Zurich, 20-K-1851-06-07; Gottfried Semper, fragmentary draft letter to Edward Falkener, undated (1851), gta Archives/ETH Zurich, 20-K-1851(S):1; Joanna Hilary Bonham Carter, letters to Gottfried Semper, 6 and 20 June 1851 and undated (August 1851), gta Archives/ETH Zurich, 20-K-1851-06-06, 20-K-1851-06-20:1, and 20-K-1851-08:1; Gottfried Semper, fragmentary draft letter to Joanna Hilary Bonham Carter, undated (1851), gta Archives/ETH Zurich, 20-K-1851(S):4.

_48. Gottfried Semper, *Avis*, 1 April 1851, gta Archives/ETH Zurich, 20-DOK-1851:9e, edited in G. Semper, *London Writings*, see note 29.

_49. Walter Ruding Deverell, letter of appointment to Gottfried Semper, 11 September 1852, gta Archives/ETH Zurich, 20-K-1852-09-11, edited in G. Semper, *London Writings*, see note 29. The Department of Practical Art was expanded in 1853 to become the Department of Science and Art.

_50. Anonymous author, *Appendix F III (j): Prospectuses of the Lectures on Art*, in *First Report of the Department of Science and Art*, Eyre and

Spottiswoode for Her Majesty's Stationery Office, London 1854, pp. 218–21 (here pp. 220–21).

_51. Gottfried Semper, draft lecture, undated (1853), gta Archives/ETH Zurich, 20-Ms-122, fol. 1r, edited in G. Semper, *London Writings*, see note 29. The word "broken" is inserted in the left margin of the sentence.

_52. Semper stated: "A Foreigner must naturally feel very timid and embarrassed in addressing to You a paper written in ~~broken~~ English on a Subject, which by itself is difficult, and would be so to him, if he had to treat it in his own linguage". *Ibid.*

_53. *Ibid.*, fol. 3r–v. Cf. Gottfried Semper, draft lecture, undated (1853), gta Archives/ETH Zurich, 20-Ms-124, fols. 1r, 2r, edited in G. Semper, *London Writings*, see note 29.

_54. M. Gnehm, *Stumme Poesie: Architektur und Sprache bei Gottfried Semper*, gta Verlag, Zurich 2004, pp. 30–4, 45–6. Strangely enough, Semper had altered "topics" to "topic" in his manuscript.

_55. Gottfried Semper, draft lecture, 20-Ms-122 (see note 51), fol. 8r.

_56. *Ibid.*

_57. Semper stated: "As soon as one or some of these coefficients vary, the Result must vary likewise, and must show in its features and general appearance a certain distinct caracter; – if this is not the case, then it fails for want of Style". *Ibid.*, fol. 8r–v.

_58. Cole noted in his diary: "Stayed for Semper's lecture, his first: thoughtful & suggestive". Attaching a certain degree of importance to this note, Elizabeth Bonython and Anthony Burton have remarked: "Since Cole's diary entries are so very laconic, and so rarely deal with anything but practical matters, this entry may be interpreted as indicating some intellectual affinity between him and the German theorist". Henry Cole, diary (transcript), 20 May 1853, Victoria and Albert Museum, National Art Library, 45.C.115; E. Bonython and A. Burton, *The Great Exhibitor: The Life and Work of Henry Cole*, V&A Publications, London 2003, p. 173. Lyon Playfair was the other secretary of the Department of Science and Art. He and Cole were in practice its directors.

_59. Gottfried Semper, draft lecture, 20-Ms-124 (see note 53), fols. 5r, 6r, 9r. However, Semper now presented the equation in a slightly different form: "$Y = \Phi(x, y, z, t, v, w, ...)$" or "$Y = \Phi(x, z, t, v, w, ...)$" – he deleted the "y" in red ink at an unknown date.

_60. *Ibid.*, fol. 6r.

_61. *Ibid.*

_62. Gottfried Semper, draft lectures, undated (1853 and 1854), gta Archives/ETH Zurich, 20-Ms-122, fols. 5v, 6v, 12r, 13r; 20-Ms-124, fol. 5r; 20-Ms-129, fols. 2v, 3r, 7r–v, 8r, 11r–v; 20-Ms-133, fols. 1r, 2v, 3r, 8r, 10v; 20-Ms-134, fols. 2r–v, 3v, 5r, 6r; 20-Ms-135, fol. 4v; 20-Ms-136, fols. 1r, 3r, 4v, 5r, 6v, 7v; 20-Ms-138, fol. 11r; 20-Ms-141, fols. 6r, 9r–v, 10r; 20-Ms-142, fols. 5v, 8r–v, 9v; 20-Ms-144, fols. 1v, 11r. All manuscripts edited in G. Semper, *London Writings*, see note 29.

_63. Gottfried Semper, draft lectures, 20-Ms-122 (see note 51), fols. 5r, 9r; 20-Ms-124 (see note 53), fols. 4r, 7r, 17v, 19r.

_64. Gottfried Semper, draft lectures, undated (1853 and 1854), gta Archives/ETH Zurich, 20-Ms-129, fol. 9v; 20-Ms-131, fol. 5r–v; 20-Ms-133, fols. 2v, 12v; 20-Ms-135, fols. 2v, 4v, 5r–v, 6v, 9v, 10v; 20-Ms-144, fol. 11v. All manuscripts edited in G. Semper, *London Writings*, see note 29.

_65. Gottfried. Semper, draft lecture, 20-Ms-122 (see note 51), fols. 12v, 16r.

_66. The whole sentence reads: "I shall trie in the curse of my lectures, to give the evidences of these assertions". Gottfried Semper, draft lecture, undated (1854), gta Archives/ETH Zurich, 20-Ms-141, fol. 2v, edited in G. Semper, *London Writings*, see note 29.

_67. Anonymous author, *Gottfried Semper and His Theory of Art*, "The Architect", 32, 20 December 1884, pp. 397–98 (here p. 397). For his part, Nikolaus Pevsner has noted: "The lectures must have puzzled his [i.e. Semper's] English audiences greatly. They were profound rather than practical and just a little cranky". N. Pevsner, *Some Architectural Writers of the Nineteenth Century*, Clarendon Press, Oxford 1972, p. 260.

_68. G. Semper, *Über die formelle Gesetzmässigkeit des Schmuckes und dessen Bedeutung als Kunstsymbol*, "Monatsschrift des Wissenschaftlichen Vereins in Zürich", 1, 1856, pp. 101–30 (here pp. 101–2).

_69. G. Herwegh, *Zürich*, "Intelligenzblatt der Stadt und Landschaft Zürich", 2, no. 26, 26 January 1856, pp. 102–3. Semper gave the lecture in the Town Hall of the City and Canton of Zurich. "St. Peter's" and "Fraumünster" are references to churches in Zurich.

_70. Gottfried Semper, *Historical View of English Language*, undated manuscript (probably 1850), gta Archives/ETH Zurich, 20-Ms-149, fol. 22r–v.

_71. The watermark in the paper ("C & I Honig") does not tell whether Semper purchased the sheet in Paris or in London; it indicates paper made by the Dutch company Cornelis and Jan Honig.

_72. Intending to emigrate to North America, Semper had sent the majority of his books to New York in September 1850, and they remained there for several months. Gottfried Semper, letter to Johann Carl Semper, 30 September and 1 October 1850, gta Archives/ETH Zurich, 20-K-1850-10-01(S); Johann Carl Semper, letter to H. Bleidorn, 13 May 1851 (copy), gta Archives/ETH Zurich, 20-K(DD)-1851-05-13.

_73. M. Weishaupt, *Historischer Ueberblick der Entwickelung der englischen Sprache*, Jent and Gassmann, Solothurn 1850. A copy of the book with an old shelfmark (12982.e.3) is held by the British Library.

_74. J.W.H. Nolte and C.L. Ideler, *Handbuch der Englischen Sprache und Literatur, oder Auswahl*

103

interessanter chronologisch geordneter Stücke aus den Klassischen Englischen Prosaisten u. Dichtern, 6th ed., vol. 1, Nauck, Berlin 1844. This edition, prepared by Ideler after Nolte's death, is the only one of the first volume that is held by the British Library, with an old shelfmark (1341.l.3). The first edition, in one volume, was published anonymously under the title *Handbuch der Englischen Sprache, oder Auswahl lehrreicher und unterhaltender Aufsätze aus den besten Englischen Prosaisten und Dichtern*, Buchhandlung der Königlichen Realschule, Berlin 1793; but Nolte and Ideler only included the section on Blair in the later editions.

_75. J.W.H. Nolte and C.L. Ideler, *Handbuch*, see note 74, pp. 437–41. Cf. H. Blair, *Lecture IX: Structure of Language; English Tongue*, in H. Blair, *Lectures on Rhetoric and Belles Lettres*, 1st ed., vol. 1, Strahan & Cadell and Creech, London and Edinburgh 1783, pp. 159–82 (here pp. 169–74). Nolte and Ideler explicitly referred to this edition of the lectures, which were published in thirteen further editions before and after Blair's death. J.W.H. Nolte and C.L. Ideler, *Handbuch*, see note 74, p. 436.

_76. F.W.P. Greenwood and G.B. Emerson, *The Classical Reader: A Selection of Lessons in Prose and Verse*, 1st ed., Lincoln and Edmands, Boston 1826, pp. 223–25; 10th (?) ed., Robert S. Davis, Boston 1847, pp. 215–17; further editions 1828, 1829, 1830, 1833, 1835, 1836, 1839, and 1843; O. Behnsch, *English Made Easy: Praktischer Lehrgang zur leichten und schnellen Erlernung der Englischen Sprache*, 1st ed., Kern, Breslau 1840, pp. 70–74; 5th ed., Kern, Breslau 1849, pp. 78–81; further editions 1843, 1846, and 1847.

_77. However, Nolte and Ideler did not invent the title "Historical view of the English Language; its irregularities accounted for; its copiousness, compared with the French Language" themselves, but composed it from the index in the second volume of H. Blair's *Lectures on Rhetoric and Belles Lettres*. Under the entry "English language", the index gives: "Historical view of the English language, 169. The Celtic the primitive language of Britain, 170. The Teutonic tongue the basis of our present speech, 171. Its irregularities accounted for, 172. Its copiousness, 173. Compared with the French language, 174". H. Blair, *Lectures*, see note 75, 1st ed., vol. 2, Strahan & Cadell and Creech, London and Edinburgh 1783, after p. 550.

_78. A.C. Croll Baugh, *A History of the English Language*, Appleton-Century, New York 1935, pp. 49–312; D. Denison and R. Hogg, *Overview*, in R. Hogg and D. Denison (eds.), *A History of the English Language*, Cambridge University Press, Cambridge, MA 2006, pp. 1–42 (here pp. 8–17); D. Kastovsky, *Vocabulary*, in *ibid.*, pp. 199–270 (here pp. 216–26, 246–50, 256–59).

_79. O. Behnsch, *Ueber das Verhältniss der deutschen und romanischen Elemente in der englischen Sprache*, Max, Breslau 1844, pp. 19, 21.

_80. Gottfried Semper, *Historical View* (see note

70), fol. 22v. The sentence may be translated as follows: "This was therefore the language of the first Britons, the first inhabitants of our island so far as we know, and it remained so until the arrival of the Saxons in England in the year of Our Lord 450, who after they had vanquished the Britons did not mingle with them, but rather drove them from their dwellings and chased them along with their language into the mountains of Wales".

_81. *Ibid.*

_82. In Nolte's and Ideler's source, the phrase "in the year of our Lord 450" has a comma in front of it and a semicolon after it. J.W.H. Nolte and C.L. Ideler, *Handbuch*, see note 74, p. 438. Cf. H. Blair, *Lectures*, see note 75, p. 170.

_83. In Nolte's and Ideler's source, the phrase in question is "together with their language". It is enclosed by two commas for the sake of clarity. J.W.H. Nolte and C.L. Ideler, *Handbuch*, see note 74, p. 438. Cf. H. Blair, *Lectures*, see note 75, p. 170.

_84. H.F. Mallgrave (ed.), *Gottfried Semper, London Lecture of December 1853: "On the Origin of Some Architectural Styles"*, "RES: Anthropology and Aesthetics", no. 9, spring 1985, pp. 53–60 (here p. 53).

_85. Gottfried Semper, draft lecture, undated (1853), gta Archives/ETH Zurich, 20-Ms-117, fol. 3r, edited in G. Semper, *London Writings*, see note 29. Only correcting a minor error, Semper altered the name "Theben" to "Thebes" in pencil. Finally, he rejected the question along with the whole manuscript. In another manuscript, he repeated it almost verbatim: "But what see we on the monuments of Niniveh and Theben?" Gottfried Semper, draft lecture, undated (1853), gta Archives/ETH Zurich, 20-Ms-119, fol. 1r.

_86. Gottfried Semper, draft lecture, 20-Ms-122 (see note 51), fol. 12r.

_87. Semper's English sentence could also be translated as follows: "Wenn ein solcher bleierner Vogel in der Luft fliegt, ist er von einer Hülle atmosphärischer Luft umgeben, die vor ihm verdichtet ist und hinter ihm verdünnt ist". However, this translation is improbable because the act of flying involves dynamics. In a similar sentence, Semper used reflexive verbs to express aerodynamic effects: "Die Kugel ist gleichsam der Kolben, der sich zwischen zwei Luftnimben befindet, von denen der eine in gewissen Verhältnissen zur Geschwindigkeit sich verdichtet, der andere dagegen nach anderen Verhältnissen sich verdünnt". G. Semper, *Ueber die bleiernen Schleudergeschosse der Alten und über zweckmässige Gestaltung der Wurfkörper im Allgemeinen*, Verlag für Kunst und Wissenschaft, Frankfurt am Main 1859, p. 13.

_88. For an example mentioned by Thomas Leverton Donaldson, see below.

_89. Gottfried Semper, draft lectures, undated (1853 and 1854), gta Archives/ETH Zurich, 20-Ms-93, fol. 3v; 20-Ms-122, fol. 11v; 20-Ms-144, fol. 2v. 20-Ms-122, and 20-Ms-144, edited in G.

Semper, *London Writings*, see note 29. On the second occasion, Semper replaced the expression with the correct English words.

_ 90. Gottfried Semper, draft lectures, undated (1853), gta Archives/ETH Zurich, 20-Ms-117, fol. 3r; 20-Ms-119, fol. 1r; 20-Ms-129, fols. 5v, 6v; 20-Ms-131, fols. 1r, 2r–v; 20-Ms-137, fol. 3r; 20-Ms-138, fols. 10r, 11r. In addition, Semper also wrote "tempel" and "tabernakel". Gottfried Semper, draft lectures, undated (1853 and 1854), gta Archives/ETH Zurich, 20-Ms-118, fol. 4r; 20-Ms-131, fols. 1r, 2r–v; 20-Ms-138, fols. 9v, 12r; 20-Ms-141, fol. 8r; 20-Ms-144, fols. 16v, 20r. All manuscripts edited in G. Semper, *London Writings*, see note 29.

_ 91. Gottfried Semper, draft lectures, undated (1853 and 1854), gta Archives/ETH Zurich, 20-Ms-122, fol. 13r; 20-Ms-142, fol. 3v; 20-Ms-144, fol. 11r. All manuscripts edited in G. Semper, *London Writings*, see note 29.

_ 92. Gottfried Semper, draft lecture, undated (1853), gta Archives/ETH Zurich, 20-Ms-123, fol. 3v.

_ 93. Gottfried Semper, draft lectures, undated (1853 and 1854), gta Archives/ETH Zurich, 20-Ms-93, fol. 3v; 20-Ms-122, fols. 10v, 11v, 12v, 15r–v; 20-Ms-123, fol. 9v; 20-Ms-124, fols. 17r, 18r–v; 20-Ms-135, fols. 10v, 13r; 20-Ms-136, fol. 3r; 20-Ms-138, fols. 3r, 5r, 8r; 20-Ms-142, fols. 3r, 4r; 20-Ms-144, fols. 3r–v, 4r, 15r, 18v, 19r; 20-Ms-145, fols. 2r, 3v. All manuscripts except 20-Ms-93 and 20-Ms-123 edited in G. Semper, *London Writings*, see note 29.

_ 94. Gottfried Semper, draft lecture, 20-Ms-135 (see note 62), fols. 6v, 7r–v.

_ 95. Gottfried Semper, draft lectures, undated (1853 and 1854), gta Archives/ETH Zurich, 20-Ms-122, fols. 1r, 9v; 20-Ms-124, fol. 17v; 20-Ms-133, fol. 1r; 20-Ms-142, fol. 5r; 20-Ms-143, fol. 4r; 20-Ms-144, fol. 3r. All manuscripts edited in G. Semper, *London Writings*, see note 29.

_ 96. Gottfried Semper, draft lecture, 20-Ms-124 (see note 53), fol. 16v.

_ 97. Gottfried Semper, draft lecture, 20-Ms-122 (see note 51), fol. 12v.

_ 98. Gottfried Semper, draft lecture, 20-Ms-138 (see note 62), fol. 3r.

_ 99. Gottfried Semper, draft lecture, 20-Ms-144 (see note 62), fols. 4v, 16r. Cf. S. Luttmann, *Gottfried Sempers "Vergleichende Baulehre"*, see note 35, pp. 278, 465.

_ 100. Gottfried Semper, draft lecture, 20-Ms-124

(see note 53), fol. 2r. Cf. Gottfried Semper, draft lecture, 20-Ms-122 (see note 51), fol. 3r.

_ 101. G. Semper, *Der Stil in den technischen und tektonischen Künsten, oder Praktische Ästhetik: Ein Handbuch für Techniker, Künstler und Kunstfreunde*, vol. 1, Verlag für Kunst und Wissenschaft, Frankfurt am Main 1860, p. 7.

_ 102. Gottfried Semper, draft lecture, 20-Ms-124 (see note 53), fol. 6r. By ultimately deleting the words "but little" along with the whole sentence, Semper did not express that he regarded them as incorrect.

_ 103. Thomas Leverton Donaldson, letter to Gottfried Semper, 26 May 1853, gta Archives/ETH Zurich, 20-K-1853-05-26. Cf. G. Semper, *Das Königliche Hoftheater zu Dresden*, Vieweg, Braunschweig 1849. See also the chapter by Murray Fraser in the present volume.

_ 104. Gottfried Semper, draft letter to Henry Cole, undated (October 1854), gta Archives/ETH Zurich, 20-K-1854-10(S).

_ 105. Semper had his passport extended in London on 26 June 1855 and spent the night of 27 to 28 June in Rouen. Fletcher Wilson, passport for Gottfried Semper, 17 March and 26 June 1855, gta Archives/ETH Zurich, 20-DOK-1855:3; Hôtel de Paris, bill for Gottfried Semper, 28 June 1855, gta Archives/ETH Zurich, 20-DOK-1855:13.

_ 106. Gottfried Semper, draft letter to Henry Cole, undated (July 1857), gta Archives/ETH Zurich, 20-K-1857-07(S); Gottfried Semper, fragmentary draft letter to Henry Cole, undated (November 1857), gta Archives/ETH Zurich, 20-K-1857-11(S):2; Gottfried Semper, fragmentary draft letter to Hermann Behn-Eschenburg, undated (November 1857), gta Archives/ETH Zurich, 20-K-1857-11(S):1.

_ 107. I. Nicka and K. Pokorny-Nagel, *Preliminary Remarks*, in P. Noever (ed.), *Gottfried Semper: The Ideal Museum; Practical Art in Metals and Hard Materials*, Schlebrügge, Vienna 2007, pp. 21–22 (here p. 21).

_ 108. W. Herrmann, *Editorial Method*, in W. Herrmann, *Gottfried Semper*, see note 38, pp. xxi–xxii (here p. xxii); H.F. Mallgrave (ed.), *Gottfried Semper, London Lecture of November 18, 1853: "The Development of the Wall and Wall Construction in Antiquity"*, "RES: Anthropology and Aesthetics", no. 11, spring 1986, pp. 33–42 (here p. 33).

$$s = \frac{1}{vng} \cdot (c - c') \left(\sqrt{1 + \left(\frac{c-c''}{c-c'}\right)^2} - \sqrt{1 + \left(\frac{c-c}{c-c'}\right)^2} \right)$$

$$+ \frac{c}{vng} \cdot Arc \left(fin = \frac{a-c'}{c-c'} - Arc\, fin = \frac{c-c}{c-c'} \right)$$

$$s = \frac{1}{vng} \cdot \frac{c'}{2} \cdot \left(-\sqrt{1 - \frac{(c'-2c)^2}{c'^2}} \right)$$

$$+ \frac{c}{2\,vng} \cdot Arc \cdot \left(fin = -1 - Arc\, fin = \frac{(c'-2c)}{c'} \right)$$

$$Arc\, cos =$$

$$\frac{1}{neg} \cdot (40° + c) = 0.$$

$$c = -\frac{c'}{4}$$

Sonja Hildebrand

Gottfried Semper on Architectural Curvilinearity

_ Figure 1.
Gottfried Semper,
manuscript page for
*Ueber die bleiernen
Schleudergeschosse
der Alten* (1859), ca.
1853 (Courtesy of
the gta Archives/ETH
Zurich, 20-Ms-161).

In a footnote in his seminal work on Gottfried Semper's years of exile in London, Wolfgang Herrmann mentions fifty borrowing slips that document Semper's reading at the British Library – or rather the British Museum Library, as it was called until 1973.[1] According to a note on the corresponding archive file, Herrmann evidently looked into the matter in 1972 at the Sächsische Landesbibliothek (State Library of Saxony) in Dresden, where the slips are preserved.[2] Two of the borrowing slips are undated, and on two others the year is missing. Semper handed in the remaining forty-six slips between 8 March and 13 December 1852.[3] Most are from the period between mid-April and mid-August, when Semper was working intensely on his manuscript *Practical Art in Metals and Hard Materials; Its Technology, History and Styles* – the historical and systematic catalogue and survey of metal works commissioned by Henry Cole.[4] Herrmann mentions the borrowing slips in connection with the catalogue, but does not evaluate them in any greater depth. As part of the research project on "Architecture and the Globalization of Knowledge in the 19th Century: Gottfried Semper and the Discipline of Architectural History", Dieter Weidmann transcribed all the borrowing slips. Later he identified and provided bibliographic details for the titles, most of which Semper had only indicated in an abbreviated form.[5]

As a work that Semper was intending to use as a recommendation for his employment as a teacher in the Department of Practical Art, the metal catalogue was of the greatest importance for him as an exile who was living at barely a basic level at the time. Thanks to the bibliography compiled by Semper in the catalogue, 33 of the 41 order slips he filled out in the weeks leading up to the submission of the manuscript can be linked to the work. Four further titles, which are not cited, can be assigned to this area of research in terms of content.[6] Only four books slip through the cracks. These deserve all the more interest because Semper borrowed them during a phase when he was spending a great deal of energy and time on the manuscript.[7] One of the titles refers to an archaeological work on Athens, which falls into Semper's general archaeological field of interest.[8] More noteworthy are three fundamental works on mathematics, which Semper borrowed on three different days between 28 May and

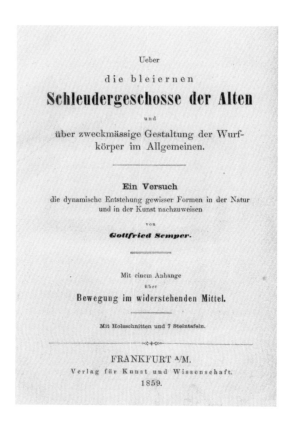

Ueber

die bleiernen

Schleudergeschosse der Alten

und

über zweckmässige Gestaltung der Wurfkörper im Allgemeinen.

Ein Versuch

die dynamische Entstehung gewisser Formen in der Natur
und in der Kunst nachzuweisen

von

Gottfried Semper.

Mit einem Anhange
über

Bewegung im widerstehenden Mittel.

Mit Holzschnitten und 7 Steintafeln.

FRANKFURT ∧/M.
Verlag für Kunst und Wissenschaft.
1859.

108

2 June. These were Georg von Vega's *Logarithmisch-trigono-metrische Tafeln*, a book that had also been in Semper's Dresden library; Joseph-Louis Lagrange's *Leçons sur le calcul des fonctions*; and Newton's *Philosophiae naturalis prinpicia mathematica*, a work that Semper had already read as a student in Göttingen.[9]

Semper's interest in mathematics is well known. His particular affinity for it was evident as early as his school years and in his choice of subjects to study in Göttingen. For Semper, this interest was initially combined with an inclination towards the military sciences, hydraulic engineering, and finally architecture.[10] However, Semper's mathematics studies with Bernhard Friedrich Thibaut had provided him not only with a subject-specific education in the narrower sense. Thibaut had also introduced him to a form of epistemology adopted from Johann Friedrich Herbart, which was based on training the students' "Anschauung" to enable them to grasp the inner – "organic" – connection among things regulated by principles.[11]

This approach, situated in the general context of Romantic thinking, became a guiding one for Semper's theoretical work, which stands out through its high degree of transdisciplinarity and its exceptionally strong focus on the interconnectivity of phenomena in human history and cultural production. It was only during the years of his London exile, however, that Semper in his theoretical work returned to the disciplinary field of mathematics itself. The research he carried out at that time resulted in the treatise *Ueber die bleiernen Schleudergeschosse der Alten* (On the Leaden Slingshot Bullets of the Ancients), which was finally published in 1859.[12] The first traces of Semper's reinvolvement in mathematics are the three books he ordered in the British Museum Library.

In this chapter, I will reconstruct the connection between Semper's reading of these three books in the late spring of 1852 and his writing on Greek slingshot bullets. Including this early episode in the genesis of the treatise on the one hand allows a more complete reconstruction of the debate that prompted Semper's work. On the other hand, it draws attention to a change in mathematical culture in mid-nineteenth-century Britain, to which Semper's development of the innovative concept of a formal aesthetic – one that expects unstable conditions of perception – corresponds. Semper

_ Figure 2.
Title page of Gottfried Semper, *Ueber die bleiernen Schleudergeschosse der Alten*, 1859 (Courtesy of ETH-Bibliothek Zürich).

Fig. 2

bridged the tension between the artist's task of defining form and the impossibility of reliably achieving that goal, due to the conditions of perception, by referring to calculation methods that operate with variables. As a result, Semper arrived at a morphological conception of form and a topological conception of space.

"Invisible Curve": debates over 'deviations' from the straight line in Greek temples

If one deciphers the cryptic allusions that Semper makes in the introduction of his 1859 book, it appears that it was a lecture by the Scottish artist and art theorist David Ramsey Hay at the Royal Institute of British Architects (RIBA) in February 1853 that prompted his study.[13] The text was delivered by architect and archaeologist Francis Cranmer Penrose; Hay was not allowed to present the lecture himself, as he was not an RIBA member. Semper attended the meeting as an invited guest. In March 1853, Hay's paper was published in the architectural journal "The Builder" under the title *An Attempt to Develope the Principle Which Governs the Proportions and Curves of the Parthenon of Athens.*[14]

Hay was a member of the Royal Society of Edinburgh and enjoyed a national reputation as an official interior designer to Queen Victoria. He was a prolific writer. Between 1828 and 1856 he published fifteen books, the success of which is documented by multiple reprints and translations into German and French. His aesthetic theory was highly original. Hay was convinced that visual beauty in terms of colours, shapes, and proportions was intimately linked to musical harmonies resulting from certain pitches, scales, and chords. He applied his visual aesthetics to various fields including colour theory, the ornamental arts, the human figure, and architecture. His aesthetic theory was modern in that it did not locate musical properties in the objects themselves, but rather regarded them as immanent to the human mind. According to Hay, aesthetic experiences are possible because the musical features that are inherent in the human mind structure perception.[15]

In his RIBA paper, Hay outlined his theory of beautiful forms in classical architecture, which he related to the Parthenon in the final section – in critical disagreement with Penrose's studies on the curvature of Greek temples. Penrose had been making known his research on the Parthenon since the end of the 1840s through lectures;[16] his seminal book *An Investigation of the Principles of Athenian Architecture* appeared in 1851.[17] Hay thus became a participant in a public discussion, sparked by Penrose's work, which proved to be a fundamental debate in various respects. It was a debate about the relationship between perception and measurable properties, as well as about what contributions could be made by which type of mathematics to the description of aesthetic phenomena. A range of evidence, including the three mathematics books borrowed at the British Museum Library (and perhaps also the archaeological work on Athens that he ordered a few days later, on 11 June), indicates that Semper had already started to look into these issues months before he attended the RIBA presentation of Hay's paper.

Very soon after his arrival in London in September 1850, Semper must have heard about the ongoing discussions about Penrose's observations and his explanation of the

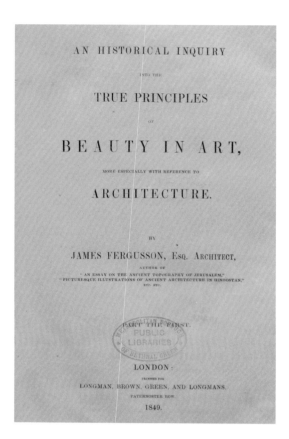

_ Figure 3.
James Fergusson, *An Historical Inquiry into the True Principles of Beauty in Art*, 1849, title page (Private ownership).

curvature, entasis, and inclination of certain building components in Greek temples as representing optical corrections. A first reaction to this can be found as early as January 1851 in a manuscript sent by Semper to Eduard Vieweg, which was published in the same year under the title *Die vier Elemente der Baukunst* (*The Four Elements of Architecture*). The brief passage shows clearly that Semper was relatively well-informed about Penrose's book project, which was still in progress at the time, since apart from Penrose's "discovered deviations", he also mentions sections dealing with ancient polychromy. It was probably precisely these "new polychrome details and a coloured restoration of the Acropolis" that drew Semper's attention to what he called "Mr. Penrose's careful study". Indeed, in the plate section of the book, Penrose published colour reconstructions of details that to some extent corroborated the results of Semper's research in ancient polychromy.

Semper discusses Penrose's discovery of the deviations in the Greek temple in a lengthy footnote, which shows that a new field was opening up for him here. He begins with an observation that can be read as the first formulation of a research subject: "The more successful we are in discovering in detail the high perfection of these creations, the more we lose sight of their full understanding". His initial, preliminary conclusion shows that he had only appreciated Penrose's reflections on optical corrections rather superficially: "As for this particular feature on the Attic-Doric temples … we will have to be content for now with observing that here a transposition of painterly effects into the field of architectural effects took place, insofar as the painterly effect consists of optical illusion".[18]

Semper may have first read about Penrose's studies on ancient curvature in James Fergusson's *An Historical Inquiry into the True Principles of Beauty in Art* of 1849.[19] This extremely broadly conceived systematic-historical work, which includes the natural sciences and the applied arts, must have been of interest to Semper in several respects. He must have seen a copy at the latest in the spring of 1851, since in his discussion of the Great Exhibition, which was published on 17 May 1851 in the German supplement of "The Illustrated London News", he clearly refers to the three catego-

Fig. 3

_ Figure 4.
Francis Cranmer Penrose,
*An Investigation of the
Principles of Athenian
Architecture*, 1851, figs. 1–6:
curve diagrams (Courtesy of
ETH-Bibliothek Zürich).

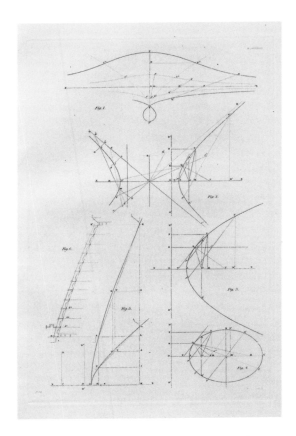

ries of technic, aesthetic, and phonetic arts established by Fergusson in the book.[20]

The *Historical Inquiry* also includes a short chapter on Penrose's observations and theories. Fergusson's attitude towards Penrose is largely critical and is based on an underlying conviction that it is only what an observer can discern spontaneously that can be aesthetically effective. Invisibility applies in particular to the curvature of the long sides of a temple, which therefore, according to Fergusson, could have been "nothing more than a drainage curve".[21] Penrose's approach appeared to him to be "the very metaphysics of art. The idea that a form, the existence of which can only be detected by the most perfect mathematical instruments, should be a cause of beauty in a visible and tangible object is what I can neither understand nor appreciate".[22] In this respect, even the title of Fergusson's chapter embodies the crux of his criticism: "Invisible Curve".

Fig. 4

In his 1851 book, Francis Cranmer Penrose emphasized to readers the mathematical aspects of his discoveries and the description of them. He already warns readers about this in the preface, drawing attention to the aids provided: in view of the many mathematical arguments used, he had taken the precaution of including a glossary of mathematical and technical terms, as well as "a summary of those properties of the Conic Sections, and some other curves" in the appendix.[23] Against this background, it is not surprising that mathematical aspects increasingly took centre stage in the debate after the book's publication.

At the beginning of February 1852, Penrose's book was reviewed positively in "The Builder". The review incidentally mentions the interpretation of curvature as a response to the landscape situation, with Emil Braun being cited as the presumed author of this interpretation: "If we remember rightly, Dr. Emil Braun suggested that it was to make the lines harmonise with the sea horizon".[24] The same hypothesis is also presented by Penrose, who may have adopted it from Braun.[25] Emil Braun was the German archaeologist employed at the Instituto di corrispondenza archeologica in Rome, whose letter had motivated Semper to move to London instead of emigrating to New York. Braun visited Semper immediately after his arrival in the British capital.[26] In London and later

111

from Rome as well, he continued to be a mentor for Semper. It is conceivable that it was through Braun that Semper first learned of Penrose's discoveries.[27]

Two weeks after the anonymous review appeared in "The Builder", a reply to it was published in the same journal, by an author who is only identified with the initials "R.R.". The author exclusively discusses Braun's suggestion, which he rebuts with the help of a series of mathematical calculations.[28] The author of a review of Penrose's book in "The Edinburgh Review" published in April 1852, on the other hand, argues against excessive mathematical reasoning. The argument is not against Penrose's study, which is assessed very favourably. Instead, it is directed against critics such as Fergusson and a similar discussion published in "The Athenæum" in March 1852, the anonymous author of which, with reference to Fergusson, raises the question of the *cui bono* of the invisible curves.[29] By contrast, the reviewer in "The Edinburgh Review" points out the "unconsciousness" or rather the "forgetfulness of consciousness with which the great artist works", in the same way that the "skilful pianist" plays automatically and without thinking. "So, the artist is vividly conscious of the laws by which he works", is the conclusion drawn from this by the reviewer, "at the instant he is acting upon them, but those laws and their modifications are so numerous, and he has so little motive for caring about them after he has done his work by them, that he is apt to overlook the fact of their independent existence".[30] It was therefore also a "grand error of sceptical philosophers, of revolutionary politicians and of German and Germanising critics" to demand "data for the data".[31]

This was approximately the point the public discussion had reached when Semper borrowed the three mathematics books mentioned above at the British Museum Library. In the context of the timing – and, I would argue, also in the context of the content – of the debate over Penrose's curves, Semper was in the summer of 1852 consulting works that could provide him with information about the calculation of spherical forms, as well as about the mathematical description of natural phenomena and ways of depicting them with the help of mathematical curves.

The curvature of the Parthenon: ellipse versus hyperbola

In February of the following year, Semper heard the lecture by David Ramsey Hay at the Royal Institute of British Architects. In his paper, Hay argued in favour of a system of harmonic proportion that was as simple as possible, based on elementary

the depression of any point below the level of the point of sight is exactly in proportion to its distance from it.

Let a' = half the length of building; x' = distance of point of sight from building (and suppose it opposite the centre); y' = distance from point of sight to ends of building. Let a, x, and y = the depressions corresponding to these lengths respectively; then $a:x:y::a':x':y'$. Now, since the triangles are right angled, $y'^2 - x'^2 = a'^2$ substituting the other proportionals

$y^2 - x^2 = a^2$, let b = actual curvature, equal difference of y and x.

$y - x = b$ divide the preceding by this.

$y + x = \frac{a^2}{b}$ subtract the former

$2x = \frac{a^2}{b} - b \therefore x = \frac{a^2 - b^2}{2b}$.

This is the depression of the building at its centre, and this subtracted from the greater depressions of every other point will give the curvature at these parts.

x' is now easily obtained from the equation $x' = \frac{a'x}{a}$. Having now obtained the distance of the point of sight, we can easily find the length of the line from it to any given point, m, in the building. Let p' = length, then p = depression, and $x - p$ = curvature at m, which being compared with the actual curvature, will show whether the real and the supposed curvature be identical.

Let us take an example. A building, 100 feet long, is placed at an elevation of 140 feet above the sea; actual curvature, at 15 feet from centre = ·0064; at 25 feet, ·0154; at the ends, ·0433 = b.

In this case the dip of the horizon is 11′ 39″, which gives in 50 feet length ·1696 depression = a. Then,—

$x = \frac{·1696^2 - ·0433^2}{2 \times ·0433} = ·3105 =$ depression on length x'.

$x' = \frac{50 \times ·3105}{·1696} = 91·6 =$ length of point

_ Figure 5.
Detail from R.R., *The Curved Lines of Greek Architecture*, "The Builder", 21 February 1852.

Fig. 5

geometrical forms and arithmetical operations, which for him was the "fundamental element of the beautiful in architecture".[32] Based on the observation that "a right line has only three directions – the horizontal, the vertical, and the oblique"[33] and that curved forms must be regarded as equivalent to angular basic shapes, Hay established a canon of six basic forms: "perfect square, oblong rectangle, isosceles triangle, circle, ellipse, and composite ellipse".[34] For Hay, simplicity in formal and proportional design was a basic condition for beauty, since it was only this that allowed beauty to be clearly represented and conveyed – or, in Hay's words, to create beautiful artefacts whose "beauty … [is] of a demonstrable and intelligible character".[35]

Hay explained in detail the way in which he had determined the basic forms:

> The elementary forms in architecture are, like the elementary sounds in music, few and extremely simple in their nature. … When a horizontal and a vertical line meet, they make a right angle, which may with safety be assumed as the fundamental angle, from the harmonic divisions of which by 2, 3, 5, 7, or multiples of these primes, the beauty of every architectural design is to arise. When two lines thus making a right angle are joined by an oblique line, the three form the right angled triangle, which is the prime element of all figures employed in architecture.[36]

The rectangle consisted of two compound triangles, and the round shapes could also be traced back to this basic shape by assigning each of them to one of its derivatives: "the circle belongs to the perfect square … the ellipse to the horizontal and vertical rectangle … and … the composite ellipse … belongs to every isosceles triangle".[37]

The reductionism of Hay's approach becomes clear not only from its strict two-dimensionality but also in its limitation to forms that can be constructed geometrically and relationships that can be expressed arithmetically. Among the basic forms, the "composite ellipse" is the most complex shape; similar to a basket arch, its individual parts are joined together in such a way that as few angles as possible are created.[38] Hay introduced it as being "new and very little understood". However, he had studied it and found that it could be described very simply on the basis of his categories of form. "I may state", he writes, "that the composite ellipse is simply a figure composed of arcs of various ellipses harmonically flowing into each other, whose foci are placed on the sides of an inscribed isosceles triangle".[39]

What then follows makes it clear that Hay was arguing on the basis of a "fundamental conviction" ("Hintergrundüberzeugung").[40] In his eyes, an object can only be beautiful if its shape can be traced back to the set of basic forms that he had identified. Thus, he writes of the "composite ellipse" that it "closely resembles the parabolic and hyperbolic curves; but it has what these curves have not, viz. the essential quality of inscribing harmonically one of the rectilinear elements of architecture". By contrast, he dismisses parabolas and hyperbolas as "merely curves of motion, which never can harmonically inscribe, nor resolve themselves into a figure of any kind".[41]

This conception determined Hay's concluding critical comment on Penrose:

> I cannot help demurring to the conclusions at which Mr. Penrose has arrived with respect to the aesthetic developments of the Parthenon; especially to his idea that the entases of the columns are hyperbolic curves, that the soffit of the corona of the pediment is a curve of the same kind … this mode of proof must at first sight seem conclusive; but it can only be so in the absence of a knowledge of the composite ellipse and of the various other modes in which ellipses may be combined. For an acquaintance with these will show that arcs of the composite, or mixed ellipse, resemble so closely those of the hyperbola and parabola, that the most careful investigator might be mistaken.[42]

113

This passage also makes it clear that Hay was concerned not with what a form looks like but rather with the question of how it is described mathematically.

The earliest – at that time still implicit – manifestation of Semper's reaction to Hay's paper and the debates preceding it was the very first lecture he delivered at the Department of Practical Art, on 20 May 1853. In the lecture, Semper addressed a series of fundamental considerations. These included what would later become known as his "style formula".[43] Semper introduced it in terms of a metaphorical representation. "Every work of art", he writes, "is a *result*, or, using a Mathematical Term, it is a *Function* of an indefinite number of quantities or powers, which are the variable coefficients of the embodiment of it. $U = \Phi x, y, z, t, v, w$. As soon as one or some of these coefficients vary, the Result must vary likewise, and must show in its features and general appearance a certain distinct character".[44] Semper repeated and specified this representation of the work of art in the form of a mathematical function in his second lecture at the department, which introduced his lecture series of autumn 1853. On this occasion – perhaps partly in response to critical remarks that had been made on his first lecture – he added to the comparison an explanatory note on the metaphorical nature of the formula:

> It will be said, that an artistical problem is not a mathematical one and that results in fine arts are hardly obtainable by calculation. This is very true, and I am the last to believe that mere reflexion and calculation may at any time succeed in filling the place of talent, and natural taste. Also I only wanted this shedula as a crutch for leaning on it in explaining the subject I therefore will kindly be allowed to prosecute my proposition and to give some real attributions and values to those letters.[45]

This commitment to artistic intuition corresponded to a fundamental conviction that Semper had already set out in 1834, in his so-called Inaugural Lecture at the Dresden Academy of Arts. On the basis of the observation that "architecture does not have its models for the representation of an idea ready-made in the forms (*Gestalten*) and formal appearances (*förmliche Erscheinungen*) of nature, but is based on indeterminable but no less certain and firm laws (which seem to agree with the fundamental laws of nature) according to which it orders all the spatial needs of human relations", he claims: "Although we are convinced of the existence of these laws, we cannot nevertheless determine them mathematically a priori and thus also not teach them scientifically (as, for instance, the laws of music), we must therefore try to practise the only criterion of their existence, the feeling for their excellence".[46]

It may have been a revisiting of such lines of thought that had prompted Semper – as early as August 1852, immediately after submitting the manuscript of the metals catalogue to Henry Cole – to order another book in the British Museum Library: Johann Nicolaus Forkel's *Ueber die Theorie der Musik* (On the Theory of Music) of 1777.[47] Forkel believed that the appreciation of musical art must be based on a thorough knowledge of the underlying rules of music, which he saw as being summarized in a "physical and mathematical theory of sound".[48] However, as the book was written for a lay audience, Forkel's introduction is not really a listing of a set of rules that can be practically applied by musicians. It is more about two aspects: firstly, a knowledge of rules that make it possible to establish common criteria, beyond subjective perception, in music (as in the sciences and the fine arts). Forkel argues that subjective perception is determined by nature and therefore is not bad per se, but that it can be detrimental to art appreciation if there is a lack of knowledge of the rules. Secondly, in his eyes the rules were basically justifiable insofar as they are the result of a careful study of nature. Forkel believed that it is only when perception has been trained and is able to recognize the rules derived from nature that a full appreciation of art is possible, devoid of misunderstandings. It is only then, for example, that one can avoid seeing a painted shadow in a painting as a mere blotch. Thus, according to Forkel, adequate aesthetic perception is dependent on a knowledge of physical and mathematical rules. However, these rules are not perceived as such but rather make it possible to recognize a beautiful melody or beautiful form.

Forkel's book may have been a reference source for Semper when he was rethinking the relationship between mathematical properties and intuition, both in artistic production and in the perception of forms. In his London lecture of 20 May 1853, he referred to mathematics and mechanics in connection with his explanations of "use". Use was one of the "coefficients" that determine the form of an artwork identified by him. The "Savages, and semi-Barbarians", Semper writes in his paper, had instinctively followed the laws of mechanics that underlay usage forms. Wherever such instinctive creation was no longer the case among more advanced civilizations, "science and calculation" could lead back to a form that corresponds to the usage of an object.[49] At this point, Semper cites the example of the Greek slingshot bullet. He argues that its almond-shaped form corresponds perfectly to its dynamic function as a projectile. The question of the way in which "these Projectiles are the Result of an instinctive feeling of their makers for fittness or if they are proofs of the high state of Mechanical Science with the Greecs"[50] is answered by Semper in his 1859 book on Greek slingshot bullets, recognizing the scientific competence of the Greeks.[51] Consistently with Forkel, and also following Bernhard Friedrich Thibaut's views on the education of *Anschauung* as being based on mathematical training, one could say that the Greeks had created the mathematical and scientific foundations for the intuitively correct (and accordingly beautiful) design of artistic forms.

115

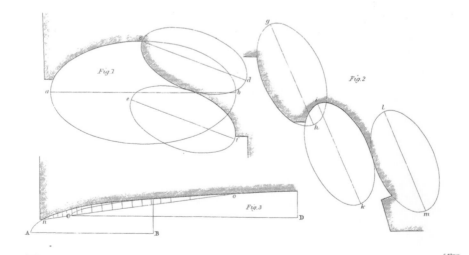

_ Figure 6.
David Ramsay Hay, *The Orthographic Beauty of the Parthenon*, 1853, plate 7 (Courtesy of Hathi Trust Digital Library, copy Cornell University).

According to Semper, the dynamic properties of the shape of the leaden slingshot bullets also characterize those forms of nature generated by the "power *of animal and vegetable Life* – and we must add", he continues, "that, the more the works of our hands have the appearances of being results of such living forces, which act against gravity and substance, the higher they stand upon the scale of artistical accomplishment". In this respect, in Semper's view the dynamic almond shape of the slingshot bullet reflects one of the bases for the beautiful, lively forms of Greek architecture: "The Greec temples and monuments in general are not constructed, they have grown".[52]

At the end of the section of the lecture on use as a coefficient of (beautiful) form, Semper addresses the ongoing debates on the curvilinearity of Greek temples. He does so largely implicitly at this point. He becomes more explicit later on, in the version he published as an introduction to his treatise of 1859, where he elaborates on what is only sketched out in the lecture. In the London paper, Semper states that the measurement of the Greek temples and the geometric descriptions of their forms based on it "will never succeed, for, if it is right in Mathematics, to consider certain surfaces as the results of revolving curves, it is not the same in Natural history and in Art. Very beautiful … forms may have sections of no proportion and beauty and beautiful sectional outlines or projections may produce by revolving them very unhappy Surfaces".[53] In Semper's eyes, it can therefore be said, objects do not have a stable form, insofar as they are dependent on perception.

But how is one to deal with the unstable conditions of perception? What answer can be given to this from the point of view of the practising and teaching artist? What Semper presented to his audience at Marlborough House as a solution represents dynamics as the correct field of mechanics and mathematics in relation to this. "Nature works not like a turner after working drawings", he explained, "its forms are alltogether dynamical productions, and it is only by way of that science, which treats of the mutual actions and reactions of forces, that we may hope to find the keys for some of the simplest material forms. What is true in Nature, has its application also for artistical forms, if they are animated by organic life, like the works of the Greeks".[54]

116

_ Figure 7.
Gottfried Semper, manuscript page with calculations concerning the form of Greek slingshot bullets, 1853 (Courtesy of the gta Archives/ETH Zurich, 20-Ms-118, fol. 1v).

Fig. 6

In this way, Semper's argumentation points in the opposite direction to David Ramsay Hay's arguments. Semper rejected design based on simple numerical operations and geometric figures. The rigid and lifeless-looking forms with which Hay illustrated his explanations fall into this category.[55] The principle that Hay had explicitly rejected – the form-generating laws of motion – was regarded by Semper as being fundamental to design. For Hay, "motion" was in itself an argument for rejecting parabolas and hyperbolas as "merely curves of motion".[56] By contrast, it was precisely these curves that Semper made the object of his investigation. In the spring of 1853, he began his mathematical study of Greek slingshot bullets. Using extensive calculations, he aimed to prove that the aerodynamic almond shape of the bullets was best suited to their function. The chronological coincidence between this study and the preparation of the lecture of May 1853 is evidenced by a manuscript page belonging to the first version of the lecture draft: on the reverse side of it are calculations that can be assigned to the study on the slingshot bullets.[57]

Fig. 7

For Semper, therefore, mathematics was more than a mere metaphor. It was at the same time a discipline that allowed him to recognize inner laws of form and, in a second step, to apply them creatively. The Greeks did the same, as Semper explains in the version of his study published in 1859. In the formal design of their buildings, Semper writes in the introduction to his book, the Greeks did not simply fol-

117

low the "inspiration of a vague artist's instinct". Instead, they had "clearly set themselves their task". The aim of his study was "to prove by means of the simplest possible example that the Greeks did not merely observe the laws of nature and endeavour to reproduce the forms that arose according to them, but rather that they had really investigated these laws and from them, independently of all imitation of nature, created their own structures, which coincided with those of nature precisely only in the commonality of the law".[58] In this way, the observation of natural forms is transferred into form-giving calculation. In his study, Semper applies an analogous method to Greek slingshot bullets. Their shape resembles that of almonds or plum pits. According to Semper, this is why the Greeks called them *balanoi*

_ Figure 8.
Gottfried Semper, manuscript page with calculations and diagrams concerning the form of Greek slingshot bullets, ca. 1853 (Courtesy of the gta Archives/ETH Zurich, 20-Ms-161).

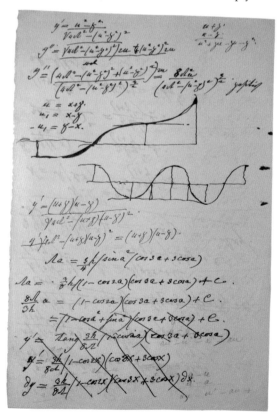

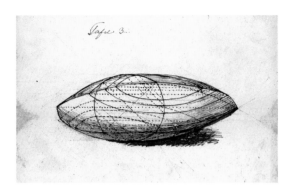

and the Romans *glandes*.[59] But the slingshot bullets are not plum pits or almonds made of lead, but man-made objects whose shape was optimized and mathematically calculated according to the requirements of dynamics.

 In the study on the aerodynamic shape of slingshot bullets, Semper was entering a field in which he was able to investigate a relational principle as a basic condition for form. The variability of the factors coincides with the perceived variability of the form of the object moving in space. Only a type of calculation that works with variables does justice to both the dynamic natural model and the relativity of aesthetic perception.[60] Morphology takes the place of a doctrine of stable forms, and topological space takes the place of metric space. At the same time, the study on the slingshot bullet makes it possible to place an instrument in the artist's hands. If we were to observe a slingshot bullet flying through the air in slow motion, we would perceive it as more or less beautiful depending on its relative position to us. As an object held in the hand, by contrast, the slingshot bullet can be reliably experienced as beautiful – provided the light is good – because the principles of movement are frozen in its form, as it were.

 The calculations made by Semper, which fill about one hundred pages in the 1859 book, are largely trigonometric.[61] This is somewhat at odds with the "style formula", in which Semper describes the work of art as being the result of a function. This divergence between claim and practice might be due to the mathematical training he had received and the disciplinary limitations that resulted from it. That modern analysis was nonetheless a frame of reference for Semper is already clear from the fact that in May and June 1852, in addition to Vega's *Logarithmisch-trigonometrische Tafeln* and Newton's *Philosophiae naturalis*, he also borrowed Lagrange's *Leçons sur le calcul des fonctions*. Semper's description of the work of art in the form of a mathematical function demonstrates an attitude; it represents a commitment to modern mathematics. The fact that he himself makes trigonometric calculations constitutes a contradiction to the "style formula" on the one hand, but on the other hand it also underlines the programmatic character of Semper's reference to calculus.

 This positioning can be seen in the context of a change in mathematical culture that became particularly virulent in Britain around the mid-nineteenth century and had an impact on a broad public.[62] Sem-

_ Figure 9.
Gottfried Semper, Greek slingshot bullet in its perfect form, drawing for plate 3 of *Ueber die bleiernen Schleudergeschosse der Alten* (1859), ca. 1858 (Courtesy of the gta Archives/ETH Zurich, 20-Ms-161).

Fig. 8

Fig. 9

Fig. 10

_ Figure 10.
Gottfried Semper, "Style formula", passage from the lecture manuscript *General Remarks on the Different Styles in Art*, 1853 (Courtesy of the gta Archives/ETH Zurich, 20-Ms-124)

118

per's work and statements on architectural curvilinearity suggest that he was aware of the epistemological dimension of modern mathematics. It cannot be assumed that his statements were a direct response to specific mathematical concepts. The same might be true for Penrose, Hay, and other authors who took part in the debate on architectural curves. But these contributions can be assessed in a context that Andrea Henderson summarizes as follows: "Victorian mathematics thus not only redefined itself as a field but also all the fields around it: inquiry centered on facts and data was increasingly distinguished from the study of the laws – or 'operations' – that structured those facts".[63]

Epilogue: Greek slingshot bullets and Prussian pointed musket balls

At the point where Semper refers to the Greek slingshot bullet in his London lecture of May 1853, he introduces a modern descendant of the Greek projectile: "The other projectile laying by them, is a Prussian pointed musket-ball".[64] It is noteworthy that Semper in his manuscript deleted an addition in the text that identified him as a fugitive from the 1848–49 revolutions: "a musket ball, which they shot into the window of my sitting Room in the Year 1849". Semper's wording suggests that he was showing the audience an example of such a musket ball as an illustration. In the frontispiece of his 1859 publication, he then depicted a Prussian pointed musket ball in addition to three Greek slingshot bullets and an Arab projectile. As a descendant of the Greek bullet, the Prussian pointed musket-ball was – according to Semper in the lecture – imperfect, as the Greek almond shape was much more expedient than the one-sided, weighted ball.

In the autumn of 1853, Semper reported to the Prussian newspaper correspondent Julius Faucher, whom he had befriended, on his studies of Greek slingshot bullets. When he found "shortly afterwards … a note about it in the Kreuzzeitung", he feared that "some Prussian engineering officer" might exploit his "idea".[65] This concern prompted Semper to seek prepublication of his study in Germany. He asked Friedrich Krause for help in achieving this. Krause ran a private school in Dresden and had supported Semper's family in many ways. Semper had thanked him for this by dedicating *The Four Elements of Architecture* to him in 1851.[66] Krause put Semper in touch with Benjamin Witzschel, a mathematics teacher at his school. Witzschel arranged for the publication of an abridged version of Semper's study, which appeared in September 1854 under the title *Von der Form der Körper, die mit geringster Resistenz in widerstehenden Mittel sich bewegen* (On the Form of Bodies That Move with Least Resistance in Resistant Media) in the Leipzig "Annalen der Physik und Chemie".[67]

Fig. 11

Fig. 12

119

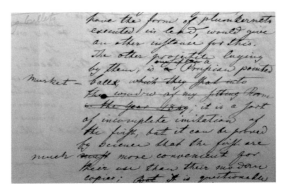

_ Figure 11.
Gottfried Semper, passage from the lecture manuscript *On the Relation of the Different Branches of Industrial Art to Each Other and to Architecture* (third version), 1853, with deleted addition (Courtesy of the gta Archives/ETH Zurich, 20-Ms-122, fol. 12r).

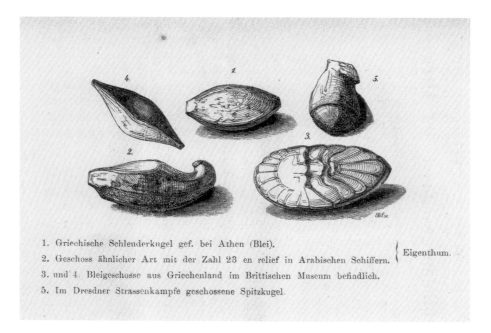

1. Griechische Schleuderkugel gef. bei Athen (Blei).
2. Geschoss ähnlicher Art mit der Zahl 23 en relief in Arabischen Schiffern. } Eigenthum.
3. und 4. Bleigeschosse aus Griechenland im Brittischen Museum befindlich.
5. Im Dresdner Strassenkampfe geschossene Spitzkugel.

_ Figure 12.
Frontispiece of
Gottfried Semper,
*Ueber die bleiernen
Schleudergeschosse der
Alten*, 1859 (Courtesy of
ETH-Bibliothek Zürich).

The article concentrates mainly on presenting the mathematical argumentation. Among other things, it explains the aerodynamic advantages of a shape that is pointed on both sides. The article's starting point, however, is a reference to a series of experiments that Prussian engineers had carried out with oval-shaped projectiles. On the basis of such experiments, according to Witzschel, Semper's "soon to be published work … 'Ueber die Schleudergeschossse der Griechen'" should be of "some interest".[68] In fact, optimizing the shape of rifle bullets was a field in which research was also being carried out outside Prussia at the time.[69] The pointed musket ball was not only the usual ammunition of the Prussian army in those days. As seen at the time, it was virtually a symbol of Prussian state power – a state power that was a culturally, politically, and existentially destructive one, especially from a postrevolutionary perspective. This is evidenced, among other things, by the *Zeit-Distichen*, a polemical reckoning with Prussia, which Hoffmann von Fallersleben published in 1849 under the title *Spitzkugeln*.[70]

In relation to Semper's attempt to illustrate the parameters of beautiful and animated form using the example of Greek slingshot bullets, a certain paradox arises from this. For the Prussian pointed musket balls, although not perfectly functional and thus also less beautiful in form, are destructive, whereas Greek slingshot bullets – perfectly formed and thus all the more certain to bring death – are associated with the lively forms of Greek architecture.

I am indebted to Michael Gnehm for suggesting the title of this chapter. "Architectural curvilinearity" is a notion borrowed from an essay by Greg Lynn, but I have not drawn on Lynn's arguments. Cf. G. Lynn, *Architectural Curvilinearity: The Folded, the Pliant and the Supple*, "AD Profile", 63, no. 102 (*Folding in Architecture*), pp. 8–15.

_1. W. Herrmann, *Gottfried Semper im Exil: Paris, London 1849–1855. Zur Entstehung des "Stil" 1840–1877*, Birkhäuser, Basel 1978, p. 68.

_2. I am grateful to Dieter Weidmann for this information.

_3. Herrmann, *Gottfried Semper*, see note 1, p. 68, erroneously gives a shorter time span (30 April –19 August 1852).

_4. Cf. the edition of a later copy of that manuscript: G. Semper, *The Ideal Museum: Practical Art in Metals and Hard Materials*, edited by P. Noever, Schlebrügge, Vienna 2007.

_5. Edited in G. Semper, *London Writings 1850–1855*, edited by M. Gnehm, S. Hildebrand, and D. Weidmann, gta Verlag, Zurich 2021.

_6. Two books by Serlio; von der Hagen, *Briefe in die Heimat*, 1818; *Indian Archipelago*, 1851. Cf. Semper, *London Writings*, see note 5.

_7. Cf. S. Hildebrand, *Gottfried Semper: Architekt und Revolutionär*, Darmstadt, wbg, 2020, pp. 119–22.

_8. Semper's borrowing slip reads: "C. Ottfried Müller, Die Alterthumer v. Athen mit Beiträgen von …, 1829". It probably refers to J. Stuart and N. Revett, *Die Alterthümer von Athen*, 3 vols. (vol. 3 entitled *Alterthümer von Athen und andern Orten Griechenlands, Siciliens und Kleinasiens, gemessen und erläutert von C.R. Cockerell, W. Kinnard, T.L. Donaldson, W. Jenkins, W. Railton*), trans. K. Wagner and F. Osann, Carl Wilhelm Leske, Darmstadt 1829–33, which contains a text by Karl Otfried Müller on the Parthenon metopes and frieze (vol. 2, pp. 657–96). Cf. Semper, *London Writings*, see note 5.

_9. Cf. Gottfried Semper, letter to his brother Johann Carl, 10 December 1823, gta Archives/ETH Zurich, 20-K-1823-12-10(S).

_10. Cf. W. Herrmann, *Sempers Weg von der Mathematik zur vergleichenden Baulehre*, in B. Wyss (ed.), *Bildfälle: Die Moderne im Zwielicht*, Artemis, Zurich 1990, pp. 73–81 (here pp. 73–77); U. Poerschke, *Architektur als mathematische Funktion: Überlegungen zu Gottfried Semper*, in M. Eggers (ed.), *Von Ähnlichkeiten und Unterschieden: Vergleich, Analogie und Klassifikation in Wissenschaft und Literatur (18./19. Jahrhundert)*, Winter, Heidelberg 2011, pp. 121–41 (here pp. 129–30); S. Hildebrand, *Gottfried Semper*, see note 7, pp. 12–20.

_11. Cf. S. Hildebrand, *"… verschiedene Anwendungen einer und derselben grossen Wissenschaft": Gottfried Semper und die Mathematik*, "Mathematische Semesterberichte", 65, no. 2, 2018, pp. 153–69 (here pp. 154–59), DOI 10.1007/s00591-018-0228-5; S. Hildebrand, *Gottfried Semper*, see

note 7, pp. 12–17. Literature on Herbart is vast. For Herbart and the training of *Anschauung* see recently: T. Teutenberg, *Die Unterweisung des Blicks: Visuelle Erziehung und visuelle Kultur im langen 19. Jahrhundert*, transcript, Bielefeld 2019, pp. 87–92; from the perspective of the history of mathematics: H.N. Jahnke, *Mathematik und Bildung in der Humboldtschen Reform*, Göttingen, Vandenhoeck & Ruprecht 1990, pp. 122–34. For Thibaut see K. Reich, *Bernhard Friedrich Thibaut, der Mathematiker an Gauß' Seite*, "Mitteilungen der Gauß-Gesellschaft", 34, 1997, pp. 45–62.

_12. G. Semper, *Ueber die bleiernen Schleudergeschosse der Alten und über zweckmässige Gestaltung der Wurfkörper im Allgemeinen: Ein Versuch, die dynamische Entstehung gewisser Formen in der Natur und in der Kunst nachzuweisen*, Verlag für Kunst und Wissenschaft, Frankfurt am Main 1859, reprinted in G. Semper, *Gesammelte Schriften*, edited by H. Karge, vol. 1.1, Olms-Weidmann, Hildesheim 2014, pp. 660–778.

_13. Cf. S. Hildebrand, *Towards an Expanded Concept of Form: Gottfried Semper on Ancient Projectiles*, in S. Hildebrand and E. Bergmann (eds.), *Form-Finding, Form-Shaping, Designing Architecture: Experimental, Aesthetical and Social Approaches to Form in Recent and Postwar Architecture*, Mendrisio Academy Press and Silvana Editoriale , Mendrisio and Milan, 2015, pp. 131–43 (here p. 136); S. Papapetros, *Ornament as Weapon: Ballistics, Politics, and Architectural Adornment in Semper's Treatise on Ancient Projectiles*, in G. Necipoglu and A. Payne (eds.), *Histories of Ornament: From Global to Local*, Princeton University Press, Princeton 2016, pp. 46–61 (here p. 50); S. Hildebrand, *"… verschiedene Anwendungen einer und derselben grossen Wissenschaft"*, see note 11, pp. 162–63; S. Hildebrand, *Mathematische Kurven in der Architekturtheorie um 1850: Gottfried Semper, David Ramsay Hay und die Ästhetik der invisible curves des Parthenon*, "figurationen", no. 2, 2020, pp. 55–76 (here p. 60). The present chapter follows on from the author's own work listed above, partly incorporating some of the formulations presented there.

_14. D.R. Hay, *An Attempt to Develope the Principle Which Governs the Proportions and Curves of the Parthenon of Athens*, "The Builder", 11, 1853, pp. 162–64. The text is identical with the reprint of the lecture in the "RIBA Papers" under the date of the meeting on 7 February 1853.

_15. C. Raz, *Music of the Squares: David Ramsay Hay and the Reinvention of Pythagorean Aesthetics*, "The Public Domain Review", 16 May 2019, https://publicdomainreview.org/essay/music-of-the-squares-david-ramsay-hay-and-the-reinvention-of-pythagorean-aesthetics (accessed 20 August 2020).

_16. Cf. J. Fergusson, *An Historical Inquiry into the True Principles of Beauty in Art, More Especially with Reference to Architecture*, Longman, Brown, Green, and Longmans, London 1849, p. 396, note.

121

_17. F.C. Penrose, *An Investigation of the Principles of Athenian Architecture; or the Results of a Recent Survey, Conducted Chiefly with Reference to the Optical Refinements Exhibited in the Construction of the Ancient Buildings in Athens*, Society of Dilettanti, London 1851.

_18. G. Semper, *The Four Elements of Architecture: A Contribution to the Comparative Study of Architecture (1851)*, in G. Semper, *The Four Elements of Architecture and Other Writing*, trans. H.F. Mallgrave and W. Herrmann, Cambridge University Press, Cambridge, MA 2010, pp. 74–129 (here p. 80).

_19. J. Fergusson, *An Historical Inquiry*, see note 16.

_20. G. Semper, *Die große Ausstellung: Die Völker von europäischer und nicht europäischer Bildung*, "The Illustrated London News", 18, 17 May 1851, German supplement, no. 3, pp. 34–35, reprinted in G. Semper, *Gesammelte Schriften*, see note 11, pp. 369–70, and edited in G. Semper, *London Writings*, see note 5.

_21. J. Fergusson, *An Historical Inquiry*, see note 16, p. 396.

_22. *Ibid.*, p. 397.

_23. F.C. Penrose, *An Investigation*, see note 17, p. v.

_24. Anonymous author, without title, in "The Builder", 10, 7 February 1852, pp. 81–82 (here p. 82).

_25. F.C. Penrose, *An Investigation*, see note 17, p. 79.

_26. Cf. S. Hildebrand, *Gottfried Semper*, see note 7, pp. 103–4.

_27. Another possible source is Thomas Leverton Donaldson. Semper knew him from an earlier stay in London and visited him as early as October 1850, shortly after relocating. Donaldson was one of the founders and secretaries of the Royal Institute of British Architects. As early as 1847 he was the addressee of a letter on *The Necessity of Numerous Correct Examples of Mathematical Lines, as Specimens of Forms to Instruct the Eye in Truth and Beauty, and to Suggest Applications to Designs*, published by its author Joseph Joplin (London 1847), in which Penrose's work on the curvature of the Parthenon was discussed. I thank Elena Chestnova for pointing me to this publication. On Semper's relationship with Donaldson cf. D. Weidmann, *Through the Stable Door to Prince Albert? On Gottfried Semper's London Connections*, "Journal of Art Historiography", no. 11, December 2014, pp. 1–26 (here pp. 14–18).

_28. R.R., *The Curved Lines of Greek Architecture*, "The Builder", 10, 21 February 1852, pp. 121–22.

_29. Anonymous author, *Fine Arts: An Investigation of the Principles of Athenian Architecture, &c. By Francis Cranmer Penrose. Published by the Dilettanti Society*, "The Athenæum", 291, no. 1272, 13 March 1852, pp. 304–5 (here p. 304).

_30. Anonymous author, *An Investigation of the Principles of Athenian Architecture; or the Results of a Recent Survey, Conducted Chiefly with Reference to the Optical Refinements Exhibited in the Construction of the Ancient Buildings of Athens. By Francis Cranmer Penrose, Architect, M.A., &c. Illustrated by Numerous Engravings. Published by the Society of Dilettanti. London: 1852 [sic]*, "The Edinburgh Review", 95, no. 194, April 1852, pp. 395–405 (here p. 404).

_31. *Ibid.*, pp. 404–5. It is not clear who is being referred to in the groups of persons asking for data that are listed. For reasons that will be outlined in the following part of this chapter, however, Semper should not have been included in it.

_32. D.R. Hay, *An Attempt*, see note 14, p. 162.

_33. *Ibid.*

_34. *Ibid.*, p. 163.

_35. *Ibid.*, pp. 162–63.

_36. *Ibid.*

_37. *Ibid.*, p. 163.

_38. I am grateful to Klaus Volkert of the University of Wuppertal for the analysis of Hay's "composite ellipse", on the basis of D.R. Hay, *The Orthographic Beauty of the Parthenon Referred to a Law of Nature*, Blackwood and Sons, Edinburgh 1853, plate 7.

_39. D.R. Hay, *An Attempt*, see note 14, p. 163.

_40. This term is used following W. Detel, *Wissenskulturen und universelle Rationalität*, in J. Fried and M. Stolleis (eds.), *Wissenskulturen: Über die Erzeugung und Weitergabe von Wissen*, Campus, Frankfurt am Main 2009, pp. 181–214.

_41. D.R. Hay, *An Attempt*, see note 14, p. 163.

_42. *Ibid.*, p. 164.

_43. Cf. H.F. Mallgrave, *Gottfried Semper: Architect of the Nineteenth Century*, Yale University Press, New Haven 1996, pp. 217–18; U. Poerschke, *Architektur als mathematische Funktion*, see note 10; U. Poerschke, *Architecture as a Mathematical Function: Reflections on Gottfried Semper*, "Nexus Network Journal", 14, 2012, pp. 119–34, DOI 10.1007/s00004-011-0101-5.

_44. G. Semper, *On the Relation of the Different Branches of Industrial Art to Each Other and to Architecture: Third Version*, gta Archives/ETH Zürich, 20-Ms-122, fol. 8r, edited in G. Semper, *London Writings*, see note 5; emphasis in the original.

_45. G. Semper, *General Remarks on the Different Styles in Art*, gta Archives/ETH Zürich, 20-Ms-124, fol. 6r, edited in G. Semper, *London Writings*, see note 5. In research, the manuscripts 20-Ms-122 and 20-Ms-124 have hitherto been erroneously treated as two variants of the lecture of autumn 1853; cf. the commentary on *General Remarks on the Different Styles in Art*, in G. Semper, *London Writings*.

_46. "[A]ber d. Architektur hat ihre Vorbilder zur Darstellung einer Idee nicht fertig in den Gestalten und förmlichen Erscheinungen der Natur, sondern sie beruht auf unbestimmbaren aber nicht desto weniger sicheren und festen Gesetzen, (die mit den Grundgesetzen der Natur übereinzustimmen scheinen,) nach denen sie alle räumlichen Bedürfnisse der menschlichen Verhältnisse ordnet. … Obwohl wir vom Dasyn dieser Gesetze überzeugt sind, so können wir sie dennoch nicht mathematisch a priori bestimmen und also auch nicht wissenschaftlich beibringen (wie etwa d. Gesetze der Musik), wir müssen also das einzige Criterium ihres Vorhandenseyns, das Gefühl für ihre Vorzüglichkeit, zu üben suchen". G. Semper, *Dresdner Antrittsvorlesung* (1834), transcription in H. Laudel, *Gottfried Semper: Architektur und Stil*, Verlag der Kunst, Dresden 1991, pp. 221–34 (here pp. 223–24).

_47. J.N. Forkel, *Ueber die Theorie der Musik, insofern sie Liebhabern und Kennern nothwendig und nützlich ist: Eine Einladungsschrift zu musikalischen Vorlesungen*, Vandenhoeck, Göttingen 1777.

_48. *Ibid.*, p. 11.

_49. G. Semper, *On the Relation*, see note 44, fol. 11v–12r.

_50. *Ibid.*, fol. 12r.

_51. G. Semper, *Ueber die bleiernen Schleudergeschosse*, see note 12, p. 6.

_52. G. Semper, *On the Relation*, see note 44, fol. 13r.

_53. *Ibid.*, fol. 13r–v.

_54. *Ibid.*, fol. 13v.

_55. D.R. Hay, *The Orthographic Beauty*, see note 38. Cf. S. Papapetros, *Ornament as Weapon*, see note 13, pp. 50–51.

_56. D.R. Hay, *An Attempt*, see note 14, p. 163.

_57. 20-Ms-118, fol. 1, gta Archives/ETH Zurich.

_58. G. Semper, *Ueber die bleiernen Schleudergeschosse*, see note 12, p. 5. The belief that the Greeks had precisely calculated the proportions of their buildings had already been held by James Stuart. Accordingly, Stuart had felt legitimized to measure the dimensions of the Parthenon with the help of trigonometric calculations. Cf. D. Mondini, *La storia come archivio di exempla: Stuart & Revett e le raccolte illustrate di antichità tra Sette e Ottocento*, in S. Hildebrand, D. Mondini, and R. Grignolo with B. Pedretti (eds.), *Architettura e saperi / Architecture and Knowledge*, Mendrisio Academy Press and Silvana Editoriale , Mendrisio and Milan 2018, pp. 73–89 (here p. 83).

_59. G. Semper, *Ueber die bleiernen Schleudergeschosse*, see note 12, p. 6.

_60. Cf. the analogous observations presented by S. Papapetros, *Ornament as Weapon*, see note 13, pp. 50–51.

_61. S. Papapetros, *Ornament as Weapon*, see note 13, p. 52.

_62. Cf. J.L. Richards, *Mathematical Visions: The Pursuit of Geometry in Victorian England*, Academic Press, Boston 1988; A.K. Henderson, *Algebraic Art: Mathematical Formalism and Victorian Culture*, Oxford University Press, Oxford 2018.

_63. A. Henderson, *Algebraic Art*, see note 62, p.8.

_64. G. Semper, *On the Relation*, see note 44, fol. 12r.

_65. Gottfried Semper, draft of a letter to Friedrich Krause, 6 Mai 1854, gta Archives/ETH Zürich, 20-K-1854-05-06(S). Cf. D. Weidmann, *Gottfried Sempers "Polytechnikum" in Zürich: Ein Heiligtum der Wissenschaften und Künste*, PhD diss., ETH Zurich, 2010, vol. 1, pp. 282–83; D. Weidmann, *Through the Stable Door*, see note 27, pp. 17–18. Dieter Weidmann was the first to reconstruct the story reported below.

_66. Cf. S. Hildebrand, *Gottfried Semper*, see note 7, pp. 95–96, 107–8.

_67. B. Witzschel, *Von der Form der Körper, die mit geringster Resistenz in widerstehenden Mitteln sich bewegen*, "Annalen der Physik und Chemie", 93, no. 10, 18 September 1854, pp. 297–305.

_68. *Ibid.*, p. 297.

_69. Cf. for instance Sinner, *Ueber die Spitzkugeln*, "Allgemeine schweizerische Militärzeitung", 3=23, 1857, pp. 262–63.

_70. A.H. Hoffmann von Fallersleben, *Spitzkugeln: Zeit-Distichen*, Leske, Darmstadt 1849.

123

Elena Chestnova

Vessels of Character

"How strikingly is symbolised the light spiritual and lucid nature of the monteneer inhabitants of Greece in this form [of the Hydria], opposed to the Nile Pail, which is a true representative of the national Genius of the Aegyptians".
Gottfried Semper[1]

_ Figure 1.
Gottfried Semper,
Hydria, ca. 1853
(Courtesy of the gta
Archives/ETH Zurich).

Figs. 2, 3

The hydria of the Greeks and the situla of the Egyptians are among the most famous of Gottfried Semper's example artefacts. The two vessels feature in several of his texts from the 1850s, culminating in the magnum opus *Der Stil*, and Semper presents them throughout as instances of national character embodied in things. He invokes the hydria and situla at a time when the idea of the nation is looming large in European thought, when material culture is appearing in travel reports and early ethnographies as a key characteristic of peoples. Artefacts, including ceramics, are increasingly used at this time as tools for constructing identities and differences.

The very familiarity of these two containers and the way in which they appear to slip naturally into the national classifications of material culture of their period put them almost beyond questioning. What else can you say about the situla and hydria? They do, after all, make consistent appearances in almost every piece of scholarly work on Semper. But tracing the path of these renowned vessels through his London manuscripts reveals that their early incarnations have scarcely been studied. Moreover, the paradigms, metaphors, and exclusions that are found in the context of their first public appearance tell us much about discourse on the national artefact in general – both in discussions on design education and in the public sphere at large.

Manufactures, archaeology, and anatomy

The situla and the hydria made their first public appearance on 25 November 1853, in a lecture delivered by Semper in London's Marlborough House. It was the first in a series of three talks focusing on "the potters industry" as "The most important of all the different branches of industry for the general history of art and for artistical science".[2] These lectures, delivered on 25 November and on 2 and 9 December 1853,[3] are preserved in what appear to be three manuscript drafts. The venue in which they were held – an elegant mansion on Pall Mall – at the time housed the London School of Design, which was part of the newly formed Department of Science and Art, a net-

_ Figure 2.
Gottfried Semper, Hydria, ca. 1853 (Courtesy of the gta Archives/ETH Zurich).

_ Figure 3.
Gottfried Semper, Situla, ca. 1853 (Courtesy of the gta Archives/ETH Zurich).

work of institutions dedicated to the education of designers for industry. The department was part of the government's Board of Trade and operated under the leadership of Henry Cole and Richard Redgrave from 1852 onwards. Its schools ran a regular schedule of public lectures, and the instructors, among them Semper, were expected to contribute to the programme.

The manuscripts of Semper's lectures cover a great expanse of material. This testifies to the extent of his fascination with ceramics, which grew considerably while the talks were in preparation. When he initially planned the cycle in the spring of 1853, Semper was intending to devote just one talk to potteries: *Connexion of Ceramic Art with the Art of Metal Casting: Its Influence on Architecture and the Other Arts.*[4] The title refers to his ideas about the relative place of ceramics among the other decorative arts, which had formulated in his catalogue *Practical Art in Metal and Hard Materials* in the spring and summer of the previous year.[5] It is in this catalogue that the hydria and situla appear on paper for the first time, as part of one of the sequences of artefacts in different materials that Semper presented in order to demonstrate the formal origins of metalwork. As part of this scheme, he linked ceramics with metal casting, while speaking about vessels as a category: "the prototypes of this ... Series of Objects lie beyond the reach of the Art of Metal Working. In this Instance, Plastic Art, namely the Art, which employs itself in the production of forms in clay, presents to us the prototypes required".[6]

The fact that Semper draws a link between ceramics and metalwork through the process of casting suggests that observation of industrial processes could have played some part in the formation of his theories. Casting was indeed a key technique in the 1850s – not only in metals but also in the manufacturing of pottery. Semper would have seen this at first hand when, just before compiling *Practical Art in Metal*, he spent several weeks on a study visit to the ceramics manufactory of Herbert Minton in Stoke-on-Trent,[7] observing "all the new and astonishing things … in this centre of English and Universal industry".[8] In order to produce forms for which moulding was not possible (too detailed, complex, or partly undercut), plaster formwork was filled with very liquid clay called "slip". The absorption of water by the plaster meant that a layer of clay formed on the surface of the mould, while the rest of the slip could be poured away.[9] One of the famous design creations by Henry Cole – Semper's direct superior at the Department of Science and Art – was in fact produced using exactly this method.[10] Under the pseudonym Felix Summerly,[11] Cole had designed this ceramic teapot as part of a set, to be made by Minton's, for the Society of the Arts competition in 1845. The tea set and other artefacts from the series of Felix Summerly's Art Manufactures went on to become exemplars of Design Reform – a project for improving the artistic quality of British goods.[12] Semper's ceramics lectures, and *Practical Art in Metal*, which predated them, were both compiled under the auspices of Design Reform and with impetus from Cole.

The trip to Stoke – also suggested by Cole, who was a friend of Herbert Minton – was in part a result of Semper's ongoing interest in ceramics, which went back to the time before his exile from Dresden in 1849.[13] But the methodical analyses of specific clay pieces, supported by painstaking research on particular artefacts, that appear in *Practical Art in Metal* were carried out in 1852. Semper's primary aim at this point was to create a systematic overview of decorative artefacts:

Fig. 4

127

_ Figure 4.
Teapot from the Felix Summerly tea service, designed by Henry Cole, manufactured by Minton, 1846 (designed), 1846–1890 (made), bone china, slip-cast body and spout, press-moulded handle, painted in enamels (© Victoria and Albert Museum, London).

The Range of this Series ["Vessels"] is extremely wide, and a Survey of the same can only be gained by Classification. … This may probably be accomplished by first dividing into principal Classes the objects according to the fundamental Ideas manifested in the Objects themselves. After which the Materials and means employed in the representation of those Objects, must furnish a second principle of order and arrangement. Thirdly, the historical and ethnographic Arrangement must be considered; showing how the original forms are, at all times essentially the same: but subjected, according to circumstances to variety in their different appearances.[14]

These words follow a general introduction to ceramics and to the idea that forms of vessels and sculptures in different materials are still essentially ceramic forms. Semper's first ceramics lecture paraphrases this and goes on to highlight the historical importance of ceramic vases. This, again, is a development of a remark from *Practical Art in Metal* where Semper draws attention to the ceremonial significance of the hydria and the situla: "Nile Bucket, in Egypt, is a symbolical & National Emblem, whose form has a religious and mystical Signification. In like manner, the Hydria of the Greeks was the sacred Vessel carried by Virgins in religious Processions".[15]

In the first ceramics lecture, Semper explains that the religious role played by ceramic items extended to their use as funerary containers and other grave goods. In this view, he follows on from the thoughts of his Göttingen teacher, archaeologist Karl Otfried Müller,[16] although the further development of the idea in Semper's text owes much more to the French scientist and director of the porcelain manufactory at Sèvres, Alexandre Brongniart.[17] It is the latter who envisages pots as cultural fossils, proposing an unclear position for clay artefacts in the divide between naturalia and artificialia:

Deux seules matières, riches d'instruction pour l'histoire des sociétés et pour celle du globe, peuvent traverser des milliers de siècles en nous apportant les premiers éléments de l'histoire la plus ancienne des peuples et de la terre; ce sont, d'une part, les terres cuites façonnées en vases ou en ustensiles, et de l'autre les parties solides des animaux et des végétaux réduit à l'état fossile; après ces deux matières, tout est périssable ou muet.[18]

In his lecture, Semper refers to these words indirectly when he states that "Terra Cotta vases, which come from the excavations of tombs are for history of mankind, what are the fossil remains of plants and animals for history of nature. They are the most ancient and the most speaking documents for history of civilization".[19]

Partly from Müller, but especially from Brongniart, Semper inherits a clearly biological understanding of ceramics. Clay is regarded in Brongniart's writings as a quasi-organic material. Ceramic shards are fossils that are capable of speech, inasmuch as they are bodily remains and are therefore subjected to similar procedures of comparative classification. After this, it comes as no surprise that Semper chooses to continue his lecture by paraphrasing what has been attributed in popular idiom to Georges Cuvier: "Show me what sort of potteries a nation has produced and I shall tell you what nation it was".[20]

Cuvier, one of the leading comparative anatomists of his generation, said the same of fossils and species in the 1820s. An effective showman, as well as a gifted scientist, he sought to strengthen his position within the controversial disputes that rocked the discipline of comparative anatomy in the first quarter of the nineteenth century.[21] When Semper speaks of pottery shards and nations, the controversy is

128

no longer related to the fossils of long-dead organisms, but to living human beings. The larger question is whether the races of mankind developed as different species or as constituent parts of a single species. By 1853, several authors had spoken out in favour of a polygenesis theory of race, in which white, black, Asian, and Native American people were all regarded as representing separate species.[22] Many others rejected this idea because it was incompatible with the Christian story of Creation, but nonetheless believed that "skin color was destiny"[23] and that what they called "nations" had fixed and unchangeable characteristics.

Much of this is reflected in Semper's lectures, although little of it is consistent enough for any real ideological intention to be assigned to it.[24] Nevertheless, ceramics appear as clearly national objects in his analyses: he thinks of vessels, including the hydria and the situla, as directly constituent of nations, almost literally as body parts. As an apparent implication of the biological perception of ceramics that he inherits from Brongniart, Semper conceives of nations, at least in this instance, as being akin to species of animals: clearly defined, different from one another, and apparently static. His ideas about the relationship between people and material culture are subject to an array of influences: his observations of manufactures, his study of archaeology, and the emulation of the principles of classification used in comparative anatomy. But whichever the area, in an effort to categorize systematically, Semper embraces an approach that focuses on constructing differences. These in turn are conceived as sufficiently static to be enshrined as laws of art, or of nature.

129

Real and symbolic uses

In order to clarify how Semper manages to fold ceramic pots into the body of the nation, it must be noted that his key sources – both Müller and Brongniart – highlight not only the functionality of ceramic artefacts but also their ability to engage the human spirit. It is their interaction with both the physical and the immaterial aspects of humanity that makes ceramic pots into vessels of memory. Müller is particularly succinct when he describes special classes of art "that create and represent appliances, vessels and buildings in accordance with the needs and purposes of outward life, on the one hand, but on the other also in accordance with the inner demands of the human spirit".[25] Thus, when Semper speaks of "national" pots, he – like his sources – not only has in mind the formal properties of shards and the relative locations of archaeological finds but also the way in which the spirits of nations are embodied within ceramic artefacts. When he introduces the examples of the Greek hydria and Egyptian situla in his lecture, he is trying to explain how this embodiment takes place.

As part of his first lecture on pottery, Semper compares the merits of two alternative classification systems: one based on the geometric forms of vessels[26] and one that looks at the uses of pots. He finds the second system more suitable and proposes to "consider Ceramic forms ... and their ornamentations as the results ... of their real or supposed uses and applications".[27] Although this formula can be easily misread as a functionalist prescription, it is in fact intended as an attempt to make sense of the multifariousness of artefacts. The "supposed uses", introduced as a correction of "symbolical uses", extend the notion of functionality as a purely material application into the spiritual and cultural domains.

Semper spends the remainder of the first lecture addressing the requirements of purely physical uses of ceramic vessels: containing, dipping, collecting, and pouring out. Even these pragmatic aspects of form are for him connected with national spirit through the contingencies of living conditions: the situla is intended to bail water out of the Nile by dipping, while the hydria is adapted for catching the mountain stream. But these "real" uses, in Semper's terms, were intertwined with what he calls "supposed" or "symbolical" uses, which addressed the social and cultural roles of artefacts. When, at the end of the first lecture, he begins to discuss the ornamentation of ceramics, his ideas become focused on the symbolism of "use" in both senses: "Like it is necessary for a monument to show its immouveability, the same a mouveable thing must show its mouveability. Therefore, the stands of the Ancient mouveable things are so often ornamented with feet of animals or sometimes are pure imitation of feet".[28] Similarly, handles must express the symbolism of carrying a vessel and are therefore not redundant, even in vases that are obviously too large to lift. In both cases, "real" and "symbolical" uses are entwined, since the former come to be expressed by allegorical means, and the latter are represented through the ornamental use of pragmatic elements.

Fig. 5

Semper's category of "symbolic" use makes it possible to rationalize aspects of the form and iconography of artefacts that are otherwise hard to subject to classification. In his scheme of things, it enables two alternate nations – the Greeks and the Egyptians – to employ very different vessels for the same basic need of containing and conveying water. The differences of form and ornamentation come down to a differentiation of symbolic use, which in turn implies that the two groups of people are not only distinct in the ways in which they physically interact with their environment and resources but also in "symbolic" traits and factors that express their thoughts, perceptions, and emotions. In speaking of "symbolic" use, Semper explicitly establishes clay artefacts as vessels for human subjectivity, and he firmly believes in the possibility of its systematic division into static categories. This is what Semper understands as a "historical and ethnographic arrangement" of forms.

130

_ Figure 5.
Tripod stand, bronze, Etruscan, 500–475 BCE, Vulci, Italy (© Trustees of the British Museum).

Advanced nations

Semper's second lecture focuses on the subject of ornament in pottery. This is not only a reflection of his own obsession but also a measure of the interest in the topic among his audience. Another immigrant in England, Leon Arnoux, summarizes the main concerns of the ceramics industry by stating that "in pottery, the material is of little value, and it is only with the art displayed in shaping and decorating it, that its price can be increased".[29] Arnoux worked as both a chemist and an artistic director at the manufactory of Herbert Minton in Stoke, where Semper met him in the spring of 1852 and described the Frenchman as a "man, who combines uncommon knowledge, practice and strength with true artistical taste and feeling".[30]

Arnoux had joined Minton's in 1848 – at the beginning of the period when the budding culture of international exhibitions was beginning to display British pottery and porcelain in direct comparison with continental and North American competitors. The issue of decorative value was starting to be related specifically to the quality of British wares in relation to foreign things. The deliberations of the Special Parliamentary Committee of 1835 already revealed a great deal of worry about the quality of design of British manufactures. From that time onwards, ornamented artefacts became the central element in a project to improve domestic products and elevate national taste.[31]

Semper addresses the question of the relative merits of national pottery directly in the second ceramics lecture when he states that "The more advanced the artistic feeling of a nation is, the more we observe on its productions of industrial art a strong distinction between the two principles of ornamentation while the same are confounded and pass gradually over one into the other with other nations of less artistical and perhaps more poetical and religious tendency".[32] The two categories of ornamentation he is referring to address "real" and "symbolical" uses. He describes the ornaments in the first category as those expressing "dynamic function". Those in the second are called by Semper, after British art writer James Fergusson, "phonetic ornaments".[33]

Ornaments with a "dynamic function" are largely non-figurative:

> Every part of a work as well as the Ensemble of it, must tell what dynamical function it has to fullfill, not only by its form but also by its ornaments. When the last have no other significations but that, to be symbols taken from nature or borrowed from other arts, with the sole intention to awake in our minds in a agreable manner a clear conception of the dynamical function of a whole or a part of a work of art.[34]

As an example of such ornaments, Semper cites the "beautiful Greec ornaments" and various natural features that underline structural properties of form, such as the ribs on the surface of pumpkins and gourds, "chalices [calyces] of flowers, with their stalks", bands, and nets.[35] He links these features with the growth and liveliness of organic forms, extending the biological metaphor to consider decorative artefacts as living bodies. If the animal-like feet of vases and cabinets are regarded as suggesting a potential for movement, "dynamic ornaments" underline the ability of ceramics to grow and bloom. On Semper's illustration of the hydria seen from the side, the leaf-like pattern surrounding the bottom of the vessel just above the base is a "dynamic"

Fig. 2

_ Figure 6.
Chestnut dish, made by
Minton, Hollins & Co., 1855,
lead-glazed earthenware
with metal heater (©
Victoria and Albert Museum,
London).

_ Figures 7a–c.
"Two Drivers, Past, Present",
beer jug, designed by
Henry James Townsend
for Felix Summerly's Art
Manufactures, made by
Minton, 1848, moulded
stoneware (© Victoria and
Albert Museum, London).

ornament. It accentuates the swelling form of the pot and "grows" upwards, stressing its vertical movement. Similar devices were used in ceramic artefacts contemporary with Semper's lectures. In Minton's majolica chestnut dish, for example, the stylized leaves in relief that surround the base and the rim would have qualified as "dynamic" ornaments underlining the roundness of the object. However, the realism of the foliage forming the cover of the dish and the spoon would probably have been considered excessive by Semper and his Design Reform colleagues.

Fig. 6

The hydria also shows us the ideal configuration of "dynamic" ornaments. According to Semper, they should be formed into bands and stripes, leaving "neutral" fields between them for "phonetic" ornaments – "those which, while agreeably variating the elementary form of a work or part of a work, by means of outlines and colours, are representing thin[g]s, actions and circumstances, which are not immediately connected with the dynamical or structiv idea of a thing".[36] In other words, he is describing the figurative decorations of pots that may indicate their broader cultural context. Here again, the Greeks reign supreme in Semper's opinion, with the "beautiful pictures" on their vases "representing Heroic battles and objects relating to the destinations of the Vases".[37] The illustration of the hydria, again, provides an example in which the main group shows women using hydrias to collect and carry water, while the bottom panel presents a mythological scene of lion-wrestling (possibly Hercules or Cyrene).

It might be useful to consider a contemporary example of this type of ornamentation: the *Two Drivers* jug, another of Felix Summerly's manufactures. The pot is a

Figs. 7 a–c

decorative take on a popular type of vessel that was used to collect beer from a pub, and the decoration shows old-fashioned coach travellers seeking refreshment at an inn, while a modern locomotive passes by with greater speed and comfort on the other side of the jug. The unpainted surface of the vessel signals at least an intention to market it as a cheap product, while the obvious association of beer drinking with old-fashioned modes of travel carries a temperance message likely addressed to the lower classes. This makes the jug a good example of the issues encompassed by the discussions on design to which Semper is contributing in his lectures.

There may also be grounds for speculating that, in his choice of illustrations, Semper was displaying something of the priggishness of his colleagues. The hydria in figure 2 is the one that Semper included as an illustration in *Der Stil*, and therefore the one that is referred to in scholarship. Among Semper's papers, however, there is another illustration of a hydria – drawn in similar style, in the same size, and on the same paper as the one that is typically cited. This one shows an Attic hydria found in the British Museum, depicting two sirens surrounded by grapevines and bunches of grapes on the body, with the figure of a seated Dionysus on the shoul-

Fig. 1

der.[38] The "phonetic ornaments" of this vessel refer undoubtedly to the storage and consumption of wine rather than water. Using this hydria as an example would thus have weakened Semper's argument about national types and destinations of ornaments. But one wonders also if he might have decided to omit it because it clearly contradicted the moral message that the Design Reform, in part, was seeking to convey.

133

In Semper's opinion, the vessels of the Greeks demonstrate the highest achievement in the ornamentation of ceramics, of which the Egyptians fall short. Theirs is a less "advanced" art, with a stronger "poetical and religious tendency":

> the monumental art in Egypt shows no ornament properly speaking; every decoration is a religious or a political or a topographical Symbol, every colour employd is the same; The Egyptian style of composition is a writing the Egyptian Style of Colouring is not a music with colours, it is a prosody.[39]

_ Figure 8.
Inlaid jade vase, Lahore, nineteenth century (© Victoria and Albert Museum, London). This is one of the Indian artefacts that Semper singles out for praise in his comments for the catalogue of the Museum of Ornamental Art.

The relative backwardness of Egyptian art does not, in Semper's eyes, mean that it is lacking in merit, a view that is consistent with the positions of his London colleagues. Ralph Nicholson Wornum, for example, who could on occasion be very harsh in his dismissal of non-European decorative artefacts,[40] described Egyptian ornament as "pleasing and tasteful" in the simplicity of its arrangement and "eminent in its complete adaptation of its own natural productions".[41] He also notes that the understanding of art seen in the monuments and artefacts of the ancient Egyptians rivals that of the capitals of modern Europe.

Wornum's ranking of ancient Egyptian, and especially Greek, art as superior to modern productions is consistent with the view of his Design Reform colleagues and with that of Semper. The latter draws particular attention to the excellence of ancient creations and to the "unquestioned superiority of half barbarous nations, especially of India with her gergeous products of industry".[42] He presents this as a "mortifiing truth",[43] since the cultural and technological supremacy of Europeans should in theory lead to them turning out finer designs than their primitive counterparts. Although Wornum would have disputed the artistic merit of Indian artefacts, many of the Design Reform protagonists would have agreed with Semper – including Henry Cole, Richard Redgrave, and Owen Jones.

The apparent conundrum that was presented to Semper and his contemporaries by the British decorative artefact rested on the assumption that different 'nations' represented different stages of human progress. This idea, with its origins in the European Enlightenment, had by the nineteenth century acquired a new interpretation that not only placed various races and ethnicities on different steps of the ladder of human development but dictated that they remain there in perpetuity.[44] Europeans, with their technological supremacy, put themselves at the top and forefront of human progress. Was it therefore contradictory for Semper and his colleagues to be denouncing European decorative artefacts as inferior to those of the "half-barbarous nations"? Or is this to be read as an indication of liberalism on their part that was exceptional in the context of mid-Victorian scientific racism?

Fig. 8

Common vessels

Semper's third ceramics lecture examines different techniques and processes of pottery manufacture and briefly mentions what he sees as the causes of decline in the artistic quality of ceramic goods. These include mainly the technologies that enabled serialization of ceramics, a decrease in their price, and the consequent availability of pottery items to wider audiences: the potter's wheel, the mould, and the lathe. The application of such tools must, in Semper's view, be heavily moderated. The potter's wheel should "be manipulated everwhere by intelligent hands and not as it often happens by an other machine, which knows nothing but what he was teached by his master".[45] He is referring here to a "jigger" or a "jolly" machine – an apparatus intended to replace the labour of the thrower or presser. These devices were introduced in the 1830s[46] or 1840s[47] but were only beginning to become widespread around the time of Semper's lecture. He similarly disapproves of the lathe and templates, which were both commonly used in nineteenth-century potteries to divide labour and speed up production.[48]

Moulding, which was commonly used to turn out identical forms, should in Semper's eyes be employed for its potential inaccuracies, rather than the possibilities of serialization: "the imperfection of this process, is its power, The modeller must know and *submit* to these imperfections and remember, that a moulded piece of pottery can not, and must not appear like a piece which is turned on the wheel or on the lath[e]".[49] This type of product, in Semper's view, is intended specifically for the more general market: "The Moulded works have generally the destination of being multiplied frequently, whence the symbols and ornaments for the decoration of the moulded works must show a sort of Market type and be of more general applications".[50] He is therefore advocating variation in exactly the kinds of ware in which manufacturers of the time were trying to achieve greater uniformity, speed, and cheapness.

Although the Design Reform enterprise was premised specifically on the possibility of achieving beauty in industrially produced artefacts and was not characterized by a rejection of the machine, it remained prejudiced against the commonplace and the cheap. The analyses of pottery by its protagonists remained distant from the realities of the ceramics market of their time, and they were exclusive in reserving their praise for luxurious and expensive products. Theirs was a highly reified view, since even in the 1850s, British pottery items ranged widely in material, technique, and the intended consumer. It has in fact been observed that historical studies of ceramics from this period still tend to misrepresent the subject by perpetuating the bias of Semper's contemporaries and focusing on top-of-the-range examples.[51] The suggestion that this is at odds with historical reality is supported by the reflections of Arnoux:

> None of the specimens above mentioned [della Robbia, Palissy ware, etc.], however, could serve as the basis for a manufacture sufficiently large to become an extensive branch of commerce. A moment's consideration of the subject would lead us to point to earthenware as the kind of pottery which is actually produced in larger quantities than all others, and it is in Great Britain that the most important seat of this manufacture is to be found.[52]

135

In other words, if one is to speak of the national British pottery in the 1850s, it is precisely the cheap mass manufactures that should be placed centre stage. However, most accounts of ceramics from this time demonstrate a reluctance to acknowledge this. When Herbert Minton died in 1858, his friend Matthew Digby Wyatt, a member of Henry Cole's circle, gave a commemorative lecture praising the late manufacturer's achievements:

> The excellence of the bodies, glazes, gilding, and colours of the old establishments of Bow, Chelsea, Derby, and Worcester, left but little room for novelty and improvement, so far as excellence is concerned to Staffordshire manufacturers. The only path open to them was by greater economy in every process, and by carefully recognizing and discriminating the talents of their workpeople, to endeavour to convert the class of goods which had been previously of altogether exceptional demand and production, into objects of ordinary commercial supply and demand.[53]

Wyatt acknowledges that Minton was forced to concentrate his efforts on cost cutting and division of labour to produce cheaper wares for larger markets, but he goes on to ignore these completely in the rest of his address. He hardly mentions, for example, the common printed earthenware made by Minton's and other manufacturers in Stoke, which from the 1830s onwards became an increasingly important export to North America, as well as a popular product at home.[54] He concentrates instead on the firm's luxury productions and its innovations in the processes of encaustic tile-making and majolica, della Robbia and Palissy wares, among others.

Semper is equally exclusive in his third lecture on ceramics, where he gives an overview of some of the common clay mixes and glazes, as well as methods of working them. He comes close to pointing out that common forms, in their simplicity, can result in better designs when he praises the work of "great founders of art in times gone by" who "carried out a popular motive to its higher significance by treating it artistically".[55] But he nonetheless dedicates most of the lecture to exactly the same luxury wares as Wyatt: majolica and historical faience.

Both Semper and Wyatt, as well as the more practical Arnoux, ignore completely the depth of the commonplace engagement with ceramics that is revealed to us in Victorian literature. George Eliot's Mrs. Tulliver, for example, laments the impeding loss of her "chany" in view of her husband's bankruptcy:

> "O dear, O dear", said Mrs Tulliver, "to think o' my chany being sold i' that way – and I bought it when I was married, just as you did yours, Jane and Sophy: and I know you didn't like mine, because o' the sprig, but I was fond of it; and there's never been a bit broke, for I've washed it myself – and there's the tulips on the cups, and the roses, as anybody might go and look at 'em for pleasure. You wouldn't like your chany to go for an old song and be broke to pieces, though yours has got no colour in it, Jane – it's all white and fluted, and didn't cost so much as mine".[56]

Her china cups are treasured possessions, her mark of identity in relation to the world and to her sisters, to whom she addresses her short monologue. The effort that went into amassing enough money to actually purchase the china, rather than trading in used clothes for it as was the common practice,[57] is a mark of its status, a profound emotional as well as economic investment. Henry Mayhew, in his article on the *Street-Sellers of Crockery and Glass-Wares*, confirms what George Eliot tells us through the words of Mrs. Tulliver. He writes that the "trade" of the numerous itinerant sellers of ceramics in London was almost equally divided into what may be called "fancy" and "useful" articles. A lodging-letter will "swop" her old gowns and boots, and drive keen bargains for plates, dishes, or wash-hand basins and jugs. A housekeeper, who may be in easier circumstances, will exchange for vases and glass wares. Servant maids swop clothes and money for a set of china "gainst they get married".[58]

For many women in Britain, like Mrs. Tulliver, purchasing a set of china was a rite of passage, a key element in the status of a married woman, and a segment of a newly established home.

Moreover, the consumption of ceramics in the 1850s could become a fully fledged obsession. Wilkie Collins's protagonist in his short story *My Spinsters* proclaims "pottery mania" to be in line with such compulsions as "saving money", "good living", "music", "smoking", and "angling".[59] Other writers confirm that a passion for ceramics could be entertained with relatively modest means: "We ... need not be very rich before we have it in our power to drink tea and coffee out of porcelain. Indeed, there is scarcely a dust-heap in the country that does not contain fragments of European pottery".[60]

Semper acknowledges the depth of Victorian engagement with ceramics implicitly when he recognizes the role of the hydria, the situla, and other containers as vessels for human subjectivity. His Design Reform colleagues premise their entire project on the intensity of this engagement by assigning to the decorative artefact an ability to effect 'improvement' – to alter human character and achieve what they saw as a more enlightened aesthetic disposition, fitting for the level of European technological progress. Hence, the notion of the 'national artefact' contains a double set of prejudices: it designates as technologically primitive even those non-European artefacts that it recognizes as artistic exemplars, and it rejects the notion of the commonplace as the national, suggesting instead an exclusive aesthetic ideal as the ornament of the nation.

137

Material differences

The drafts of Semper's ceramics lectures break off just after a short commentary on the most quintessential of European ceramic obsessions: porcelain. His notes concentrate on the persistent otherness of this material: "We will in our taste in China pottery be allways more or less followers of the Chinese; And I am excusing this direction for this special kind of industry, more than for any other".[61] Yet this condition remains lamentable: "But the better will be that [direction] of following our own way and of taking for guides the nature of the materials, the idea of that which is to be represented, and the traditions of our own European Pottery works, which, well applied, will allways afford good precedents".[62]

Despite recognizing the quality of design in non-European artefacts, Semper returns to a kind of aesthetic protectionism in calling for the creation of properly native forms. After all, he is looking at ceramics primarily as decorative objects and as artefacts in the interior, which, from the 1830s onwards, increasingly permeated European domesticity and identity.[63] The interior was created not just by the inside spaces of architecture but by the artefacts that filled them. As early as 1835, we can read Thomas Hope's definition of a home as an extended body of possessions:

> In all regions man has felt the necessity of adding to the covering which is carried about with the person, and which we call attire, another covering, more extended, more detached, more stationary, for the purpose of ampler comfort and of greater security, and which might be able, with his body, to include such goods as he possessed.[64]

Hope defines the decorated interior as no less than the mark of civilization that distinguishes the cultured man from the "savage". Those peoples who forego the construction of permanent dwellings are described in his text as little more than animals.

Semper had read Hope's text as early as 1849 or 1850 while compiling an early draft of his magnum opus and researching ideas about the origins of architecture.[65] It was at this time, and in the context of archaeology, that he began to develop an interest in decorative artefacts and in interiorized domestic structures. Thus, in Semper's preference for European porcelain rooted in local traditions, it is possible to read a distant call for a distinctly European interior, at a time when domestic settings were full of colonial things.[66] This reminds us that, despite the recognition of Indian artistic exemplars, the discourse on the national artefact into which the hydria and situla emerged remained profoundly territorial.

Another aspect of the national artefact that is worth recalling in the conclusion of this chapter is its apparent stasis. The hydria and situla, as well as other artefacts in Semper's theory of applied art, were conceived as firm parts of the body of the nation and actively constitutive elements of its spirit. As such, they were never supposed to change. After all, Semper did claim to be able to identify a nation by the fragments of its pottery. His Design Reform colleagues similarly believed in the static character of artefacts. A well-conceived object was to exercise an improving influence upon its owner. The character of this influence was up to the designer to create and, once properly inculcated, it became an inalienable property of the artefact. The possibility that the same object might improve one person and then go on to degrade another was simply not on the Design Reform horizon. And yet, this is exactly how many artefacts behave. Material culture studies have made us aware of the fact that things have biographies, in the course of which their meaning, value, and status can change radically.[67] Simply put, artefacts carry an amazing potential to mean many things to many people.

Material culture, including the built environment, readily plays an active and constantly shifting role in the performance of human identities, which are themselves transitory and dynamic.[68] Despite this, contemporary design disciplines such as architecture often appear to perpetuate the assumption of a stasis of meaning on the part of their products that does not advance far from the ideas of nineteenth-century Design Reformers and art theorists. Given the foundational role that Semper's age has played in defining the paradigms of modern design disciplines, this is perhaps not surprising. But seeing how close the notion of a static identity of artefacts lies to the idea of a static identity of people and to the deterministic views that went on to perpetuate many of the worst prejudices of the nineteenth century in the tragic events of the twentieth, further examination of its history is certainly warranted and timely.

_ 1. Gottfried Semper, *Classification of Vessels*, draft of a lecture given in London on 25 November 1853, gta Archives/ETH Zurich, 20-MS-133, fol. 3r, edited in G. Semper, *London Writings 1850–1855*, edited by M. Gnehm, S. Hildebrand, and D. Weidmann, gta Verlag, Zurich 2021. (Titles and quotations from Semper in this chapter preserve his original spelling.)

_ 2. *Ibid.*, fol. 1r.

_ 3. *Ibid.* Gottfried Semper, *On Vessel Parts*, draft of a lecture given on 2 December 1853, gta Archives/ETH Zurich, 20-MS-134; Gottfried Semper, *Influence of the Materials and Their Treatments upon the Development of Ceramic Types and Style*, draft of a lecture given on 9 December 1853, gta Archives/ETH Zurich, 20-MS-135, all manuscripts are edited in G. Semper, *London Writings*, see note 1. See *Second Report of the Department of Science and Art*, Eyre and Spottiswoode for Her Majesty's Stationery Office, London 1855, p. 162.

_ 4. G. Semper, *Prospectuses of the Lectures on Art*, in *First Report of the Department of Science and Art*, Eyre and Spottiswoode for Her Majesty's Stationery Office, London 1854, pp. 220–21 (here p. 220).

_ 5. There are two surviving copies of this document: one in London at the National Art Library and one in Vienna at the MAK; references here are to Gottfried Semper, *Practical Art in Metal and Hard Materials: Its Technology, History and Styles* (London 1852), National Art Library, London, 86.FF.64. There is a published transcript of the Vienna copy in G. Semper, *The Ideal Museum: Practical Art in Metals and Hard Materials*, edited by P. Noever, Schlebrügge, Vienna 2007.

_ 6. G. Semper, *Practical Art in Metal* (see note 5), fols. 175r–176r.

_ 7. W. Herrmann, *Gottfried Semper im Exil: Paris, London 1849–1855. Zur Entstehung des "Stil" 1840–1877*, Birkhäuser, Basel 1978, pp. 64–66.

_ 8. Gottfried Semper, letter to Henry Cole, 9 April 1852, London, National Art Library, 55.BB Box 10, published in W. Herrmann, *Semper im Exil*, see note 7, pp. 128–30 (here p. 128).

_ 9. L. Arnoux, *Pottery*, in *British Manufacturing Industries*, edited by G.P. Bevan, 2nd ed., Stanford, London 1877, reprinted HardPress, Los Angeles 2016, pp. 1–74 (here p. 28); G.A. Godden, *Victorian Porcelain*, Jenkins, London 1961, pp. 152–54.

_ 10. Parian wares, which mainly comprised small statuettes, were for the most part also made in this way and were regarded by Cole and his colleagues as an important means of disseminating knowledge of art. The statuettes were often copies of larger works, frequently made for institutions such as the Art Union, and distributed as a means of making sculpture available to people who might not have the chance to visit the originals. See Arnoux, *Pottery*, see note 9, p. 48. See reviews for statuettes in the "Journal of Design and Manu-

factures" and *The Use and Abuse of "Parian"*, "Journal of Design and Manufactures", 4, no. 20, 1851, pp. 45–59.

_ 11. "Felix Summerly" was an alias of Henry Cole, used by the reformer in the 1840s and 1850s when he was directing improving enterprises such as the series of "Art Manufactures" and a number of cheap guidebooks to places of artistic interest. See A. Burton and E. Bonython, *The Great Exhibitor: The Life and Work of Henry Cole*, V&A, London 2001.

_ 12. For a comprehensive account of the Design Reform, see, for example, L. Kriegel, *Grand Designs: Labor, Empire, and the Museum in Victorian Culture*, Duke University Press, Durham, NC 2007.

_ 13. See the German translation of Semper's 1850 essay in French on porcelain painting: G. Semper, *Ueber Porzellanmalerei*, in G. Semper, *Kleine Schriften*, edited by M. and H. Semper, Spemann, Berlin 1884, pp. 58–75. See also W. Herrmann, *Semper im Exil*, see note 7, pp. 63, 127; W. Herrmann, *Gottfried Semper: Theoretischer Nachlass an der ETH Zürich. Katalog und Kommentare*, Birkhäuser, Basel 1981, p. 85 (MS 47). For Semper's early designs for ornamental ceramics, see B. von Orelli-Messerli, *Gottfried Semper (1803–1879): Die Entwürfe zur dekorativen Kunst*, Imhof, Petersberg 2010.

_ 14. G. Semper, *Practical Art in Metal* (see note 5), fols. 176r–177r.

_ 15. *Ibid.*, fol. 199r.

_ 16. This is apparent in Müller's deliberations on tectonics, in K.O. Müller, *Handbuch der Archäologie der Kunst*, Max, Breslau 1830, pp. 314–64. This issue is beyond the scope of the present chapter but has been explored by the author elsewhere. See E. Chestnova, *History in Things: Gottfried Semper and Popularization of the Arts in London 1850–55*, PhD diss., Università della Svizzera italiana, Mendrisio 2017, pp. 39–46 (a revised version of the dissertation will be published in 2022: *Material Theories and Objects: Gottfried Semper and the Mid-nineteenth Century*, Routledge, Abingdon).

_ 17. A. Lajoix, *Alexandre Brongniart: Scholar and Member of the Institut de France*, in D.E. Ostergard (ed.), *The Sèvres Porcelain Manufactory: Alexandre Brongniart and the Triumph of Art and Industry, 1800–1847*, Yale University Press, New Haven 1997, pp. 25–41.

_ 18. A. Brongniart, *Traité des arts céramiques, ou Des poteries considérées dans leur histoire, leur pratique et leur théorie*, vol. 1, Béchet Jeune, Paris 1844, p. x.

_ 19. G. Semper, *Classification of Vessels* (see note 1), fol. 2r–v.

_ 20. *Ibid.*, fol. 2v.

_ 21. D. Outram, *Georges Cuvier: Vocation, Science and Authority in Post-revolutionary France*, Manchester University Press, Manchester 1984, pp. 180–84.

_ 22. R.J.C. Young, *Colonial Desire: Hybridity in*

Theory, Culture and Race, Routledge, London 1995, pp. 47–50.

_23. S. Stuurman, *The Invention of Humanity: Equality and Cultural Difference in World History*, Harvard University Press, Cambridge, MA 2017, p. 351.

_24. It is quite possible that Semper's biological analogies were intended as rhetorical flourishes rather than as structural metaphors. On the inconsistencies of Semper's parallels to comparative anatomy, see A. Hauser, *Der "Cuvier der Kunstwissenschaft": Klassifizierungsprobleme in Gottfried Sempers "Vergleichender Baulehre"*, in T. Bolt (ed.), *Grenzbereiche der Architektur: Festschrift für Adolf Reinle*, Birkhäuser, Basel 1985, pp. 97–114.

_25. "Welche Geräthe, Gefässe, Gebäude einerseits den Bedürfnissen und Zwecken des äussern Lebens gemäss, andrerseits aber auch nach innern Forderungen des menschlichen Geistes erschaffen und darstellen". K.O. Müller, *Handbuch der Archäologie der Kunst*, see note 16, p. 314.

_26. Semper is referring to the ideas of French potter Jules Ziegler in the latter's *Études céramiques: Recherche des principes du beau dans l'architecture, l'art céramique et la forme en général, théorie de la coloration des reliefs*, Mathias, Paulin, Paris 1850.

_27. G. Semper, *Classification of Vessels* (see note 1), fol. 6v.

_28. *Ibid.*, fol. 12r.

_29. L. Arnoux, *Pottery*, see note 9, p. 7.

_30. Gottfried Semper, letter to Henry Cole, 9 April 1852, quoted in W. Herrmann, *Semper im Exil*, see note 7, p. 128 (Semper's emphasis).

_31. See the review of sources and interpretations in M. Romans, *Living in the Past: Some Revisionist Thoughts on the Historiography of Art and Design Education*, "International Journal of Art & Design Education", 23, no. 3, 1 October 2004, pp. 270–77.

_32. G. Semper, *On Vessel Parts* (see note 3), fol. 2r.

_33. The term comes from a work on aesthetics by James Fergusson in which he identifies phonetic ornaments as those relating to "Speech, or Power of communicating Thoughts or Ideas". J. Fergusson, *An Historical Inquiry into the True Principles of Beauty in Art, More Especially with Reference to Architecture*, Longman, Brown, Green and Longmans, London 1849, pp. 115–24 (here p. 115).

_34. G. Semper, *On Vessel Parts* (see note 3), fols. 1v–2r.

_35. *Ibid.*, fols. 2r, 3r–4v.

_36. *Ibid.*, fol. 2r.

_37. *Ibid.*

_38. British Museum Collection Online, Hydria 1837, 0609.73 (accessed 22 October 2018).

_39. G. Semper, *On Vessel Parts* (see note 3), fol. 2r–v.

_40. See R.N. Wornum, *The Exhibition as a Lesson in Taste*, in *The Art Journal Illustrated Catalogue: Industry of All Nations 1851*, George Virtue, London 1851, pp. i–xxii.

_41. R.N. Wornum, *Analysis of Ornament: The Characteristics of Style: An Introduction to the Study of the History of Ornamental Art*, Chapman & Hall, London 1856, p. 35.

_42. G. Semper, *Influence of the Materials and Their Treatments* (see note 3), fol. 1r.

_43. *Ibid.* See G. Semper, *Science, Industry, and Art: Proposals for the Development of a National Taste in Art at the Closing of the London Industrial Exhibition (1852)*, in G. Semper, *The Four Elements of Architecture and Other Writings*, trans. H.F. Mallgrave and W. Herrmann, Cambridge University Press, Cambridge, MA 1989, pp. 130–67 (here p. 134, on "The same, shameful truth").

_44. S. Stuurman, *Invention of Humanity*, see note 23, pp. 352–53.

_45. G. Semper, *Influence of the Materials and Their Treatments* (see note 3), fol. 3r. The passage "which knows … his master" was deleted by Semper and replaced by an alternative formulation.

_46. J. Thomas, *The Rise of the Staffordshire Potteries*, Adams and Dart, Bath 1971, p. 56.

_47. D. Barker, *The Industrialization of the Staffordshire Potteries*, in D. Barker and D. Cranstone (eds.), *The Archaeology of Industrialization: Papers Given at the Archaeology of Industrialization Conference, October 1999*, Maney, Leeds 2004, pp. 203–21 (here p. 215).

_48. J. Thomas, *Rise of the Staffordshire Potteries*, see note 46, pp. 22–29.

_49. G. Semper, *Influence of the Materials and Their Treatments* (see note 3), fol. 5v.

_50. *Ibid.*, fol. 6r.

_51. D. Barker, *Industrialization of the Staffordshire Potteries*, see note 47.

_52. L. Arnoux, *On Ceramic Manufactures*, in *Reports on the Paris Universal Exhibition*, part 2, Eyre and Spottiswoode, London 1856, pp. 351–72 (here p. 358).

_53. M.D. Wyatt, *On the Influence Exercised on Ceramic Manufactures by the Late Mr. Herbert Minton, Being a Paper Read before the Society of Arts, on May 26th, 1858*, printed for private distribution only, London 1858, p. 8.

_54. See references in A. Anderson, *The Romance of Old Blue: Collecting and Displaying Old Blue Staffordshire China in the American Home c. 1870–1938*, "Interpreting Ceramics", 15, 2013, http://www.interpretingceramics.com/issue015/articles/03.htm#b015 (accessed 5 May 2019).

_55. G. Semper, *Influence of the Materials and Their Treatments* (see note 3), fol. 1r.

_56. G. Eliot, *The Mill on the Floss* (1860), edited by G.S. Haight, Clarendon Press, Oxford 1980, p. 178.

_57. H. Mayhew, *London Labour and the London Poor: A Cyclopaedia of the Condition and Earnings of Those That Will Work, Those That Cannot Work, and Those That Will Not Work*, vol. 1, Office, 16 Upper Wellington Street, Strand, London 1851, pp. 365–69; B. Hillier, *Pottery and Porcelain 1700–1914: England, Europe and North America*,

140

Weidenfeld & Nicolson, London 1968, pp. 191–92; B. Hillier, *Two Centuries of China Selling*, "ECC Transactions 7", no. 1, 1968, http://www.englishceramiccircle.net/index.php/ECC_Transactions/article/view/634 (accessed 5 May 2019).

_ 58. H. Mayhew, *London Labour and the London Poor*, see note 57, vol. 1, p. 366.

_ 59. W. Collins, *My Spinsters*, in "Household Words", edited by C. Dickens, 14, no. 335, 23 August 1856, pp. 121–26 (here p. 121).

_ 60. H. Morley, *Pottery and Porcelain*, in "Household Words", edited by C. Dickens, 4, no. 80, 4 October 1851, pp. 32–37 (here p. 32).

_ 61. G. Semper, *Influence of the Materials and Their Treatments* (see note 3), fol. 12r.

_ 62. *Ibid*.

_ 63. The interior emerged at this time on the one hand as a coherent intentional whole and on the other as a collective artefact that simultaneously reflected and created the character of its owner. See C. Rice, *The Emergence of the Interior: Architecture, Modernity, Domesticity*, Routledge, London 2007, pp. 2–3; S. Muthesius, *The Poetic Home: Designing the 19th-Century Domestic Interior*, Thames & Hudson, London 2009.

_ 64. T. Hope, *An Historical Essay on Architecture*, 2nd ed., Murray, London 1835, p. 1.

_ 65. S. Luttmann, *Gottfried Sempers "Vergleichende Baulehre": Eine quellenkritische Rekonstruktion*, PhD diss., ETH Zurich, 2008, p. 406; Gottfried Semper, *Vergleichende Baulehre*, Paris 1849–50, gta Archives/ETH Zurich, 20-MS-58, fol. 46v.

_ 66. See, for example, D. Cohen, *Household Gods: The British and Their Possessions*, Yale University Press, New Haven 2006.

_ 67. See various contributions in A. Appadurai (ed.), *The Social Life of Things: Commodities in Cultural Perspective*, Cambridge University Press, Cambridge, MA 1986.

_ 68. D. Harris, *Social History: Identity, Performance, Politics, and Architectural Histories*, "Journal of the Society of Architectural Historians", 64, no. 4, 2005, pp. 421–23, DOI 10.2307/25068193.

141

Kate Nichols

Remaking Ancient Athens in 1850s London: Owen Jones, Gottfried Semper, and the Crystal Palace at Sydenham

_ Figure 1.
South side corridor
of the Greek Court,
showing painted
Parthenon frieze to
the rear and painted
Egyptian sculpture to
the left, date unknown
(detail, Courtesy of
Bromley Historic
Collections, CP2B).

Athens was the site of the first, somewhat inauspicious, encounter between Gottfried Semper and the Welsh designer Owen Jones. It is not known whether the two men actually met at that time, but they certainly had a mutual friend in Athens in the French architect Jules Goury. Goury had been travelling with Semper to examine architectural polychromy in what is now Italy, and in Greece, since October 1830. In spring 1832 the two parted in Athens, and Goury set out for Egypt with Jones.[1] Athens reunited Jones and Semper during the latter's London exile, when in January 1852 the two were present at discussions over architectural polychromy at the Royal Institute of British Architects (RIBA). Both displayed illustrations of the Parthenon on the walls of RIBA's meeting room, developed out of the research they had undertaken in Athens in the 1830s.[2] In this chapter, Athenian sculpture and architecture (or rather reproductions of Athenian sculpture and architecture) bring Jones and Semper into conversation once again.

Here I examine the debates on ancient Greek sculpture and architecture to which Jones and Semper contributed in 1850s London and the communication of these debates to new mass exhibition–visiting audiences of Londoners. My aim is to provide some background about the modes of displaying and viewing plaster casts of classical Greek sculpture that were prominent in the 1850s design-reforming South Kensington circles within which Semper moved.[3] I focus on Greek sculpture exhibited for mass consumption at the Sydenham Crystal Palace, offering a perspective on classical art quite different from that which appears in intellectual histories of the history of art, architecture, and archaeology. This is an important aspect of the 1850s life of sculpture and a discourse to which, I contend, Semper contributed through his involvement with Jones. When Semper was appointed director and professor at the Eidgenössisches Polytechnikum (Swiss Federal Polytechnic) in 1855, he assembled a collection of plaster casts for teaching. Here I explore some of the ideas about plaster casts and their potential for shaping contemporary design to which Semper might have been exposed in London.

Semper, Jones, and Crystal Palaces

The prime setting for this discussion is the Greek Court at the Crystal Palace *after* the Great Exhibition, when the building was purchased by the Crystal Palace Company and moved to the South London suburb of Sydenham. The palace reopened in June 1854, with an entirely different set of exhibits from its precursor in 1851, its directorate boasting that it was "an illustrated encyclopaedia of this great and varied universe".[4] The Sydenham Palace sought to localize global knowledge, bringing the world under one glass roof in the Victorian metropole. Divided into two halves, the structure of the new palace building separated its Fine Arts Courts, in the north nave, from industrial and manufacturing displays in the south – although, as I will discuss, art and industry were not deemed philosophically distinct in the palace directorate's endeavours. Owen Jones and Matthew Digby Wyatt were responsible for the vast undertaking of designing and populating with plaster casts the Fine Arts Courts of the new palace.

Fig. 6

Fig. 2

Semper's involvement in and responses to the Sydenham Palace's "parent building", the Great Exhibition of 1851, have been well documented.[5] His much-delayed Mixed Fabrics Court at Sydenham, and his never-realized design for a Pompeian theatre for the second palace's Central Transept, tend to appear in the historiography as further underwhelming and disappointing episodes during his time in London, his failure to secure more substantial commissions at the Sydenham Palace additional testimony to his difficult relationship with British architecture in general and with Owen Jones in particular.[6] My focus on Semper at Sydenham offers a new perspective on these relations. Although Semper may have despaired at the ways in which British architects snaffled up the majority of jobs at Sydenham, his writings were foundational to what was to become one of the lasting, and most controversial, aspects of the Sydenham Palace: its display of brightly painted copies of the Parthenon frieze. Semper's work arguably gained its widest British audience through this experiment undertaken by his purported rival, Owen Jones.

Semper's considerations on the Crystal Palace were written on the eve of its opening in Hyde Park in 1851. "What a contrast between the noisy scene below", he notes, "and the majestic silence with which nature completes her works" – referring here to the elm trees contained by the palace, which "fill out the lofty canopy of the transept, blending their verdant foliage with the bars of its airy lattice work". He continues to claim that "The whole picture breathes all the youthful yet antique life and freshness of a Pompeian fresco".[7] Like Semper, this chapter is concerned with the curious relationships between ancient art, modern manufacture, and the new conditions for display to mass audiences evinced by glass and iron architecture.[8] The Greek Court at Sydenham is a particularly apposite setting for such an exploration. It contained freshly made plaster casts of a wide range of Greek (and some Roman) sculpture and architectural reconstructions – objects that its directorate hoped would transmit a variety of different sorts of knowledges to the first modern mass audiences for Greek and Roman sculpture. At its peak in the first few years of opening, it hosted over 1.3 million visitors yearly, suggesting that at least twice as many people could have seen the painted plaster casts of the Parthenon frieze in Sydenham as the originals in the British Museum.[9] In what follows I discuss two key aspects of the Crystal Palace Greek and Roman exhibits: the idea of an art-manufacture crossover and the vexed question of polychromy, which had first brought Jones and Semper into contact in 1830s Athens. Greek sculpture appears in these guises not just as something reserved for an aristocratic elite, a university teaching collection, or a fine art school. At the Crystal Palace it had a social and political life and was intertwined with debates over sex, racial difference, and good design as much as were its archaeological or artistic credentials.

Greek sculpture, art, and industry

In his 1853 lectures to the Department of Practical Art, later the Department of Science and Art, Semper stressed the vital relationships between architecture and what he calls "the different branches of industrial art" and "ornamental art"; "the history of Architecture begins", he emphasized, "with the history of practical art … the laws of beauty and style in Architecture have theyr paragons in those which concern Industrial art".[10] The instinct for art, and thus the origins of architecture, lay in industrial art, objects of daily use.[11] A year later, when the Sydenham Crystal Palace opened, Greek sculpture and architecture were implicated in the Palace Company's founding mission to improve public taste and national design and manufacture. This mission was grounded in the belief that there was an inherent connection and generative potential among sculpture, ornamental art and industrial art, both in antiquity and for the present day. The Greek Court in the north nave was in dialogue with the Sheffield Court in the south.

Fig. 2

This connection between art and industry at the palace, and in Semper's writing, is particularly interesting because it stands outside the dominant narrative of nineteenth-century culture – albeit one which is currently being reassessed in recent work on British Design Reform, the world in which Semper found himself when lecturing at the Department of Science and Art.[12] In the twentieth century, the notion of an 'industrial culture' in Britain seemed paradoxical in the wake of Raymond Williams's 1958 publication *Culture and Society 1780–1950* and (writing from a very different political perspective) Martin J. Wiener's 1981 *English Culture and the*

145

_ Figure 2.
Ground plan of the Crystal Palace at Sydenham, illustration from "The Illustrated London News", no. 688, 17 June 1854 (Author's collection).

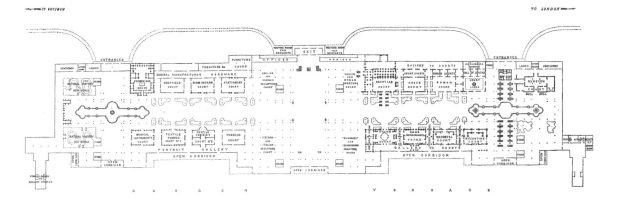

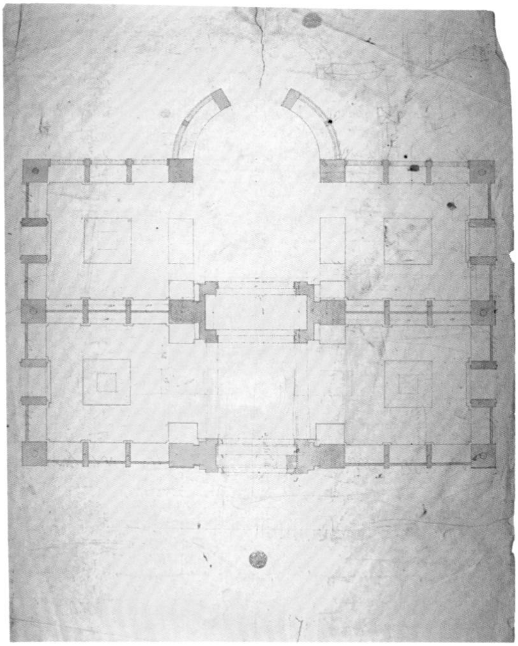

_Figure 3.
Gottfried Semper, ground plan of the Mixed Fabrics Court, Crystal Palace at Sydenham, 1854 (Courtesy of Kustodie der Hochschule für Bildende Künste Dresden, photo HfBK Dresden).

Decline of the Industrial Spirit. Both suggest a seemingly non-negotiable opposition between culture and industry. They emphasize those writings of John Ruskin, and later William Morris, which decry the crossover of art and mechanical or industrial production. More recent scholarship, however, has modified Williams's concerns. Joseph Bizup, for example, looks beyond Ruskin and Morris to analyse the development of a 'pro-industrial rhetoric' among nineteenth-century critics, scientists, and authors. In Bizup's account, the 1830s–60s design reformers play a significant role in the establishment of 'industrial culture'.[13] Here, I want to emphasize the important, and sometimes surprising, role that Greek sculpture played in this 'pro-industrial' art culture.[14]

Classical sculpture's place in the loosely defined Design Reform movement was as a teacher of good taste. It had occupied this position from the outset of the movement, habitually dated to the 1835–36 Select Committee on Connections between Art and Manufactures. During the Select Committee debates, key witnesses maintained that Greek sculpture was the ultimate arbiter of good taste, "archetypes of art … a foundation of pure and elegant taste".[15] One even called for manufacturers to set up plaster cast galleries for workers to peruse in their breaks.[16] Greek sculptors had attained such excellence, these witnesses claimed, because they lived in a society where sculpture played a public role. This was agreed across the board at mid-century by design reformers, archaeologists, manufacturers and sculptors alike.[17] The Greek Court at Sydenham stimulated new discussions and aspirations regarding public taste, ancient and modern. "Taste became intuitive" according to an "Art Journal" article on *Sculpture at the New Crystal Palace*, since ancient Greeks "worshipped and lived amid statues".[18] This excellent taste impacted upon all aspects of production and consumption in antiquity, and it had lessons about good design to communicate to the contemporary British public as well.[19]

Referring to the ancient cultures of Egypt and Greece in his handbook to the Alhambra Court at Sydenham, Owen Jones attributed present low standards of art and design to "the ignorance of the public".[20] Bringing the acknowledged excellence of Greek sculpture before the populace thus became a matter of urgency. The physical presence of such works would elevate taste, cultivating a "feeling" for the beautiful in Victorian society, as there had been in antiquity. Its architects and

_ Figure 4.
Gottfried Semper, façade
of the Mixed Fabrics
Court, Crystal Palace at
Sydenham, 1854 (Courtesy
of Kustodie der Hochschule
für Bildende Künste
Dresden, photo HfBK
Dresden).

contemporary commentators promoted the Sydenham Palace as a prime location for such an undertaking.[21] It would become the nineteenth-century equivalent of public displays of sculpture in antiquity.[22]

At the palace, ancient Greek sculptural practice was evoked as a model for rethinking the relationship between the "fine" and "useful" arts. Owen Jones and Matthew Digby Wyatt, along with witnesses in the 1835–36 Select Committee, the "Art Union", and the "Journal of Design and Manufactures", were keen to assert that Greek sculptors were artisans, combining the fine and useful arts in their work. Seeking established historical precedents, mid-nineteenth-century discussions found examples in the Renaissance but drew ultimately from what was understood of ancient Greek sculptural practice.[23] Semper, too, situated revered fifth-century BCE sculptor Phidias as a practitioner of "Hellenic industrial art" and drew a line across the centuries between Athenian shield sculpting and that undertaken in the Renaissance by Leonardo da Vinci, Michelangelo, and forward into the nineteenth century to Bertel Thorvaldsen and John Flaxman.[24] An 1851 "Journal of Design and Manufactures" article on the connections between "High Art and Ornamental Art" made much of its claim to "call on the Athenian for his authority".[25] It went on to refer to Pausanias to back up its ideas; others cited Pliny.[26] Most, however, simply asserted the unity of the arts in antiquity as a given. Owen Jones noted in 1852 that "the architect, the upholsterer, the paper-stainer, the weaver, the calico-printer, and the potter" were all artists. In "all ages but our own" the fine and useful arts had been united; "the painted vases of the Greeks are but the reflex of the paintings of their temples".[27] In 1854 he proposed the "art-collections of the Crystal Palace" as a force for their reconciliation.[28]

This crossover between the "fine" and "useful" arts and between architectural and what are usually called "decorative" arts is fundamental to Semper's writings on the origins of architecture. It is also manifest in his involvement in designing the Mixed Fabrics Court at Sydenham. This sat in the south, industrial and commercial nave of the palace, opposite the Birmingham Court, and next door to another textile court, the Printed Fabrics Court designed by Charles Barry Jr. and Robert Richardson Banks (see figure 2, where Semper's court is labelled as "Textile Fabrics Court no. 2").[29]

Commissioned in February 1854, Semper's court was finally completed some six months after the palace opened, in December 1854.[30] Semper's design was unusual for the industrial courts, since it divided the court into two, as is visible on the plans. Entering from the nave, visitors would encounter first an open room with no ceiling, day-lit through the glass roof of the palace, displaying "hosiery, shawls, and other textile fabrics" in glass cases.[31] Light-sensitive fabrics were housed in the second half of the court beneath a roof, its oak-panelled ceiling decorated with imagery of the production of textiles and the names of "the principal continental and English manufacturing towns".[32] Ancient Greece's productive role in the textile arts was emphasized by the bust of Minerva ("traditional inventress of spinning and weaving") topping the tympanum of the covered half of the court, continuing the crossover of Greek and commercial nineteenth-century cultures outlined above.[33] The official guide emphasizes the scholarly credentials of the architect of the Mixed Fabrics Court and carefully describes the symbolic and textual referents of the architecture – as it does for the Fine Arts Courts.[34]

In an article on what it called the "Modern Courts" at the Crystal Palace, literary periodical the "Athenaeum" compared the two fabrics courts. While the Printed Fabrics Court was "scarcely much more than an elegant shop", Semper's, although mocked for its "uncalled for Genii" decorating the exterior, was praised for its ambition and sensitivity to the needs of viewers – who were, of course, also potential consumers: "To see the colour of silks we need light; to judge of cloths and velvets we want room and air". According to the "Athenaeum", the palace industrial courts offered "new conceptions of the possibility of shops. We see that they need not be mere booths, cellars, dens, or sheds". The periodical emphasized that art had much to offer to commerce in the good design of tasteful shops – and that such aesthetic improvement had an explicitly financial motivation: "Let Trade, then, fly to Art, and ask her to look over his books, and help him in filling the till".[35] In such comments, it is possible to identify an explicitly commercial extension of the design-reforming claims towards the bettering of national taste through well-designed commodities, with which Semper had been so intimately involved at the Department of Science and Art.

Further connections between the Mixed Fabrics Court in the south nave and the art and architectural courts in the north can be found in Semper's London writings of the 1850s. In *The Four Elements of Architecture* (1851), Semper elaborates on the importance of fabric in the early development of the fourth element of architecture, vertical enclosure. Rush mats were the most primitive forms of walls. As solid walls emerged, they were dressed by textiles of increasing complexity, replicating the interlacings of rushes. Tapestries and carpets were replaced by other wall

Figs. 3–5

148

dressings, from mosaics, metal work, stucco through to painted relief sculpture. Semper argued that these new forms of decor evoked the form of their earlier fabric counterparts, and the role played by painted sculpture is of particular significance for my concerns here.[36] It seems that Semper took on the Mixed Fabrics Court as a step towards garnering further architectural practice in London. But the connections between its brightly painted and carved interior (visible in figure 5) and its textile objects of display, so central to his architectural theories, should not be overlooked.

Although the Mixed Fabrics Court was located in the "industrial" south side of the palace, it was intimately linked to the history of art and architecture that the Fine Arts Courts in the north nave attempted to demonstrate, and especially with Owen Jones's brightly painted Parthenon frieze in the Greek Court. At the Sydenham Palace, and in microcosm in Semper's Mixed Fabrics Court, art and industry were not inherently distinct. They might contribute to each other in productive new ways, transmitting knowledge about ancient forms into new contexts and possibilities.[37]

Fig. 6

149

Polychromy on display

Owen Jones's use of bold primary colours in the courts at the 1851 Great Exhibition had already attracted a great deal of attention.[38] Jones's polychromatic undertakings in the Greek Court at Sydenham generated even greater outrage. In the corridor at the back of the Greek Court, bordering on the Egyptian Court, was a cast of sections of the north frieze of the Parthenon. The original of this section of the frieze was on display in the British Museum. It depicts a cavalcade of horsemen galloping to the left, and because it contained so many figures and such activity it was selected as the

_ Figure 5.
Interior of Semper's Mixed Fabrics Court (at this point the Ceramics Court), figure from *The Crystal Palace, as a Teacher of Art and Art-Manufacture*, "Art Journal", 2, no. 19, 1 July 1856, p. 217 (Courtesy of Barber Fine Art Library, Library Services, University of Birmingham).

test case for what Jones proudly called "our experiment": a restored and fully painted frieze.[39] The palace was the first place in Britain to exhibit a painted piece of one of nineteenth-century Britain's most treasured possessions. It went defiantly against the conclusions of a committee called by RIBA in 1836, which had concluded that the Parthenon frieze had not been painted. With its blue background, golden hair, white flesh, pale blue and pink drapery, and red and grey horses (all taken from archaeological precedents, Jones was keen to emphasize), the frieze was a bold statement in favour of polychromy.[40]

Figs. 1, 6

The painted frieze roused commentators to feverish expressions of disgust. In 1855, Samuel Leigh Sotheby, a Crystal Palace shareholder, deemed it "as great a deformity to the natural marble as the concealment of the most beautiful portions of the human face, by its assuming the appearance of a Skye Terrier", a significant (if surreal) affront to conventional expectations.[41] Sotheby was anxious that inaccurate archaeological information was irresponsibly being put before the public. The "Morning Chronicle"'s editorial was similarly censorious, deeming the palace to have ideas above its station: "let it not claim what it does not, or ought not, to pretend to. ... As a people, we do not wish the classical and archaeological reputation of English scholarship to be committed to ... all the vivid fancies of Mr Owen Jones".[42] Yet Jones's "vivid fancies" were deeply rooted in contemporary archaeological and architectural debate. They became such a *cause célèbre* at Sydenham because these ideas were put before a new mass audience.

The "Art Journal" noted the "gaudy", "over-decorated" courts and lambasted the "bedaubed frieze ... which has lowered the finest work in the world to the level of a print sold at a penny plain and twopence coloured".[43] Sculptor Richard Westmacott Jr. branded the painted horsemen on the frieze at Sydenham "tawdry toys".[44] In 1857, American author Herman Melville deemed the entire venue, the Crystal Palace, a "vast toy. No substance", appropriate for an audience who were often described as infantile.[45] Art critic Lady Eastlake added her voice to the claims that polychromy was a crudely populist and ill-advised attempt to please the "ignorant":

> An element which may be familiar to the sailor in his figure-head, to the mechanic in his tea-garden, and to the child of five years old in the picture-book he has polychromed for himself, but which is simply a puzzle to the ignorant and a torture to the enlightened.[46]

For these critics, the attempts to please a poorly educated 'vulgar audience' by painting casts transformed great works of the past into disposable, cheap, childlike commodities. Painted sculpture was perceived as superficially naturalistic, and as such deemed attractive to those without an art-historical education. The apparent naturalism of painted sculpture was also a source of anxiety for those worried about its potential to transgress boundaries between the ideal and the real. For some contemporaries, the display of painted, and thus apparently lifelike, naked ancient Greek men was morally dangerous for an audience of women and children.[47] In the British context painted sculpture was even more abhorrent, since it was also associated with Catholicism.[48]

It was thus not entirely surprising that Jones felt compelled to respond to critics with *An Apology for the Colouring of the Greek Court* (1854). This strident defence featured a chapter in which Jones set out his arguments and described the colouring he had undertaken at Sydenham. This was followed by a section on "Historical Evidence", with essays on ancient literary descriptions of painted sculpture by critic, philosopher, and novelist George Henry Lewes and classical scholar William Watkiss Lloyd. Under the heading "Material Evidence", Jones reprinted extracts from the 1836 RIBA committee called to debate polychromy. The final section was a stand-alone ten-page essay, the longest section (excepting Jones's introduction), extracted from chapter five of Semper's 1851 *The Four Elements of Architecture* – the first time that an English translation of this section of the text was put before an Anglophone public.

Jones makes no reference to why he chose to publish Semper over any of the other well-known contemporary writers on polychromy, such as Jacques Ignace Hittorff, the "most diligent labourer in the field", as Jones put it.[49] Jones makes the briefest of mentions of Semper's connection with their mutual friend Jules Goury and their early investigations into architectural polychromy in his introduction to the *Apology*.[50] He does not explain the decision to publish the particular selection of extracts from chapter five of *The Four Elements*. In many ways, the extract was a strange choice. Bound up with Semper's complex argument about the elements of architecture, it was more theoretical than any of the other essays contained in the *Apology*. Further, Semper does not mention paint on Greek architecture until the seventh page and explicitly refuses to discuss the matter of paint on the Parthenon, the very subject which Jones's *Apology* sets out to defend.[51] As I explore below,

151

_ Figure 6.
South side corridor of the Greek Court, showing painted Parthenon frieze to the rear and painted Egyptian sculpture to the left, date unknown (Courtesy of Bromley Historic Collections, CP2B).

however, Semper's argument fitted in well with Jones's wider systematic thinking on painted architecture. For now, it is sufficient to note that by 1854, Semper had clearly picked up on the British interest in polychromy as an area of increasingly public debate to which he might contribute and which might garner publishers' interest – no insignificant matter in his impecunious London period.[52]

Semper had a long-standing interest in polychromy. In 1834, he published (in German) *Preliminary Remarks on Polychrome Architecture and Sculpture in Antiquity*, a result of his studies in Greece in the early 1830s. Polychromy was the hub of the argument in his 1851 German publication of *The Four Elements of Architecture*, the first two chapters of which were already printed in English in the short-lived archaeological journal "Museum of Classical Antiquities" in 1851. An extract from the "Museum" was also reprinted for a rather different audience in Henry Cole's "Journal of Design and Manufactures" in the same year.[53] As mentioned in the introduction, Semper and Jones had also both participated in debates on polychromy at RIBA in January 1852. Although Jones apparently protested at Semper being given any architectural commissions at Sydenham, he seems to have respected his scholarship and to have acknowledged his growing reputation on the subject of polychromy in British architectural and archaeological circles. Their appearance in Jones's *Apology* thrust Semper's learned theoretical texts on polychromy into the ribald responses to painted sculpture at Sydenham. They became a scandalous part of public discourse, associated with anxieties about moral conduct and sexuality – and also racial difference.

Greek sculpture and other cultures

The "illustrated encyclopaedia" at Sydenham also contained plaster casts of non-European peoples, displayed in tableaux with taxidermied animals in its Natural History Department.[54] The Natural History Department added an extra dimension to public anxieties about paint and undress in the classical courts. Both were explicitly connected with ideas about 'savagery' in nineteenth-century thought and fed into broader fears about the impact of the palace displays on an audience spanning the class divide.[55] A satirical piece from the "Idler" in the 1890s comments that "the directors have two kinds of statues in stock – plain and coloured".[56] Greek sculpture and ethnological models are referred to here in the same breath, the symbolic connection between "coloured" statuary and "coloured" skin emphasized. Charmaine Nelson has demonstrated the raced and gendered implications of white marble, a "privileged racial signifier", as a material for sculpture in the mid-nineteenth century.[57] Its opposite, painted sculpture, was not only associated with popular culture but also definitively associated with 'primitive', non-Western, and what contemporaries identified as underdeveloped or declining art. The outrage of Jones's painted Parthenon frieze moved sculptor Richard Westmacott Jr. and archaeologist Hodder Michael Westropp to denounce painted sculpture as works of "[b]arbarous and uncultivated nations", "practised at the worst period of art" in "Assyria, India, and Mexico".[58] Extra-European people were painted at the palace, just as these 'primitives' painted sculpture themselves. According to Westmacott and Westropp, the Greeks were too civilized to have ever painted their sculpture, and the sculpture that represented them at Sydenham ought to be similarly unpainted and untainted with any possible connections to the non-Western.

This is where Jones's displays are even more distinct – and where further connections between his displays at Sydenham and Semper's writings emerge. In his *Apology*, Jones positions Greece in the context of the rest of world art at the palace. Jones held that the Greek use of colour would seem quite ordinary once it was seen alongside painted sculpture from other time periods and locations such as Egypt and Assyria.[59] This is not to deny what Stacey Sloboda has called the "explicitly imperialist agenda" of Jones's cosmopolitan outlook, but to suggest the complexity of his engagements with various pasts and presents.[60] The British Museum definitively separated the Parthenon marbles from non-Western art by presenting them as pure, uncoloured, and the culmination of the evolution of art.[61] The architect of the Greek Court at Sydenham sought to reintegrate them with the art of Egypt and Assyria.

In this context, the choice of selections from chapter five of Semper's *The Four Elements* makes more sense. Here Semper makes his most radical claims regarding the "composite character" of Greek culture, made up out of the "humus of many past traditions".[62] The achievements of Greek architecture could only be understood in relation to other cultures.[63] The formatting of Semper's text in the *Apology* places even greater emphasis on Greece among these diverse cultures. Whereas the original German is continuous prose, the text in the *Apology* is divided into capitalized and clearly legible subsections: "THE ASSYRIANS", "THE PERSIANS", "THE EGYPTIANS", "THE CHINESE", "THE INDIANS", "THE JEWS AND PHENICIANS", and finally, "THE GREEKS".

Fig. 6

153

Conclusion

With the London polychromy debates fresh in his mind, and with his connections to the celebrated painted frieze at Sydenham, it is all the more remarkable that Semper seems not to have attempted to paint the casts collected in 1855 when he began his tenure at the Polytechnic. This explicitly technical-educational collection had entirely different purposes from that at Sydenham, although both had their bases in the ways in which new technologies might interact with ancient sculpture and architecture.[64] Perhaps after all his tribulations in London, Semper feared a similar backlash to painted sculpture in his new home and preferred to develop his ideas in academic publications rather than in more visible experiments in cast collections.

To return to the theme of architecture and the globalization of knowledge, I would like to look briefly to another cast collection, initiated in the late 1850s far from London. Its founders referred often, and with derision, to the Sydenham Palace. Melbourne, Australia, needed a cast gallery in order to teach, according to its founders, "the historic development of art".[65] It was launched by judge Redmond Barry and professor of natural sciences Frederick McCoy, whose professions are testimony to the wide variety of interest in Greek sculpture beyond art and architectural history in the nineteenth century. In Melbourne, casts were presented as

Fig. 7

_ Figure 7.
Greek and Roman plaster
cast collection at the
Swiss Federal Polytechnic
in Zurich, photograph
1915 (Courtesy of the gta
Archives/ETH Zurich).

objects of fine art-historical, rather than art-industrial, knowledge. And, notably, nothing was painted.

Casts certainly offered an opportunity to transmit knowledge about architecture and sculpture to anywhere on earth that wished to cast in plaster.[66] But the knowledge they might transmit was always related and transformed by the context in which they were examined. At Sydenham in the 1850s, discourses – some fearful, some hopeful – about sex, race, and class emerged around the display of classical sculpture. Greek sculpture was one part of a larger living spectacle in what Jason Edwards thinks of as the "ecosystem" of the palace. Edwards emphasizes the importance of appreciating the relations of its exhibits – ancient architectural and sculptural, natural-historical, and contemporary industrial. Such an approach resounds intriguingly with Semper's own description of the meeting of present-day visitors, new glass and iron architecture, and the natural and ancient historical present in his description of the 1851 palace.[67] Jones and Semper might have had only elusive, and, from the sound of things, rather antagonistic encounters in the historical archive. Here, I bring together their writings under the auspices of Jones's public art experiments wrestling with the unity of the arts and polychromy of ancient sculpture. This offers further insight into the London culture – intellectual, practical, and public – in which their ideas and practices developed.

_ 1. On Semper's travels, see H.F. Mallgrave, *Gottfried Semper: Architect of the Nineteenth Century*, Yale University Press, New Haven 1996, pp. 39–46. His mournful comment on Goury's departure from Jones and his untimely death in 1834 appears in G. Semper, *The Four Elements of Architecture: A Contribution to the Comparative Study of Architecture (1851)*, in G. Semper, *The Four Elements of Architecture and Other Writings*, trans. H.F. Mallgrave and W. Herrmann, Cambridge University Press, Cambridge, MA 1989, pp. 74–129 (here p. 76, note).

_ 2. D. Van Zanten, *Architectural Polychromy: Life in Architecture*, in R. Middleton (ed.), *The Beaux-Arts and Nineteenth-Century French Architecture*, Thames and Hudson, London 1982, pp. 197–215 (here p. 211); D. Weidmann, *Through the Stable Door to Prince Albert? On Gottfried Semper's London Connections*, "Journal of Art Historiography", no. 11, December 2014, pp. 1–26 (here pp. 15–16). See the chapter by Murray Fraser in the present volume.

_ 3. On Semper's position in 1850s Design Reform, see E. Chestnova, *"Ornamental Design Is … a Kind of Practical Science": Theories of Ornament at the London School of Design and Department of Science and Art*, "Journal of Art Historiography", no. 11, December 2014, pp. 1–18.

_ 4. S. Laing's speech, cited in "Illustrated Crystal Palace Gazette", 1, no. 11, 17 June 1854, p. 132; also published in *The Sydenham Crystal Palace Expositor*, James S. Virtue, London 1855, p. 3. For a general history of the Crystal Palace at Sydenham, see J.R. Piggott, *Palace of the People: The Crystal Palace at Sydenham, 1854–1936*, Hurst and Company, London 2004.

_ 5. See, for example, M. Hvattum, *"A Complete and Universal Collection": Gottfried Semper and the Great Exhibition*, in M. Hvattum and C. Hermansen (eds.), *Tracing Modernity: Manifestations of the Modern in Architecture and the City*, Routledge, London 2004, pp. 124–36; C. Leoni, *Art, Production and Market Conditions: Gottfried Semper's Historical Perspective on Commodities and the Role of Museums*, "Journal of Art Historiography", no. 11, December 2014, pp. 1–14.

_ 6. See W. Herrmann, *In Exile: Semper in Paris and London, 1849–1855*, in W. Herrmann, *Gottfried Semper: In Search of Architecture*, MIT Press, Cambridge, MA 1984, pp. 9–83 (here p. 77); H.F. Mallgrave, *Gottfried Semper*, see note 1, p. 213; D. Weidmann, *Through the Stable Door*, see note 2, p. 11.

_ 7. G. Semper, *A Foreign Architect's Views of the Building*, "Edinburgh Review", 94, no. 192, October 1851, pp. 575–78 (here p. 576), edited in G. Semper, *London Writings 1850–1855*, edited by M. Gnehm, S. Hildebrand, and D. Weidmann, gta Verlag, Zurich 2021.

_ 8. For an exploration of the tension between past traditions and contemporary architectural theory and practice in Semper's work, see M.

Hvattum, *Gottfried Semper and the Problem of Historicism*, Cambridge University Press, Cambridge, MA 2004. On the relationships between past and present at the Sydenham Palace, and in Jones's work in particular, see S. Moser, *Designing Antiquity: Owen Jones, Ancient Egypt and the Crystal Palace*, Yale University Press, New Haven 2013; K. Nichols, *Greece and Rome at the Crystal Palace: Classical Sculpture and Modern Britain, 1854–1936*, Oxford University Press, Oxford 2015.

_ 9. "The Times", 13 December 1859, p. 10; R. Cowtan, *Memories of the British Museum*, Bentley, London 1872, p. 305.

_ 10. G. Semper, *General Remarks on the Different Styles in Art*, draft of a lecture given on 11 November 1853 (second version), gta Archives/ETH Zurich, 20-Ms-122, fol. 5r, edited in G. Semper, *London Writings*, see note 7.

_ 11. See A. Payne, *From Ornament to Object: Genealogies of Architectural Modernism*, Yale University Press, New Haven 2012, pp. 33–46. Chestnova emphasizes the importance of Semper's involvement with the Great Exhibition and the Department of Science and Art in the development of his interest in industrial art in relation to architecture. See E. Chestnova, *Ornamental Design*, see note 3, p. 6.

_ 12. See, for example, T. Barringer, *Men at Work: Art and Labour in Victorian Britain*, Yale University Press, New Haven 2005; L. Kriegel, *Grand Designs: Labor, Empire, and the Museum in Victorian Culture*, Duke University Press, Durham, NC 2007; K. Nichols, R. Wade, and G. Williams (eds.), *Art versus Industry? New Perspectives on Visual and Industrial Cultures in Nineteenth-Century Britain*, Manchester University Press, Manchester 2016.

_ 13. J. Bizup, *Manufacturing Culture: Vindications of Early Victorian Industry*, University of Virginia Press, Charlottesville 2003, pp. 5–8 on Raymond Williams.

_ 14. For a more detailed exploration, see K. Nichols, *Greece and Rome at the Crystal Palace*, see note 8, pp. 127–63.

_ 15. *Report from the Select Committee on Arts and their Connexion with Manufactures*, House of Commons Paper 568, His Majesty's Stationery Office, London 1836, vol. 2, p. 23. For further discussion of the role of Greek sculpture in this select committee, see M. Romans, *A Question of "Taste": Re-examining the Rationale for the Introduction of Public Art and Design Education to Britain in the Early Nineteenth Century*, in M. Romans (ed.), *Histories of Art and Design Education: Collected Essays*, Intellect, Bristol 2005, pp. 41–54.

_ 16. *Report from the Select Committee on Arts*, see note 15, vol. 2, p. 29.

_ 17. *Report from the Select Committee on Arts*, see note 15; E. Falkener, *Daedalus; or, the Causes and Principles of the Excellence of Greek Sculpture*, Longman, Green, Longman & Roberts, London 1860, pp. 37–39; F. Pulszky, *On the Progress and Decay of Art; and on the Arrangement of a National*

155

Museum: A Lecture Delivered at University Hall, London, "The Museum of Classical Antiquities", 2, no. 5, March 1852, pp. 1–15 (here pp. 2–5); D. Raoul-Rochette, *Lectures on Ancient Art*, trans. H.M. Westropp, Hall, Virtue & Co., London 1854, pp. 120–21; R. Westmacott, *Handbook of Sculpture, Ancient and Modern*, Black, Edinburgh 1864.

_18. *Museum of Sculpture at the New Crystal Palace*, "Art Journal", New Series, 5, 1 September 1853, pp. 209–11 (here p. 209).

_19. See, for example, J. Gardner Wilkinson, *On Colour and on the Necessity for a General Diffusion of Taste among All Classes*, Murray, London 1858, p. 186.

_20. O. Jones, *The Alhambra Court in the Crystal Palace*, Bradbury and Evans, London 1854, p. 16.

_21. *The Crystal Palace, as a Teacher of Art and Art-Manufacture: Part V*, "Art Journal", 2nd Series, 2, 1 November 1856, pp. 345–48 (here p. 345).

_22. P. Mérimée, *De l'état des beaux-arts en Angleterre en 1857*, "Revue des deux mondes", 2nd series, 11, 15 October 1857, pp. 866–80 (here pp. 874–75); *Museum of Sculpture at the New Crystal Palace*, see note 18, p. 209; *The New Era of Industry and Art*, "Illustrated Crystal Palace Gazette", 1, no. 2, November 1853, pp. 13–14 (here p. 14).

_23. On the Renaissance as a model, see D. Irwin, *Art versus Design: The Debate 1760–1860*, "Journal of Design History", 4, no. 4, 1991, pp. 219–32 (here pp. 228–30).

_24. G. Semper, *On the Relations of the Different Branches of Industrial Art to Each Other and to Architecture*, draft of a lecture given on 20 May 1853 (first version), gta Archives/ETH Zurich, 20-Ms-118, fols. 2v–3r, edited in G. Semper, *London Writings*, see note 7.

_25. *"High Art" and Ornamental Art*, "Journal of Design and Manufactures", 4, no. 24, February 1851, pp. 161–64 (here p. 163).

_26. *Report from the Select Committee on Arts*, see note 15, vol. 1, p. 111; vol. 2, pp. 23, 88.

_27. Owen Jones, *An Attempt to Define the Principles Which Should Regulate the Employment of Colour in the Decorative Arts, with a Few Words on the Present Necessity of an Architectural Education on the Part of the Public*, Barclay [printer], London 1852, pp. 4–5. This passage also in Jones, *Alhambra Court*, see note 20, pp. 15–16.

_28. Jones, *Alhambra Court*, see note 20, p. 16.

_29. Barry and Richardson Banks's court is engraved in "The Builder", 7 October 1854, p. 523. See also J.R. Piggott, *Palace of the People*, see note 4, p. 129. It later became the Manchester Court and is one of the few areas outside of the Fine Arts Courts to have been photographed by Philippe Delamotte. See I. Leith, *Delamotte's Crystal Palace: A Victorian Pleasure Dome Revealed*, English Heritage, Swindon 2005, p. 95. There is comparatively little documentation of Semper's court in Crystal Palace publicity material.

_30. See W. Herrmann, *In Exile*, see note 6, pp. 74–76.

_31. S. Phillips, *Guide to the Crystal Palace and Park*, Bradbury and Evans, London 1854, p. 117.

_32. *Ibid.*

_33. *Ibid.*

_34. *Ibid.*

_35. *The Modern Courts at the Crystal Palace*, "Athenaeum", no. 1501, 2 August 1856, pp. 965–66.

_36. G. Semper, *Four Elements of Architecture*, see note 1, pp. 103–4.

_37. In 1856, the Mixed Fabrics Court became the Ceramics Court, widely praised for its bringing together of "fine art" and "manufactures". This seems peculiarly apposite in the light of the *Plan for an Ideal Museum* in Semper's 1852 manuscript *Practical Art in Metal and Hard Materials: Its Technology, History and Styles*. Here objects are divided into four categories according to production; the first, twisting, weaving, spinning, was linked to textiles; the second, ceramics or the kneading of soft, plastic materials. See H.F. Mallgrave, *Gottfried Semper*, see note 1, p. 211. On the Ceramics Court at Sydenham, see K. Nichols, *Greece and Rome at the Crystal Palace*, see note 8, pp. 146–48.

_38. C.A. Hrvol Flores, *Owen Jones: Design, Ornament, Architecture, and Theory in an Age in Transition*, Rizzoli, New York 2006, pp. 82–89.

_39. O. Jones, *An Apology for the Colouring of the Greek Court*, Bradbury and Evans, London 1854, pp. 17–18.

_40. *Ibid.*, pp. 20–22.

_41. S.L. Sotheby, *A Few Words by Way of a Letter Addressed to the Directors of the Crystal Palace Company*, Smith, London 1855, p. 25.

_42. "Morning Chronicle", 12 June 1854, p. 6.

_43. *The "Future" of the Crystal Palace*, "Art Journal", New Series, 6, 1 September 1854, pp. 280–81 (here p. 281).

_44. R. Westmacott, *On Colouring Statues*, "The Archaeological Journal", 12, 1855, pp. 22–46 (here p. 35).

_45. J. Leyda (ed.), *The Melville Log: A Documentary Life of Herman Melville, 1819–1891*, vol. 2, Gordian Press, New York 1969, p. 576.

_46. [E. Eastlake], *The Crystal Palace*, "Quarterly Review", 96, no. 192, March 1855, pp. 303–54 (here p. 311).

_47. See K. Nichols, *Greece and Rome at the Crystal Palace*, see note 8, pp. 187–88.

_48. See A. Yarrington, *Under the Spell of Madame Tussaud: Aspects of "High" and "Low" in Nineteenth-Century Polychromed Sculpture*, in A. Blühm and P. Curtis (eds.), *The Colour of Sculpture 1840–1910*, Van Gogh Museum e Waanders, Amsterdam e Zwolle 1996, pp. 83–92.

_49. O. Jones, *Apology*, see note 39, p. 6.

_50. *Ibid.*, pp. 5–23 (here p. 6).

_51. G. Semper, *On the Origin of Polychromy in Architecture*, in O. Jones, *Apology*, see note 39, pp. 45–56 (here p. 56), edited in G. Semper, *London Writings*, see note 7.

_52. H.F. Mallgrave, *Gottfried Semper*, see note 1, pp. 182–83.

_53. For a detailed review of Semper's polychromatic thought, see H.F. Mallgrave, *Introduction*, in G. Semper, *The Four Elements of Architecture*, see note 1, pp. 1–44 (here pp. 12–19).

_54. See S. Qureshi, *Peoples on Parade: Exhibitions, Empire, and Anthropology in Nineteenth-Century Britain*, University of Chicago Press, Chicago 2011, pp. 194–208.

_55. "Morning Chronicle", 12 June 1854, p. 6.

_56. A. Upward, *The Horrors of London: The Crystal Palace*, "Idler: An Illustrated Monthly Magazine", 9, no. 5, June 1896, pp. 756–58 (here p. 756).

_57. C.A. Nelson, *"So Pure and Celestial a Light": Sculpture, Marble, and Whiteness as a Privileged Racial Signifier*, in C.A. Nelson, *The Color of Stone: Sculpting the Black Female Subject in Nineteenth-Century America*, University of Minnesota Press, Minneapolis 2007, pp. 57–72.

_58. R. Westmacott, *On Colouring Statues*, see note 44, p. 44; H.M. Westropp, *Preface*, in D. Raoul-Rochette, *Lectures on Ancient Art*, see note 17, pp. iii–iv (here p. iv).

_59. O. Jones, *Apology*, see note 39, p. 5.

_60. S. Sloboda, *The Grammar of Ornament: Cosmopolitanism and Reform in British Design*, "Journal of Design History", 21, no. 3, 2008, pp. 223–36 (here p. 225).

_61. See I. Jenkins, *Archaeologists and Aesthetes in the Sculpture Galleries of the British Museum, 1800–1939*, British Museum Press, London 1992.

_62. G. Semper, *Origin of Polychromy*, see note 51, p. 53; G. Semper, *The Four Elements of Architecture*, see note 1, p. 101.

_63. For further exploration of Semper's ideas about Greek culture, see W.J. McGrath, *Freedom in Architecture: Gottfried Semper and the Greek Ideal*, in W.J. McGrath, *German Freedom and the Greek Ideal: The Cultural Legacy from Goethe to Mann*, edited by C. Applegate, S. Frontz, and S. Marchand, Palgrave Macmillan, Houndsmills, Basingstoke 2013, pp. 43–74 (here pp. 52–59).

_64. C. Wilkening-Aumann and A. von Kienlin, *"Zum Umgange mit dem Schönen gezwungen" – Die Gipsabguss-Sammlungen der ETH und Universität Zürich*, in U. Hassler and T. Meyer (eds.), *Kategorien des Wissens: Die Sammlung als epistemisches Objekt*, vdf Hochschulverlag AG an der ETH Zürich, Zurich 2014, pp. 193–207.

_65. R. Barry, *Address of the Trustees of the Melbourne Public Library* (1859), quoted in A. Galbally, *The Lost Museum: Redmond Barry and Melbourne's "Musée des Copies"*, "Australian Journal of Art", 7, 1988, pp. 29–49 (here p. 30).

_66. On classical plaster cast collections across Europe, in Mexico, New Zealand, the USA, and Russia, see R. Frederiksen and E. Marchand (eds.), *Plaster Casts: Making, Collecting, and Displaying from Classical Antiquity to the Present*, De Gruyter, Berlin 2010.

_67. J. Edwards, *The Cosmopolitan World of Victorian Portraiture: the Crystal Palace Portrait Gallery, c. 1854*, in K. Nichols and S.V. Turner (eds.), *After 1851: The Material and Visual Cultures of the Crystal Palace at Sydenham*, Manchester University Press, Manchester 2017, pp. 47–72; G. Semper, *Foreign Architect's Views*, see note 7, p. 576.

157

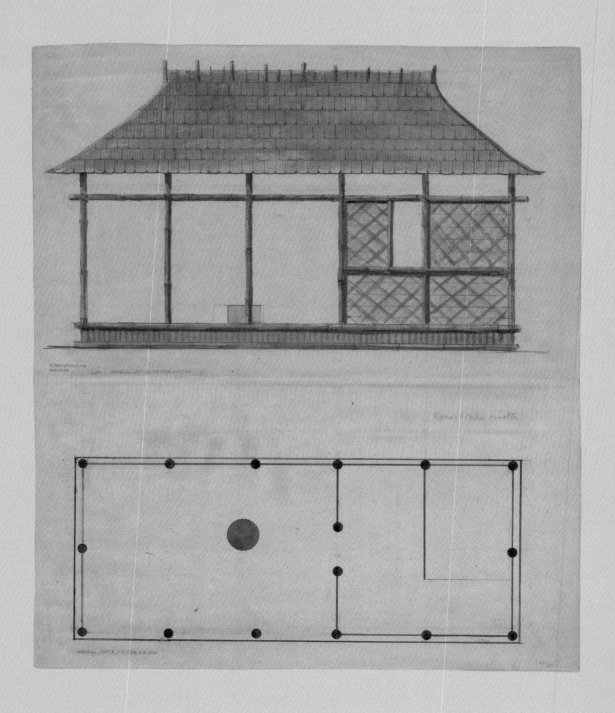

Caroline van Eck

Masking, Dressing, Tattooing, and Cannibalism: From Architectural History to the Anthropology of Art

_ Figure 1.
Gottfried Semper,
Caribbean hut, ca.
1853 (Courtesy of
the gta Archives/ETH
Zurich).

In § 60 of *Der Stil*, Semper reaches the heart of his argument: in its essence, architecture is not structure but dressing. Its origins are not to be found in the construction of walls, columns, roofs, or vaults, made to protect man from the elements, as Vitruvius and his successors until the end of the eighteenth century had argued, but in the primitive craft of weaving, and in particular in the use of textile to separate interior space from the exterior.[1] This section is also one of the most dense, compressed, and mysterious passages in a book that in itself ranks among the most difficult and inaccessible of nineteenth-century architectural treatises. Much has already been written about Semper's arguments that, in true art, materials and reality should be denied; or that, as he put it: "der Karnevalskerzendunst ist die wahre Atmosphäre der Kunst" ("the haze of carnival candles is the true atmosphere of art").[2] His repeated quotation of Hamlet's "Was war ihm Hekuba?" ("What was Hecuba to him?") is perhaps even more intriguing[3] but has largely been ignored by the more architecturally minded of his commentators. This fits in with the dominant tendency of Semper scholarship until recently to concentrate on his work as an architect, designer, and architectural theorist. The anthropological aspects of his work, their implications for a global history of art, and their historical context have received far less attention.[4] In this chapter, I will first analyse § 60, to show how practically all the key themes of *Der Stil* are brought together here into a coherent but programmatic statement. These are: the concept of style itself; the four basic crafts common to all mankind that together make up the cradle of art; the complex of notions circling around representation; the performative nature of apparently static arts such as sculpture, ceramics, and architecture; the transition from primitive craft to fine art and its defining characteristic: masking, dressing, negating, and even destroying material, matter, and reality. In the second part, I will consider some aspects of Semper's historical and intellectual ancestry and how he transformed the ideas of his predecessors into an anthropology of art. To conclude, I will argue that Semper developed a radically new vision of the origins of architecture and its essence as an art of representation, or *Darstellung*, in which that central concept of German aesthetics receives an entirely new meaning as well and in which anthropological data are combined with a transformation of one of the central notions of German Idealist aesthetics, viz. that representation is the defining characteristic of fine art.

The argument of § 60: space creation is the essence of architecture; its origins coincide with those of the craft of textile

The origin and essence of architecture is not construction but the visible representation of enclosed space, which in its earliest form took the shape of the partition, pen, or fence made of plaited or interwoven sticks and branches. It is thus intimately linked with weaving or textile, one of the four primitive crafts that can be found all over the world and which form the cradle of human art and industry: "[T]he beginning of building coincides with the beginning of textiles".[5]

With the invention of weaving, the first repertoire of forms was extended enormously: the crude pens made of sticks, branches, leaves, or grass to divide interior from exterior, inner life from outer life, or the hearth from the vast undefined spaces surrounding it gave way to curtains and tapestries. These did not represent the construction of walls or roofs but rather the "formale Gestaltung der Raumesidee" ("formal construct of the spatial idea").[6] Walls, fortifications, or scaffolds upholding and securing spatial enclosures are secondary elements, foreign to the origin of building, which is to enclose and thereby create space. The origin of architecture, according to Semper, is therefore not construction but dressing – *Bekleidung*, the *Urform*, one could say, of architectural *Darstellung*. *Nachahmung* (imitation) is here replaced by *Darstellung* (representation) as both the motor of architectural development and the key to a theory of architectural invention, meaning, and style.

Accepting as confirmation the re-creation of a Caribbean bamboo hut that he had seen at the Great Exhibition of 1851, Semper here breaks with the entire classical tradition of considering the *petite cabane rustique*, that is a building, as the origin of architecture and instead locates its origins in the *action* of space creation and the *craft* – weaving – that made this possible by providing woven curtains, carpets, tents, etc.[7] By the same stroke, architectural history for Semper was no longer – as it had been, for instance, in the teaching of the École des Beaux-Arts or existing handbooks such as Franz Kugler's – the story of how classical architecture had been adapted to varying times and places without changing its essence. Instead, it became a project closely allied to the new discipline of anthropology, in that it considered architecture no longer as an art based on an intellectual activity – *ratiocinatio* for Vitruvius, *disegno* for Vasari – but primarily as a craft whose products were to be investigated in the same way as all other human artefacts.

The tents, scaffolds, and funerary piles that are the first and ephemeral textile human dwellings and constructions are mysteriously transfigured, as Semper ironically puts it in one of his numerous allusions to the history of religion – which, as we shall see, so much influenced his ideas – into enduring, monumental buildings. That transformation marks the transition from building as a pre-architectural craft to the art of architecture.[8] It took place when its founders changed ephemeral festival apparatus – scaffoldings decked out with festoons and garlands, bands and trophies

Fig. 1

– into durable buildings because they wished to leave a permanent memorial of important religious or political acts. One example Semper gives of this transformation of ephemeral ritual structures that were still very close to the primitive crafts of weaving and carpentry are the two Lycian tombs in the British Museum, which he illustrates in this section. They suggest wooden structures, with painted reliefs between the joists and crowned by a sarcophagus-like top – that is, a stone representation of funeral pyres made of wood and covered with carpets, or, "a funeral pyre monumentally conceived".[9] The theatre is another instance of an ephemeral structure endowed with a monumental character: its architecture originated in the richly decorated wooden stages and proscenia described by Pliny and Vitruvius, which were highly encrusted with ornamentation. Not only were these ephemeral stages decorated – they were also dressed. We should always bear in mind, Semper stresses, that the framework, the structure of these scaffoldings and dwellings, is not the essence of architecture; that consists of the draperies, hangings, and curtains that create and demarcate space. These cases illustrate the principle of exterior decoration and dressing of the structural framework that is at work in both ephemeral and monumental architecture: "[T]he outward reason for monumental undertakings has always been, and still is, the wish to commemorate and immortalize some religious or solemn act, an event in world history, or an act of state".[10]

This transformation occurred because of the human drive to create a lasting, monumental record of important political and religious acts, situations, and rituals. The festive apparatus, as Semper calls it, of an improvised scaffold or structure is the original *Motiv* (motif) of the more permanent monument in stone, which proclaims, as he puts it, these foundational moments, rites, or situations to the following generations. Architectural monuments are therefore restitutions, in more enduring materials, of ephemeral constructions such as altars, theatres, or funeral pyres and tombs. Architecture considered as an art is no longer, as it had been in the Vitruvian tradition, primarily a building that fulfils its functions in a fitting, enduring, and beautiful manner; in yet another radical innovation, its aim and essence have become to act as performative speech.[11]

The examples of ancient theatres, altars, and tombs that Semper gives serve to show that the "Prinzip der äusserlichen Ausschmückung und Bekleidung" ("principle of the exterior decoration and dressing") of structures and frames was necessary in ephemeral festival buildings, with "festival" in the sense of marking an important event or action in the life of a society; and that hence this principle of "Verhüllung der structiven Theil*e*" ("veiling structural parts") must appear just as natural in the earliest monumental, enduring treatment of tents or hangings in the first stone appearance of monumental architecture.[12] We move here, incidentally, from a carefully supported archaeological argument to a hypothetical thesis about the development of architecture from the first, pre-architectural stages of making ephemeral structures and literally dressing them with hangings, tapestries, or carpets. *Bekleidung* was also the key concept in Carl Bötticher's *Der Baumkultus der Hellenen* of 1856, a monumental essay tracing the origins of Greek architecture to the *cultus* of trees. Unlike Bötticher, however, Semper firmly believed in the primacy of the theatrical instinct for the birth of art.[13]

161

Dressing and masking reality in the arts

At the very end of § 60, Semper adds a long footnote that is one of the most puzzling passages in the entire book.[14] It starts as an added explanation of the argument in the main text: the urge or instinct to *Bekleiden und Maskiren* (dress and to mask) are as old as humanity itself. The joy this gives to human beings makes mankind into painters, architects, poets, musicians, and playwrights. Hence both the creation and the enjoyment of art presuppose the atmosphere of carnival, with its licence to mask and disguise: "[d]er Karnevalskerzendunst ist die wahre Atmosphäre der Kunst" ("the haze of carnival candles is the true atmosphere of art"). What happens in this carnival atmosphere is not just a cheerful celebration of disguise and playacting but something more far-reaching: the negation of reality and of material, "die Vernichtung der Realität und des Stofflichen", is necessary for a form to appear as a meaningful symbol and as an independent, free human creation. The viewer should be made to forget the artistic means that were used to achieve this. *Naturmenschen* (primitive men) had an unspoiled feeling for doing this, and in more advanced cultures the great masters are capable of it as well, although they also use the mask to cover or deny matter.

Now for an architectural theorist, this is quite a surprising statement. How are we to understand this idea that art is born from the pleasure we all have in dressing and masking, that true art is born from the negation of reality in the haze of carnival candles, and that this results in forms that are both meaningful symbols and independent, free human creations? How are we to understand all the key terms in this statement – "form", "negation", "matter", "meaningful symbol", and "independent human creation"?

Let us keep these questions for a moment and see how Semper explains it. He gives the example of the sculptor Phidias, who in his statues of Greek gods for the Parthenon friezes had masked and even destroyed matter or *Stoff*. Now *Stoff* is an interestingly ambivalent term that can mean both matter in the sense of material, particularly of textiles, and also matter in the sense of subject-matter, theme, or topic. In the case of Phidias, Semper argues that he liberated his statues from all nonvisual elements and that this resulted in a series of living gods that appear to meet us as the expression or embodiment of purely human beauty. In other words, we might gloss Semper, Phidias did away with all references to what we would now call religious iconography or symbolism, preserving not the usual attributes of the gods that enable us to identify them, such as the *aegis* or the *caduceus*, but entirely human forms, dressed in human clothes – albeit of superhuman beauty, one might add.

But then, just as it seemed we might understand what Semper is trying to convey, he suddenly quotes Hamlet: "'What was Hecuba to him?'" It is a quotation from the scene in which Hamlet invites the players to perform a play about fraternal homicide and in which one of the players is invited to speak a monologue about the Trojan queen Hecuba, in which the actor is himself so overcome by emotion that Polonius makes him stop.[15] What can Semper possibly have meant by this? Semper continues that drama could be meaningful in both the earliest and the highest stages of human development. In Greece, that meant the early stages of Dionysian drama as recorded on vases and in the 'stone dramas' of Phidias, as well as in the work of Aeschylus, Sophocles, and Euripides. There the proscenium became the frame – in itself a device that transforms the reality or ontological status of what is performed within its boundaries – of a *Bild* (image) showing major episodes from the history of humanity, which by their very performance – and monumental framing, one might add – are not over and done with but keep recurring. "'What was Hecuba to them?'", Semper pursues: not only Greek drama, also the plays of Shakespeare or Mozart's *Don Giovanni* need the reality-denying devices of the gaze of carnival candles and the spirit of masks.

In other words – as perhaps the actor in Hamlet most clearly shows – in order to perform a role (just as, Semper would add, to sculpt a god or build a theatre), one has to mask and thereby transform one's materials: one's personality and appearance in the case of acting, the accidental attributes of religion in the case of Phidias, or the material reality – materials and their unworked, raw appearance, subject to the physical laws of matter – in the case of architecture. This ties in with Semper's hypothesis of dressing and masking as being not only one of the primal urges of mankind but also the origin of architecture: dressing and masking are a textile activity, one could say, and hence this primitive manual craft – one of the four basic crafts that according to Semper together constitute the reservoir of forms and techniques that produced humanity's material culture – is at the same time the material manifestation of a fundamental human trait. In other words, Semper's analysis of the development of human material culture in terms of crafts is combined here with his aesthetics of the negation of material reality and his anthropological theory of the arts as the result of this human urge.

Architectural dressing, that is, is not just an image in another medium of the four basic crafts that are the origin of architecture. It is the final step completing the transformation of a building into monumental architecture, when it becomes architecture proper and uses materials for figurative representation or "bildliche Darstellung".[16] It is also a denial of material reality that paradoxically greatly enhances the presence of the work of art, be it a drama or a building. It makes the building appear and act upon the viewer, makes it alive and humanizes it. Thus, his long excursus on tapestry and the arts of the decorator among the ancients concludes by stating that the reader is now forced to relinquish traditional views of Graeco-Roman architecture as white, uncoloured, and static, to replace them with an "image of antique architecture as colorful and lively" ("ein farbig belebtes Bild").[17] Polychromy, that is, is a variant of the principle of dressing and masking and a descendant of earlier uses of tapestry to create spaces. In that sense, the coloured walls of Pompeii are close relatives of Chinese building techniques with their combination of wooden scaffolding and hangings: "If we traveled in our imagination back to Pompeii as it was eighteen hundred years ago, many things there would seem Chinese to us".[18]

Throughout *Der Stil*, passages occur in which architecture is described as if it were a living structure, in which the artistic expression of the conflict between pressure and counterpressure animates the building's appearance. In the case of Greek temples, the use of a 'veil of paint' masks mechanical necessity and transforms them into "dynamic, even organic, forms, a matter of endowing them with a soul".[19] Masking or dressing is essential for buildings to become works of art. At the same time, the theatrical mode that Semper advocates implies both a dematerializa-

163

tion of architecture (it no longer simply is but represents itself and the events in the society that led to its creation not as a material artefact but as a cultural being) and an oscillation between presence and representation, acting and enacting that is characteristic of a theatrical performance. Semper's monumental architecture is a theatre of appearances. Dressing dramatizes architecture, makes it into a picture. In doing so, it also fictionalizes it, because masks offer a representation of human or animal faces, but at the same time also a fictive identity to the person who bears them. In that sense, the dressing of a façade denies the material reality of the construction it covers.

Hence – Semper concludes this long excursus – the chief, but also the most difficult task of a theory of style or *Stillehre*, is to show how this principle of dressing and dematerialization operates in Greek architecture so that the appearance of the work of art makes the viewer forget the technical means and materials; makes the work appear, act, and become as a form sufficient unto itself.[20] Style, one could say, does not consist in learning how to use the elements of classical architecture in a correct and appropriate way, as if it were a language – the Latin of architecture. Semper instead uses another model: that of seeing built forms as dressing and masking. Architecture started out as the monumental, enduring rendition in stone of wooden ephemeral structures erected to record important events, but gradually it becomes a much more abstract series of forms that represent the structural and formal characteristics of a building rather than referring to religious or ritual meaning. Thus, Greek art is different from its Assyrian ancestors in that it has freed itself from what Semper calls "tendentious" elements that refer to realities outside the sphere of architecture, conceived as the art of space creation and marking by means of textile techniques and its representations in more enduring materials:

> Greek art, by contrast ... conceives ornamental symbols above all in a structural-functional sense, with any reference to the tendentious meaning they still retain made as mild and faint as possible. It allocates to higher art its neutral fields, where it can develop freely, independent of the structure and the immediate material function of the system.[21]

This leaves the student of style with a very arduous task: to show, first, the transition from the earliest, textile origins of building as a way of creating inner spaces and marking the home off from the exterior world; second, to show that this process is a process of monumentalization, rooted in the desire of cultures to preserve an enduring record of major political, religious, or social events; third, to show that the major drive in transforming textile dwellings into art is the universal, innate human pleasure in dressing, covering, and masking and the attendant atmosphere of unreality; and finally – although this list of points to be argued is not complete – to show how, in the course of history, art and architecture increasingly liberated themselves from the representation of extra-architectural elements to that of elements intimately connected to construction and function. In other words, I would argue, Semper's theory of style is a highly complex mixture of a radically anthropological concept of art, on the one hand, seeing it as material culture born from the primitive craft of weaving and made to create space; and, on the other hand, a view of its development – as opposed to the origins of art – that is fuelled by a typically nineteenth-century aesthetic ideology of the essence of art as representation and the expression of human freedom, conceived by Semper above all as a freedom from all elements that to him are external – or tendentious, as he would call it – to architecture. In this respect, his long excursion on the tapestry of the ancients is illuminating because it traces the workings of the principle of dressing and negation of material from the tapestries of the Assyrians through the triumphal processions of the Romans to their mural paintings and into the Middle Ages.[22] At the same time, he presents this development as a gradual separation and rejection of what he calls tendentious ornament – that is, ornament referring to religious or cosmological views that are unrelated to the direct aims or functions of artefacts. In Assyrian art, animal forms – lions, griffins, etc. – representing the use of these objects would result in an animation of these objects:

> Just as vegetal ornament re-creates a *structure* as an *organism*, animal ornament raises dead *household furnishings* to the status of a voluntary or involuntary *domestic animal*! When I give a piece of furniture feet in the shape of lion's paws or deer's hooves, I define it as an object that moves according to my will, or at least as one that can be moved. I have the ability to adjust symbolically the degree of mobility that I wish to give it! A post's capacity for support and verticality is given living expression when I invest it with those forms that carry out a similar function in the animal world.[23]

In Graeco-Roman art, this evolution would go further. As we saw, in his statues for the Parthenon Phidias rejected all contingent external elements to achieve the animated appearance of the Greek gods in the shape of beautiful human bodies.

165

Semper's sources

Semper was not just a great theorist of art as a masking of reality but was also very adept at masking his own sources. There is one author, however, whom he mentions and quotes repeatedly: Antoine-Chrysostôme Quatremère de Quincy, and this reference leads us directly to a significant part of the complex of ideas, theories, and bodies of knowledge on which he drew in § 60 and its note.[24] Following the order of topics in these passages, I will first discuss some possible sources in eighteenth-century debates on the origin of societies and the role of art in the birth of civilization and in religion. Next, we will turn to the polychromy debate and Semper's role in it, because these are the crux, I would argue, in the development that would culminate in Semper's mature summary of his views in § 60. After that, we will zoom in on anthropological findings regarding dressing and masking among primitive people, in particular tattooing. Finally, we will return to Hecuba, which will allow us to revisit the theatrical dimensions and aesthetic implications of Semper's advocacy of an architecture that appears as the independent expression of human freedom.[25]

Eighteenth-century theories on the origins of society and the role of the arts

Although Semper rarely develops this topic in a sustained manner, *Der Stil*, like his earlier work on polychromy, is full of allusions to idolatry and fetishism and consistently speaks of buildings (and other artworks, such as tapestries) as if they are alive.[26] These two themes are related, since much late eighteenth-century and early nineteenth-century research on religion outside Europe – which continued the tradition of Protestant criticism of Catholic veneration of the Eucharist, to which Semper alludes when discussing the "Mysterium der Transfiguration" ("mystery of transfiguration") and describing the change from buildings into architecture in primitive societies[27] – centred on the belief by early societies in animated statues and objects that possessed the agency of human beings – what used to be called 'fetishism'. Fetishism, living artworks, and polychromy are related in turn, since polychromy was for a long time dismissed by its opponents as a kind of idolatry, based on a belief in the life of statues. These debates come together in one of the few books whose influence Semper acknowledged openly: Quatremère de Quincy's *Le Jupiter olympien* of 1815, one of the first manifestos in favour of polychromy, which also opens with a history of sculpture and its role in the development of primitive culture summarizing seventy years of ethnographic research and Enlightenment criticism of religion and taking it to its logical conclusion.

Fig. 2

166

_ Figure 2. *Throne and Simulacrum of Apollo at Amyclae*, plate from Antoine-Chrysostôme Quatremère de Quincy's *Le Jupiter olympien*, 1815 (Courtesy of the Institut National d'Histoire de l'Art).

In Quatremère's book on the Olympian Jupiter, art is defined and set apart from the fetish and the idol by the distance, the difference between the living model and its representation. The use of textiles or of polychromy, or of materials such as wax or ivory, indicates a lack of representational distance; they render the image too close to what it represents, so that aesthetic distance – or artistic autonomy, for that matter – cannot manifest itself.[28] Quatremère radically rejects the distinction advocated by Lessing and Winckelmann, which was to become very important for German aesthetics, between the cult object and the work of art. For Quatremère, sculpture as an art is born from religious cults:

> Pour bien apprécier et sans prévention l'art de la sculpture chez les anciens, il ne faut pas oublier qu'il fut l'art favori de la religion et le ministre le plus docile de ses volontés. Promoteur, fauteur et propagateur de toutes les opinions sur lesquelles reposait l'existence des dieux, il ne se bornait pas à en faire de simples représentations. C'est par la propriété qu'ont les signes de prendre la place des choses signifiées, que l'art de la sculpture servit très-activement la superstition, en employant les moyens les plus capables de faire prendre le change aux spectateurs ignorans. Associé ainsi à la puissance théogonique, l'art ne reproduisait pas seulement, mais il créait des dieux. Agent principal de cette puissance si prodigue d'emplois, il dut à la diversité même de ses emplois la multiplicité des formes, de goûts et de caractères qui modifièrent ses ouvrages au gré de plus d'une sorte de convenances inconnues aux arts modernes.
> … La distinction que Lessing a voulu faire entre les ouvrages exécutés en vue de la religion, et ceux qui le furent en vue de l'art, devient chimérique, lorsqu'on réfléchit que, si la religion d'un côté put détourner l'art de sa perfection, la plus grande perfection de l'art fut d'un autre côté nécessaire à la religion.[29]

We can only understand how sculpture developed if we take into account its social and above all religious roles: its origins in idolatry and the fact – always according to Quatremère – that there existed no art worthy of its name that was not made to act on the imagination and the emotions of its viewers; what subsequently he would call the moral considerations of art. In primitive society, sculpture exercises its agency thanks to its material and corporeal nature.

Polychromy

Some of Quatremère's ideas on polychromy can be traced back to one of his earliest texts, an essay on Egyptian art, which interestingly prefigures Semper's praise of Phidias's statues as pure embodiments of human beauty. In his essay on the relations between Egyptian and Greek architecture, written in 1785 for a competition held by the Académie, and published in 1788 and again in 1803, he followed received opinion and denied Egyptian art all capacity of developing towards a form of naturalism as Greek art had done.[30] The most typical variety of this art is the hieroglyph, the common element between language and figurative art. In Greece as well, writing formed the origin of sculpture, but there its development had been completely different. Because of the confluence of Egyptian political and religious institutions, its art was incapable of development:

> Symbole de l'immuabilité jusque dans les moindres parties, la sculpture égyptienne demeura constamment une écriture allégorique, dont le sens est à la vérité perdu, mais dont l'intention ne sauroit jamais se perdre …

Tous les monumens étoient des espèces de bibliothèques publiques, leurs ornemens étoient des légendes … les annales publiques du peuple; cette fonction d'historien, que la religion et le gouvernement leur imposoient … faisoient sans doute un devoir sacré de rendre éternels des monumens qui étoient sans aucune métaphore les dépositaires des rites, des dogmes, des exploits, de la gloire.[31]

Unlike French *architecture parlante*, Egyptian architecture cannot even be called art, because the Egyptians remain too close to what they represent:

ce modèle s'y confond avec l'imitation. Des soutterrains creusés dans la pierre et imités par la pierre ne doivent paroître qu'une seule et même chose … [les] Grecs … substituèrent une matière à une autre matière.[32]

Egyptian architecture for this reason was already quite incapable of development, and hence of art-historical interest; but it also suffered from another problem – defective imitation:

le vrai but de l'imitation n'est pas de se substituer tellement à son modèle que la ressemblance produise une identité capable de décevoir et de faire prendre le change. Au contraire, pour que nous en jouissions, il faut que nous apercevions que l'objet imitant n'est que l'image de l'objet imité. Là, en effet, ou par un excès d'illusion factice ou de rapprochement naturel, on croit voir la chose même imitée, dans son imitation, ce n'est plus l'image de cette chose qu'on peut prendre plaisir à voir, c'est la chose elle-meme, et là où l'on ne croit pas voir l'image d'une chose, on ne croit pas voir d'imitation. On n'en voit point.
Donc tout mode ou tout genre d'imitation qui tend le plus possible à s'approcher de ce point de similitude, dont l'effet est de faire croire que l'image qu'il présente d'une chose, est la chose même, tend aussi le plus possible à détruire ou à diminuer le plaisir qui doit résulter de l'imitation.[33]

In other words, Egyptian architecture does very well in the present-day terms of the "Uncanny Valley", but not according to the standards of late eighteenth-century artistic theory.[34]

Quatremère is already touching here on his later ideas on the confusion of the living model with its image, which for him were to become a symptom of primitive and fetishist attitudes towards art, published in his book on the polychrome statue of Jupiter in Olympia. In another text, *Sur l'idéal*, published in 1805, he further developed his view on Greek art. Whereas in Egypt statues represent abstract, general ideas rather than objects or living beings, in a semiotic system incapable of change Greek art tried to give a physical, corporeal presence to the living beings it represented:

En Grèce, le peuple se trouva porté à corporifier, ou si l'on veut à vivifier, le plus grand nombre de signes … dès que ses images cessent d'être, ou des signes ou des symboles, eurent abdiqué l'extrême simplicité des contours sans art, des lignes droites et raides, et leurs formes inimitatives, il leur faillit devenir les images des êtres … Dès lors, l'imitation corporelle doit prendre son essor.[35]

Semper may have been aware of Egyptian art either through reading Quatremère or by visiting the recently opened Egyptian Galleries in the Louvre, the Musée Charles X, whose programme of ceiling paintings was inspired by Quatremère's ideas.[36] One of them, Abel Pujol's painting of Egypt saved by Joseph, even takes the shape of a painted

_ Figure 3.
Abel Pujol, *Aegypt saved by Joseph*, ceiling painting, Louvre, 1827 (Wikimedia Commons).

169

Fig. 3

tapestry showing the scene, surrounded by a painted textile border: a triple case of the negation of material, in the trompe l'œil effect, the suggestion that the painting is in fact a textile, and the very convincing rendition of a textile border in paint.

In any case, polychromy was for Semper one of the clearest manifestations of the principle of dressing and masking at work in architecture. After he had returned from his travels to Italy and Greece in 1830–33, he argued in his first book, *Vorläufige Bemerkungen über bemalte Architectur und Plastik bei den Alten (Preliminary Remarks on Polychrome Architecture and Sculpture in Antiquity)*, that the walls and interior of Greek temples such as the Parthenon or the Temple of Theseus had been covered in washes of colour.[37] As he put it in a letter written from Athens to his brother: "The ancients not only painted the interior of their temples in the most elaborate way but they also richly covered [*bedeckt*] the exteriors. The noblest white marble was dressed [*bekleidet*] with bright colors; even the bas-reliefs were painted".[38]

To discover the system underlying the choice of colours, Semper reconstructed here – in the first of a long series of attempts – the origins of human society. The arts were born together when the first humans began to decorate their primitive abodes, because play and ornament are among the first urges of humanity. Religion was born at the same time: humans populated the earth with gods invented by themselves. Already among the Nubians, in Egypt and Etruria, painting and sculpture were combined to create painted reliefs. Next, people tried to suggest light and shadow through the illusions of colour and relief. Architecture united all these arts; it was covered in ornament from the time of its origins and shone with colour and bright materials. The preference for opulent ornament is therefore not a symptom of decadence but rather a need among primitive tribes, nourished by their fetishist religion – all according to Semper. Greek architecture was the culminating art of this period. In a reversal of conventional criticism of so-called primitive religion, Semper accused those who denied the existence of polychromy of having robbed ancient Greek architecture of its life.[39]

The ignorance of polychromy on the part of Winckelmann, or of Stuart and Revett, also robbed contemporary architecture of important means of expression. Colour was the essence of classical architecture but was rejected by Neoclassical theorists, who preferred the wax masks of ancient art and the white skeletons of temples deprived of their coloured skin. The sun and the hot climate made colour necessary to soften its effects and harmonize buildings with their brightly lit environment. But above all – and here he was following the *Lettres sur l'architecture* by Jean-Louis Viel de Saint-Maux (1787) – Semper argued that the structural parts of ancient temples only consisted of a very simple scaffolding, to which were attached flowers, sacrificed animals, festoons, or trophies. These elements subsequently came to be regarded as symbols and thus became part of temple fronts. The pearl moulding or the astragal was developed from the woollen bands tying sacrificial animals between the originally wooden columns of temples. What had started as an ephemeral textile element slowly developed from its painted representation into the mouldings that can be seen, for instance, in the Temple of Theseus in Athens.[40]

But whereas Viel de Saint-Maux regarded ancient temples as speaking poems in stone, representing the theological and cultural roots of their society, for Semper this kind of ornamentation became an almost theatrical exercise, since the monuments were the scaffolding constructed to stage ritual in a communal theatre. This is Semper's first attempt to connect the origins of theatre with those of architecture. They meet in the use of colour as a dressing, even a masking, of the material and structural reality of a building.

Tattooing

Behind polychromy lies another, much older practice that was even more repulsive to the advocates of pure, white, and colourless classical sculpture or architecture: that of tattooing the body. Karl August Böttiger, the archaeologist who defended polychromy, had already suggested in 1792 – probably influenced by Georg Forster's account of Thomas Cook's discovery of Pacific island societies – that there was a profound similarity in the earliest stages of ornament across the globe. In his essay *Cyklopen, Animaspen: Sitte der Alten, sich den Körper zu mahlen und zu punktiren*, he had suggested that the single eye of the Cyclops was in fact a tattoo of an eye.[41] In an argument that prefigures Aby Warburg's comparison of the rites of the Pueblo Indians of New Mexico with those of Periclean Athens or Medicean Florence, Böttiger suggested that this Sicilian monster was a half-brother of the Patagonians and that such practices of body ornamentation were widespread throughout the globe and typical of the earliest stages of human cultures. Semper was to construct a much more explicit anthropological connection in *Der Stil*, in the section on the development of the textile arts in New Zealand and Polynesia. In such early cultures, the tree

Fig. 4

trunks that hold up the textile hangings are decorated with painted heads, symbolized as he puts it by monstrous human heads, whose origin must be supposed to be the trophy heads of enemies killed in combat, sacrificed, or eaten. They are painted in gaudy colours, imitating the artful tattooing of the tribes:

> The fence itself consists of thick piles rammed into the ground, with branches woven between them. Yet at certain points along the fence, especially at the entrance gates, the piles are decorated with colorfully painted carvings; for that purpose, they are taller than their neighboring piles. Sculpture originated here from the carvings on the piles. The pile heads exploit the symbolism of grotesque human heads, no doubt based on the real heads of enemies killed or sacrificed and eaten. This is enhanced by a brilliant polychromy that imitates the ornaments the New Zealanders tattoo on their skin with much artistry. The polychromy is, in effect, nothing more than a tattooing of the gnarled bogey represented.[42]

The origins of ornament turn out to be slightly less benign, and more savage, than the peaceful activities of weaving and spinning. In his 1856 essay on the formal laws of adornment (*Schmuck*), he was to argue for the same origin of polychromy in canni-

_ Figure 4.
After Wilhelm Gottlieb Tilesius, *An Inhabitant of the Island of Nukahiva* [1804], plate from Karl von den Steinen, *Die Marquesaner und ihre Kunst: Studien über die Entwicklung primitiver Südseeornamentik nach eigenen Reiseergebnissen und dem Material der Museen*, 1925, vol. 1, *Tatauierungen*, p. 142 (Wikimedia Commons).

171

balism and tattooing for Greek sculpture, and in the late 1860s Semper posited this variety of body ornamentation, which combines dressing and masking with polychromy in such a suggestive way, as the origin of the Renaissance ornamental technique of *sgraffito*, which he himself was to apply in the north façade of the Eidgenössisches Polytechnikum (Swiss Federal Polytechnic, today the Eidgenössische Technische Hochschule/ETH) in Zurich.[43] One of the implications of these observations on the relations between cannibalism, tattooing, and polychromy is that they strengthen the argument Semper also presented elsewhere – for instance, in the long excursus on tapestry – against a unique and isolated development of Greek architecture. Contrary to received classical doctrine, he did not believe that Greek art or architecture originated in Greece or the Greek world but that it had evolved from earlier styles in the Middle East, among the Persians, Assyrians, and Chaldeans. This is yet another consequence of his anthropological approach to architectural history: it deprived Greek or Graeco-Roman architecture of its unique status and made it part of what we would now call the connectivity of the Middle East and Mediterranean world.[44]

172

"What was Hecuba to us?"

But how should we understand Semper's very definite reference to the monologue about Hecuba in *Hamlet*? Without going into all the potential meta-theatrical ramifications of the scene concerned, it may be helpful to recall that, in it, Hamlet invites a company of players to perform a play about rivalry and murder between brothers, in the hope of somehow triggering a chain of events that will lead to revenge for his father's murder, which he is too unresolved about to put into action himself. The players are asked to perform a monologue as well, and while one of them obliges by acting out Hecuba's plight, the other actors in the play – Hamlet and Polonius chief among them – take on the role of the chorus: they watch and comment on the actor's performance, thus serving both as intermediaries between the play and the audience and above all as a framing device, which through their comments places a distance between what is happening on the stage and the audience. In Goethe's *Wilhelm Meisters Lehrjahre*, the group of wandering actors rehearses *Hamlet* and raises the same issue as in the play itself – that of the transformation, if not negation, of the actor's personality and even appearance when he plays the role of Hecuba.

One of the possible inspirations for Semper's quotation in *Der Stil* is the preface to Schiller's play *Die Braut von Messina* (first presented on stage in Weimar in 1803), *Über den Gebrauch des Chors in der Tragödie*. In it, Schiller argues that the task of art should be to give the greatest possible happiness to the audience by setting their minds free of all their powers in the lively play. Thus, the mind is, however fleetingly, to be set free from the limitations and burdens of reality, and in the passing illusion art will awaken and exercise the human capacity to put reality at an objective distance; as Schiller puts it, to master matter by means of ideas. This already sounds quite similar to Semper's ideas on the denial of reality in the haze of carnival torches, but Schiller goes on to give an example of the way in which it is achieved in tragedy: by means of the living wall formed by the chorus, the function of which is to achieve this distancing of reality and thereby to preserve the freedom of the audience.[45] Thus the chorus, Schiller adds, acts like a beautiful, polychrome dress that enables the figures on the stage to act freely.[46] The result, Schiller adds, is that in "a higher organization", the material is no longer visible but is transformed into the incarnation of life.[47] We have come very close here to Semper's negation of matter, which, as I have argued elsewhere, can also be understood as resulting in the animation of stone, suggesting life and movement.[48] In other words, Schiller is here presenting a view of the nature and origins of theatre that unites the same elements that Semper was to use fifty years later when discussing the origins of architecture in festive ephemeral architecture – the negation of materials and reality; the innate human urge to perform, play, and mask; and polychromy as one of the main artistic means of creating this illusion of freedom.

Conclusion: a radically new concept of architecture

Semper thus unfolds a view of the nature of architecture, its origins, the laws that govern its development, and its aesthetics that is completely new. In a radical break with the Vitruvian tradition that had dominated Western architectural discourse until the 1800s, he defines the essence of architecture not as construction or structure but as the creation of space. Whereas Vitruvius had presented the column and architrave, a tectonic unity, as the starting point from which the entire edifice of architectural practice and its theory follows, Semper puts the hanging, the tapestry, or the tent cover – that is, *textile* artefacts that create and demarcate space – as its origin and essence. At the same time, the origins of architecture are no longer placed in a hypothetical primitive society that comes into being once nomadic tribes came together, learned to work together, and constructed the primitive hut – that is, in social building activity inspired or forced by the necessity of natural circumstances. Instead, Semper transforms this hypothetical primitivist aetiology into an anthropological theory that identifies the innate human urge to act and to mask reality, and thus to create art (the urge that was termed *Kunsttrieb* by Gustav Klemm), as the origin of architecture and of all other forms of art. In other words, the origins of building lie in the craft of weaving, materially speaking; whereas anthropologically speaking, the origins of the transformation of building into art are to be found in the human instinct to play and to represent.[49]

As a consequence, building no longer becomes a fine art through the correct handling of the formal vocabulary of classical architecture, an understanding of its rules such as those governing proportion, or the fulfilment of the three Vitruvian requirements of utility, solidity, and beauty, based on a sound knowledge of the best Graeco-Roman or Renaissance models. The artistic and aesthetic status of architecture is no longer derived from the way in which it fits into the classical tradition, the last spokesman for which was the Académie Royale d'Architecture. Instead, for Semper the artistic and aesthetic nature of architecture is based on *representation*. Architecture has a place among the fine arts because buildings can become meaningful symbols. But representation – which already had a quite codified meaning in Idealist and Neoclassical aesthetics – in its turn also acquires a new meaning in Semper's thought. It no longer consists of the use of religious or political iconography, which he considers to be extraneous to architecture. Instead, Semper

173

combines two elements that had not previously been brought together in artistic theory: an anthropological view of the origins of art as a commemoration (originally in ephemeral and subsequently in permanent form) of events, rites, and actions that establish and sustain cultures is combined with a transference of the Idealist and Neoclassical conception (for which Schiller and Quatremère were important sources) of representation as the sign of the aesthetic *distancing* at work in art. In *Der Stil*, this aesthetic distancing is not manifested in imitation or depiction, using different media for instance to signal that distance, but in a *negation of reality*, to remove all that is conventional or socially, politically, or religiously contingent, in order to reveal what Semper calls "purely human beauty"[50] – as in his example of Phidias's statues of Greek divinities for the Parthenon.

[This is a revised and expanded version of an article that appeared earlier as *Le cannibalisme, le tatouage, et le revêtement: de l'histoire de l'architecture à l'anthropologie de l'art*, "Gradhiva: Revue d'anthropologie et des arts", special issue: *Gottfried Semper – habiter les couleurs*, vol. 25, Summer 2017, pp. 24–49].

174

_1. G. Semper, *Der Stil in den technischen und tektonischen Künsten, oder Praktische Aesthetik: Ein Handbuch für Techniker, Künstler und Kunstfreunde*, vol. 1, Verlag für Kunst und Wissenschaft, Frankfurt am Main 1860, § 60, pp. 227–32. On primitivism in eighteenth-century and nineteenth-century architectural thought, see J. Rykwert, *On Adam's House in Paradise: The Idea of the Primitive Hut in Architectural History*, Museum of Modern Art, New York 1972 and S.D. de Jong, *Rediscovering Architecture: Paestum in Eighteenth-Century Architectural Experience and Theory*, Yale University Press, New Haven 2015, Chapter 5.

_2. G. Semper, *Der Stil*, vol. 1, see note 1, § 60, note 2, p. 231; G. Semper, *Style in the Technical and Tectonic Arts; or, Practical Aesthetics*, introduction by H.F. Mallgrave, trans. H.F. Mallgrave and M. Robinson, Getty Institute, Los Angeles 2004, p. 439. The major recent studies on Semper are: H.F. Mallgrave, *Gottfried Semper: Architect of the Nineteenth Century*, Yale University Press, New Haven 1996; M. Hvattum, *Gottfried Semper and the Problem of Historicism,* Cambridge University Press, Cambridge, MA 2004. W. Nerdinger and W. Oechslin (eds.), *Gottfried Semper 1803–1879: Architektur und Wissenschaft*, Prestel and gta Verlag, Munich and Zurich 2003, gives a good overview of research around 2000 and contains a complete catalogue of Semper's works.

_3. G. Semper, *Der Stil*, vol. 1, see note 1, § 60, note 2, p. 232; G. Semper, *Style*, see note 2, p. 439. Semper used the wrong tense in his quotation, cf. the original text in note 15.

_4. However, see H.F. Mallgrave, *Gustav Klemm and Gottfried Semper: The Meeting of Ethnological and Architectural Theory,* "Res: Journal of Anthropology and Aesthetics", 9, 1985, pp. 69–79; S. Hildebrand, *"Nach einem Systeme zu ordnen, welches die inneren Verbindungsfäden dieser bunten Welt am besten zusammenhält": Kulturgeschichtliche Modelle bei Gottfried Semper und Gustav Klemm*, in H. Karge (ed.), *Gottfried Semper – Dresden und Europa: Die moderne Renaissance der Künste*, Deutscher Kunstverlag, Munich 2007, pp. 237–50.

_5. G. Semper, *Style*, see note 2, p. 247; G. Semper, *Der Stil*, vol. 1, see note 1, § 60, p. 227.

_6. G. Semper, *Der Stil*, vol. 1, see note 1, § 60, p. 228; G. Semper, *Style*, see note 2, p. 248.

_7. See G. Semper, *The Ancient Practice of Wall Coating and Tubular Construction*, draft of a lecture given in London on 18 November 1853, edited in G. Semper, *London Writings 1850–1855*, edited by M. Gnehm, S. Hildebrand, and D. Weidmann, gta Verlag, Zurich 2021, German translation: *Die Entwicklung der Wand- und Mauerkonstruktion bei den antiken Völkern*, in G. Semper, *Kleine Schriften*, edited by M. and H. Semper, Spemann, Berlin 1884, pp. 383–93; G. Semper, *On Architectural Symbols*, draft of a lecture given in London on 22 November 1854, edited in G. Semper, *London Writings*, German translation: *Über architektonische Symbole*, in G. Semper, *Kleine Schriften*, pp. 292–303; G. Semper, *Der Stil in den technischen und tektonischen Künsten, oder Praktische Aesthetik: Ein Handbuch für Techniker, Künstler und Kunstfreunde*, vol. 2, Bruckmann, Munich 1863, § 143, p. 276.

_8. G. Semper, *Der Stil*, vol. 1, see note 1, § 60, pp. 227–29. Cf. A. Forty, *Words and Buildings: A Vocabulary of Modern Architecture*, Thames and Hudson, London 2000, Chapter "Nature", on Semper pp. 231–33.

_9. G. Semper, *Style*, see note 2, p. 249; G. Semper, *Der Stil*, vol. 1, see note 1, § 60, p. 230.

_10. G. Semper, *Style*, see note 2, p. 249.

_11. See G. Semper, *Der Stil*, vol. 1, see note 1, § 66, p. 291: "Die Plätze und Monumente waren alte geheiligte Würdenträger des Volks, die es galt, nicht zu verhüllen und unkenntlich zu machen, sondern der Gelegenheit entsprechend in überraschend festlicher und neuer Weise hervorzuheben, sie gleichsam durch den ihnen geliehenen Schmuck eine improvisierte, die Veranlassung des Festes betreffende Allokution an das Volk halten zu lassen. Daher blieb die möglichste Sorge für die Erhaltung der Individualität der alten welthistorischen Monumente für die dekorirenden Aedilen und die unter ihm wirkenden Architekten und Dekorateurs erste Pflicht und Regel. Durch den Ornatus und die ihm eingefügten Argumente wurden sie nur festlich beseelt, wurde ihnen das Organ, sich als alte Bekannte vernehmlich mit dem Volke über die Zeitumstände zu unterhalten, geliehen". G. Semper, *Style*, see note 2, p. 285: "Squares and monuments were ancient and sacred bearers of a people's dignity. As such they were not to be veiled or made unrecognizable but were to be enhanced in a surprisingly festive and new way appropriate to the occasion. Through this added decoration, as it were, they could address the people in an improvised manner about the event that occasioned the festivity. To preserve as much as possible the individuality of old world-historical monuments was therefore the first rule and task of the aediles in charge of decoration, as it was for the architects and decorators working under them. Only through their *ornatus* [ornamentum] and the themes applied to them did these monuments become festively animated, were they endowed with an organ to converse – as with an old acquaintance – with the people about their times".

_12. G. Semper, *Der Stil*, vol. 1, see note 1, § 60, p. 231; G. Semper, *Style*, see note 2, p. 250.

_13. C. Bötticher, *Der Baumkultus der Hellenen nach den gottesdienstlichen Gebräuchen und den überlieferten Bildwerken dargestellt*, Weidmann, Berlin 1856, pp. 16–24, 44, 56.

_14. G. Semper, *Der Stil*, vol. 1, see note 1, § 60, pp. 231–32; G. Semper, *Style*, see note 2, pp. 438–39.

_15. In S. Greenblatt, W. Cohen, J.E. Howard,

175

and K.E. Maus (eds.), *The Norton Shakespeare, Based on the Oxford Edition*, Norton, New York 1997: *The Tragedy of Hamlet, Prince of Denmark*, 2.2, lines 530–37, p. 1703: [the actor] "Could force his soul so to his own conceit / That from her working all his visage wanned, / Tears in his eyes, distraction in's aspect, / A broken voice, and his whole function suiting / With forms to his conceit? And all for nothing. / For Hecuba! / What's Hecuba to him, or he to Hecuba, / That he should weep for her?"

_16. G. Semper, *Der Stil*, vol. 1, see note 1, § 61, p. 233.

_17. G. Semper, *Style*, see note 2, p. 303; G. Semper, *Der Stil*, vol. 1, see note 1, § 66, p. 322.

_18. G. Semper, *Style*, see note 2, p. 264; G. Semper, *Der Stil*, vol. 1, see note 1, § 63, p. 256: "Würden wir phantasmagorisch nach Pompeji zurückversetzt, wie es war vor 1800 Jahren, manches würde uns dort chinesisch vorkommen".

_19. G. Semper, *Style*, see note 2, p. 379; G. Semper, *Der Stil*, vol. 1, see note 1, § 76, p. 444.

_20. G. Semper, *Der Stil*, vol. 1, see note 1, § 60, p. 232: "Wie auch die griechische Baukunst das Gesagte rechtfertige, wie in ihr das Prinzip vorwalte, das ich anzudeuten versuchte, wonach das Kunstwerk in der Anschauung die Mittel und den Stoff vergessen macht, womit und wodurch es erscheint und wirkt, und sich selbst als Form genügt, dieses nachzuweisen ist die schwierigste Aufgabe der Stillehre". G. Semper, *Style*, see note 2, p. 439: "How Greek architecture too supports what has been said, how it was dominated by the principle that I have sought to convey, according to which the appearance of a work of art should make us forget the means and the materials by which and through which it appears and works and be sufficient to itself as form – to demonstrate this is the most difficult task of a theory of style".

_21. G. Semper, *Style*, see note 2, p. 343; G. Semper, *Der Stil*, vol. 1, see note 1, § 68, p. 386: "Die hellenische Kunst dagegen ... fasst die ornamentalen Symbole vorzugsweise in struktiv-funktionellem Sinne, mit möglichst gemildeter und leisester Anspielung auf tendenziöse Bedeutung, die ihnen noch bleibt; der höheren Kunst weist sie ihre neutralen Felder an, wo sie, von der Struktur und dem nächsten materiellen Dienste des Systemes unabhängig, sich frei entfaltet".

_22. G. Semper, *Der Stil*, vol. 1, see note 1, § 66; G. Semper, *Style*, see note 2, § 68.

_23. G. Semper, *Style*, see note 2, p. 343; G. Semper, *Der Stil*, vol. 1, see note 1, § 68, p. 386–87: "Wie das Pflanzenornament die Struktur zu einem Organismus umschafft, so erhebt das animalische Ornament den todten Hausrath gleichsam zu einem freiwillig oder unwillig dienenden Hausthiere! Das Möbel wird dadurch, dass ich ihm Füsse in Gestalt von Löwentatzen oder Rehläufen gebe, als ein Gegenstand bezeichnet, der nach meinem Wille sich fortbewegt oder doch bewegbar ist. Den Grad der Bewegbarkeit, den ich ihm bei-

legen will, symbolisch zu nuanciren, habe ich in meiner Hand! Die Fähigkeit des Stützens und das Aufrechte eines Ständers erhält einen lebendigen Ausdruck dadurch, dass ich ihm diejenigen Formen leihe, die in der animalischen Welt aehnliches verrichten".

_24. G. Semper, *Der Stil*, vol. 1, see note 1, § 59, p. 221, note 1. On Quatremère de Quincy, see D. Knipping, *Le Jupiter Olympien and the Rediscovery of Polychromy in Antique Sculpture: Quatremère de Quincy between Empirical Research and Aesthetic Ideals*, "Monuments and Sites", 3, 2001, pp. 89–97; S. Lavin, *Quatremère de Quincy and the Invention of a Modern Language of Architecture*, MIT Press, Cambridge, MA 1992; R. Schneider, *L'esthétique classique chez Quatremère de Quincy (1805–1823)*, Hachette, Paris 1910.

_25. On Semper's views on polychromy, see most recently S. Pisani, *"Die Monumente sind durch Barbarei monochrom geworden": Zu den theoretischen Leitmaximen in Sempers "Vorläufige Bemerkungen über bemalte Architectur und Plastik bei den Alten"*, in W. Nerdinger and W. Oechslin (eds.), *Gottfried Semper 1803–1879*, see note 2, pp. 109–16. On the polychromy debate in nineteenth-century sculpture and Semper's role in it, see A. Blühm (ed.), *The Colour of Sculpture, 1840–1910*, Waanders, Zwolle 1996, esp. 18–19.

_26. See for instance G. Semper, *Der Stil*, vol. 1, see note 1, § 61, p. 234.

_27. G. Semper, *Der Stil*, vol. 1, see note 1, § 60, p. 229; G. Semper, *Style*, see note 2, p. 248.

_28. A.-C. Quatremère de Quincy, *Le Jupiter olympien, ou l'art de la sculpture antique considéré sous un nouveau point de vue; Ouvrage qui comprend un essai sur le goût de la sculpture polychrome ...*, Didot, Paris 1815, p. 68. See also C.A. van Eck, *Art, Agency and Living Presence: From the Animated Image to the Excessive Object*, De Gruyter and Leiden University Press, Munich and Leiden 2015, pp. 141–44.

_29. A.-C. Quatremère de Quincy, *Le Jupiter olympien*, see note 28, p. xxiii.

_30. "Quel fut l'état de l'architecture égyptienne et ce que les grecs paroissent avoir emprunté", submitted to a competition organized in 1785 by the Académie des Inscriptions et Belles Lettres. Quatremère de Quincy recycled large parts of this text in his entry on Egypt in the *Dictionnaire d'architecture* (1788), but he also republished the text, with minor changes but a different title, in 1803 under the title: *De l'architecture égyptienne, considérée dans son origine, ses principes et son goût, et comparée sous les mêmes rapports à l'Architecture Grecque: Dissertation qui a remporté, en 1785, le Prix proposé par l'Académie des Inscriptions et Belles-Lettres*, Barrois l'aîné et Fils, Paris 1803, see S. Lavin, *Quatremère de Quincy*, see note 24, pp. 160–70.

_31. A.-C. Quatremère de Quincy, *De l'architecture égyptienne*, see note 30, pp. 51, 59.

_32. *Ibid*, p. 207.

176

_33. *Ibid.*, p. 206.

_34. The principle of the 'Uncanny Valley' was first identified by Masahiro Mori. See N. Kageki, *An Uncanny Mind: Masahiro Mori on the Uncanny Valley*, Spectrum.ieee.org, posted on 12 June 2012.

_35. A.-C. Quatremère de Quincy, *Sur l'idéal*, n.p., n.d. [Paris 1805], p. 118.

_36. See, for instance, his *Essai sur la nature, le but et les moyens de l'imitation dans les beaux-arts*, Didot, Paris 1823, pp. 3, 11: "*Imiter dans les beaux-arts, c'est produire la ressemblance d'une chose, mais dans une autre chose qui en devient l'image … Il est au contraire de l'essence de l'imitation des beaux-arts, de ne faire voir la réalité que par l'apparence*".

_37. G. Semper, *Vorläufige Bemerkungen über bemalte Architectur und Plastik bei den Alten*, Johann Friedrich Hammerich, Altona 1834.

_38. Gottfried Semper, letter to his brother, 11 April 1832, quoted in H.F. Mallgrave, *Gottfried Semper*, see note 2, p. 45.

_39. G. Semper, *Vorläufige Bemerkungen*, see note 37, p. 10.

_40. *Ibid.*, pp. 29–30.

_41. First published in "Der Teutsche Merkur", 6, 1792, pp. 139–64. See R. Leucht, *Griechische Wilde: Vergleiche zwischen Antike und Neuer Welt, 1752–1821 (Lafitau, Böttiger, Winckelmann, Bougainville, Forster, Chamisso)*, "Euphorion", 109, no. 4, 2015, pp. 375–401.

_42. G. Semper, *Style*, see note 2, p. 254; G. Semper, *Der Stil*, vol. 1, see note 1, § 62, pp. 239–40: "Der Zaun selbst besteht aus starken eingerammten Pfählen zwischen denen Zweige eingeflochten sind, die Pfähle aber sind an gewissen Stellen der Zaunwand, besonders an den Eingangsthoren, mit buntgemalten Schnitzwerken verziert und zu diesem Zwecke überragen sie die Reihe der Nachbarpfähle. Die Skulptur ist hier aus dem Pfahlschnitzwerke hervorgegangen. Die Pfahlköpfe sind durch fratzenhafte Menschenköpfe symbolisirt deren Typus wohl ohne Zweifel die wirklichen Köpfe erlegter oder geopferter und gefressener Feinde waren. Dazu tritt eine bunte Polychromie, eine Nachahmung der Ornamente die sich die Neuseeländer mit vieler Kunst auf die Haut tättowiren, in der That nichts weiter als die Tättowirung der dargestellten knorrigen Popanze". See also G. Semper, *Der Stil*, vol. 1, pp. 217–31.

_43. See G. Semper, *Über die formelle Gesetzmässigkeit des Schmuckes und dessen Bedeutung als Kunstsymbol* (1856), reprinted in G. Semper, *Gesammelte Schriften*, edited by H. Karge, Olms-Weidmann, Hildesheim 2014, vol. 1.2, pp. 591–622 (here pp. 591–96); G. Semper, *Die Sgraffito-Dekoration* (1868), reprinted in the same volume, pp. 793–96. On the background to Semper's ideas on tattooing, see H.-G. von Arburg, *Archäodermatologie der Moderne. Zur Theoriegeschichte der Tätowierung in der Architektur*

und Literatur zwischen 1830 und 1930, "Deutsche Vierteljahresschrift für Literatur und Geisteswissenschaft", 77, 2003, pp. 407–45 (esp. pp. 417–20, with many references to earlier studies).

_44. G. Semper, *Der Stil*, vol. 1, see note 1, § 66, pp. 276–322.

_45. F. Schiller, *Über den Gebrauch des Chors in der Tragödie*, in F. Schiller, *Sämtliche Werke*, 3rd ed., Hanser, Munich 1962, vol. 2, p. 818: "Die Einführung des Chors wäre der letzte, der entscheidende Schritt – und wenn derselbe auch nur dazu diente, dem Naturalismus in der Kunst offen und ehrlich den Krieg zu erklären, so sollte er uns eine lebendige Mauer sein, die die Tragödie um sich herumzieht, um sich von der wirklichen Welt rein abzuschliessen und sich ihren idealen Boden ihre poetische Freiheit zu bewahren".

_46. *Ibid.*, p. 819: "Aber ebenso, wie der bildende Künstler die faltige Fülle der Gewänder um seine Figuren breitet, um die Räume seines Bildes reich und anmutig auszufüllen, um die getrennten Partien desselben in ruhigen Massen stetig zu verbinden, um der Farbe, die das Auge reizt und erquickt, einen Spielraum zu geben, um die menschlichen Formen zugleich geistreich zu verhüllen und sichtbar zu machen, ebenso durchflicht und umgibt der tragische Dichter seine streng abgemessene Handlung und die festen Umrisse seiner handelnden Figuren mit einem lyrischen Prachtgewebe, in welchem sich, als wie in einem weit gefalteten Purpurgewand, die handelnden Personen frei und edel mit einer gehaltenen Würde und hoher Ruhe bewegen".

_47. *Ibid.*, p. 820: "In einer höhern Organisation darf der Stoff oder das Elementarische nicht mehr sichtbar sein, die chemische Farbe verschwindet in der feinen Carnation des Lebendigen".

_48. C.A. van Eck, *Figuration, Tectonics and Animism in Semper's* Der Stil, "Journal of Architecture", 14, no. 3, 2010, pp. 153–70.

_49. See, for instance, G. Klemm, *Allgemeine Culturwissenschaft: Die materiellen Grundlagen menschlicher Cultur*, vol. 1: *Einleitung: Das Feuer, die Nahrung, Getränke, Narkotika*, Romberg, Leipzig 1855, p. 55: "Die Darstellung der Erfahrung führt den Menschen zur Kunst. … Die Darstellung von Ereignissen mit Hilfe von Musik und Tanz rief schon bei den Jägerstämmen Amerikas das Drama ins Leben". In his *Allgemeine Cultur-Geschichte der Menschheit*, Teubner, Leipzig 1843–51, vol. 1, p. 214, Klemm uses the term "Darstellungstrieb". Cf. M. Hvattum, *Gottfried Semper*, see note 2, p. 43. The idea of a theatrical essence of human nature and society was widespread in the 1860s; Charles Garnier, for instance, observed in the introduction of his book on the theatre that "all that happens in the world is, in essence, only theatre and representation". Cf. H.F. Mallgrave, *Gottfried Semper*, see note 2, p. 345.

_50. G. Semper, *Style*, see note 2, p. 439; G. Semper, *Der Stil*, vol. 1, see note 1, § 60, note 2, p. 232.

177

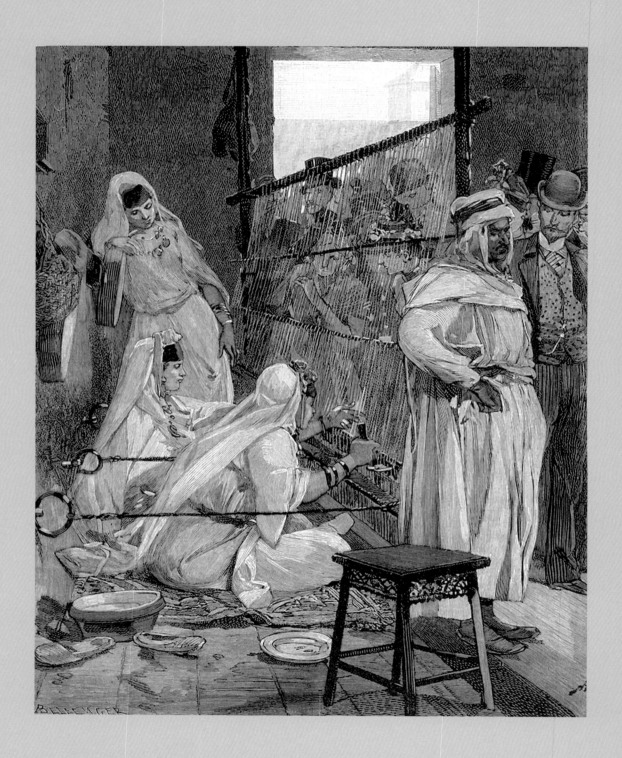

Beat Wyss

Origins of Architecture and the Textile Paradigm

_ Figure 1.
*Les tisseuses Kabyles
à l'Esplanade des
Invalides*, illustration
from "L'Exposition de
Paris de 1889", 1,
no. 17, 22 June 1889
(Wyss, *Bilder von der
Globalisierung*, 2010,
p. 83).

Fig. 2

In 1875, Eugène Emmanuel Viollet-le-Duc published a novel on the world history of architecture. The amazingly coloured frontispiece mirrors the aesthetic of *katazome*, the Japanese screen-printing textiles fabricated out of paper starched by natural resin. The technique of reproduction became better known as silk-screening, used for advertising art. It entered the Western market during the Paris World Fair in 1878, three years after Viollet-le-Duc's publication, when *japonisme* dominated Parisian taste for a decade. A manifold pasticcio of textile-like samples of tapestry from all over the world is laid out here: kilim patterns from the Middle East; grotesque amphibians in Mayan style; Egyptian papyrus blossoms; acanthus, meander, volute ornaments from Persia and Greece; noblemen dressed in an oriental manner; a fruit tree in a medieval floral style.

Viollet-le-Duc's frontispiece matches three of Gottfried Semper's issues: polychromy, textiles, and global handcraft. Was *L'histoire de l'habitation humaine* influenced by Semper's *Der Stil*, whose first volume on *Textile Kunst* (textile art) appeared in its second edition in the same year as the already mentioned Paris World's Fair (the second volume was re-edited in 1879)? One should not overrate the mechanism of 'influence' within the history of ideas. The manifest stylistic profile of the two architects was somehow idiosyncratic: Semper, the *classiciste*, versus Viollet-le-Duc, the *gothiciste.* They might have contradicted on a programmatic level, but they both share unavoidably one denominator: contemporariness. During the same time period they both worked on their encyclopaedic *opera magna*: the ten-years-elder Semper on *Der Stil in den technischen und tektonischen Künsten, oder Praktische Ästhetik*, his French colleague on his ten volumes of *Dictionnaire raisonné de l'architecture française du XIe au XVIe siècles.* While both were still working on their comprehensive volumes, a relatively slim book advanced to the status of an epistemic leitmotiv of the century: Charles Darwin's *On the Origin of Species by Means of Natural Selection* (1859). Epistemically and methodologically, the two architects worked out an 'evolution' of architecture like the English natural scientist. A transdisciplinary key word of the time was 'origin', Semper and Viollet-le-Duc as architects both traced

the origin of human building. Both of their approaches had an anthropological perspective that means in our terms: universal, global.

Viollet-le-Duc outlines his encompassing effort with a novel retelling the history of human habitation. The narrative is developed Platonically by a dialogue between two figures, Épergos and Doxi, two superhuman beings, *Übermenschen*: able to stroll through time and space, they both explore the transhistorical and transgeographic space of architectural history. The author depicts their flight by a couple of birds of prey in one of the vignettes with which each chapter of the book concludes. The travellers are interacting with the personnel they discover on their way, dialoguing, acting as omniscient consultants on questions of architecture and the true way of living.

_ Figure 2.
Frontispiece of Eugène Emmanuel Viollet-le-Duc, *Histoire de l'habitation humaine depuis les temps préhistoriques jusqu'à nos jours*, 1875 (Courtesy of Biblioteca dell'Accademia di architettura, USI).

Fig. 3

Fig. 4

Their starting point is the unsheltered savage whom Épergos teaches to construct the primordial tent, fabricated with branches of trees. The helpful supermen are doubtful whether these dull creatures have deserved their aid:

> Pourquoi modifier ainsi l'œuvre du créateur? – Qui sait! reprend Épergos; revenons ici dans cent mille jours et nous verrons si ces êtres ont oublié mes instructions pour vivre comme ils vivaient hier. S'il est ainsi, j'ai tort de me mêler de leurs affaires, et je n'ai pas trouvé; mais s'ils ont profité de mes avis, si les huttes que nous verrons alors sont mieux faites que celles-ci, j'ai trouvé, car alors ces êtres ne sont pas des animaux.[1]

Viollet-le-Duc, the omniscient narrator and draughtsman, does not hide his doubt whether the dark-skinned savage of apish physiognomy has learned his lesson in the spirit of *architectura perennis*, whose rules are canonically valid worldwide troughout human history, from the colonial missionaries.

_ Figure 3.
Birds of prey, vignette from Viollet-le-Duc, *Histoire de l'habitation humaine*, 1875 (Courtesy of Biblioteca dell'Accademia di architettura, USI).

_ Figure 4.
The primordial tent,
illustration from Viollet-le-
Duc, *Histoire de l'habitation
humaine*, 1875 (Courtesy of
Biblioteca dell'Accademia di
architettura, USI).

_ Figure 5.
The Aryan's stone building,
illustration from Viollet-le-
Duc, *Histoire de l'habitation
humaine*, 1875 (Courtesy of
Biblioteca dell'Accademia di
architettura, USI).

Next stop is the house of the Aryan, who shows his diligence in learning to reconstruct his dwelling, whose wooden fabric had been destroyed by a thunderstorm. Épergos teaches the Aryans how to work with solid stone and how to bake bricks. Contrary to the Neanderthal-like savage (title: *Sont-ce des hommes?*),[2] the Aryans show intelligence and readiness in learning. When the Aryan woman breaks out in tears for the loss of their habitat, her husband and master admonishes her:

Fig. 5

> Point de larmes inutiles, dit l'Arya. Mettons-nous à l'œuvre avant que le soleil ait disparu derrière la montagne. Viens avec nous, mère, et dis à cet étranger ce que tu désires de plus que ce que nous possédions, puisqu'il montre la volonté de nous aider.[3]

And the wife, obeying her husband, asks the teacher for a children's corner, a salon, and a master bedroom – proving the desires of an Aryan woman to be in tune with the modern nuclear family.

The Aryan stone dwelling represents the prototype of architecture as descending from the natural form of a cave. The stone building is quasi-birthed by a rock slope. The rustically inclined jambs foreshadow the Doric portal, so Aryan architecture gives already evidence of *Greekness* in its pedigreed genes. The handsome physiognomy of the white-skinned Aryan matches an architectural future already in the hands and minds of the European genius.

The third stop of the two supermen is the housing of the yellow man. Épergos appreciates its elaborated construction in bamboo and the vessels made of porcelain. But he admonishes the fat landlord for his laziness and lack of curiosity. "Nous avons admiré ton habitation et tes jardins; mais quand on possède une demeure pareille, on est peu disposé à la quitter. Ne vas-tu jamais dehors?"[4] He should take care of his physical health by moving more and eating less. But the yellow man is unteachable; he brushes off the unbidden guests harshly.

_Figure 6.
Aryan physiognomy, vignette from Viollet-le-Duc, *Histoire de l'habitation humaine*, 1875 (Courtesy of Biblioteca dell'Accademia di architettura, USI).

_Figure 7.
Chinese physiognomy, vignette from Viollet-le-Duc, *Histoire de l'habitation humaine*, 1875 (Courtesy of Biblioteca dell'Accademia di architettura, USI).

_Figure 8.
Porche de la maison chinoise primitive, illustration from Viollet-le-Duc, *Histoire de l'habitation humaine*, 1875 (Courtesy of Biblioteca dell'Accademia di architettura, USI).

Eh bien, dit Doxi quand son compagnon et lui furent dehors, tu as perdu ici ta peine, et, toi parti, les choses demeureront en l'état où nous les avons trouvées. Je n'ai pas perdu mon temps, lui répondit Épergos. J'ai laissé ici des paroles de vérité. Si le gros Faun n'en tire pas profit pour lui-même, qui te dit que sa femme, ses enfants, ses serviteurs, les oublieront.[5]

Fig. 7

The Chinese physiognomy is depicted as inscrutable and ignorant, with bulging lips greedy for food. From the eyes of the yellow race, you will never get a frank, straight-forward gaze. Racial prejudice of this type was considered common sense, stemming from the time of the Opium Wars. It denigrated a culture as apathetic, inertial, and isolationist just because imperial China resisted colonization, rejecting the benefits of Euro-American standards.

I bring up this aspect of postcolonial critique as a way to address the globalization of knowledge in the nineteenth century. This first wave of exporting Western standards on a global scale is flanked by the new discipline of anthropology, whose primary concern was the scientific justification of racial hierarchies. The non-European subject appears in the Western commercial universe as the colonized Other, performed at world's fairs as the colourful exotic whose political appropriation was in tune with the authority to dispose of merchandise in the mode of global circulation. I do stress this connection

Fig. 9

between race and globalization: first, because average nineteenth-century architectural theory mirrors the contemporary colonialist mentality; second, because Semper's approach was remarkably different, even if he, herein following Quatremère de Quincy, believed Chinese architecture to have no evolutionary potential.[6]

183

Before expanding upon this issue, let us first step back to the epochal meaning of 'origin', starting with the origin of architectural theory. The invention of architecture as a transcultural phenomenon has been a commonplace since Vitruvius. The Roman writer links the origin of human building to the invention of linguistic communication and the formation of social communities.[7] The textile paradigm, even, cannot be

_ Figure 9.
Le grand tonneau d'Épernay et quelques types exotiques, illustration from *L'Exposition de Paris de 1889*, no. 17, 22 June 1889: a page advertising champagne from Épernay, adorned with pictures of foreign legionnaires from the French colonies (Wyss, *Bilder von der Globalisierung*, 2010, p. 180).

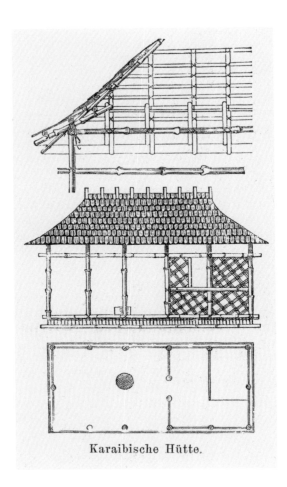

Karaibische Hütte.

ascribed as Semper's original finding. It would not have been necessary to travel geographically as far away for identifying the *Urphänomen* (primordial phenomenon) of architecture in the Caribbean hut. In order to find traces of building as a 'dress',[8] Semper simply could have had consulted the library and opened the second book on architecture by Vitruvius, as he did, of course, calling the Caribbean hut "a highly realistic specimen of a wooden structure borrowed from ethnology that corresponds to the Vitruvian primitive hut in all its elements".[9] For Vitruvius, the first manner of building was completed "with upright forked props and twigs put between, they wove their walls". Such primary building practice, Vitruvius mentions, was still observable among contemporary south-western nations, in Gaul, Spain, Lusitania, and Aquitaine. The woven hut follows the primary building model of the tent.

The Far Eastern nations of Colchi, settling between the Caucasus and Black Sea, profited from an abundance of forests by inventing the second primary model: the wooden hut by post construction. The Phrygians in the plains of Asia Minor, today's Turkey, where the raw material wood was lacking, perfected the shelter in rocky mounds and caves, covered with straw, reeds, and branches, the third primary model of architecture. By naming these three destinations and primary building types, Vitruvius

Fig. 10

Fig. 11

_ Figure 10.
Gottfried Semper, Caribbean hut, illustration from *Der Stil*, vol. 2, 1863 (Private ownership).

_ Figure 11.
The origin of architecture in Vitruvius, *On Architecture*, II.1: "Ex prima mundi hominum aetate aedificatio", illustration from the edition by Cesare Cesariano, 1521 (Marcu Vitruvius Pollio, *Baukunst*, transl. by A. Rode, edited by B. Wyss, 1987).

184

extended his Roman view up to the western and eastern fringes of the world known and partly colonized during the Augustinian era.

The origin of architecture is used here to inscribe the borderlines of civilization. We find this theoretical pattern, so dear to the modern notion of historical progress, already in the narratives of antique reports. But there is a significant difference between the Roman colonizers and nineteenth-century colonialism. Vitruvius mentions primary buildings found even in the contemporary centres of cultural and political powers, like the Areopagus in Athens, where there was an ancient building "to this day covered with mud", and the Casa Romuli at the foot of Palatino in Rome, "covered by straw".[10]

185

Absolutely modern in architectural theory, instead, is straightforward racial stratification. The view back to the origins gets exploited: nineteenth-century history of building types constructs a pedigree of architecture, consisting, on one hand, of a pure-blooded parentage, and, on the other hand, the inferior branches of architectural development – or better: degeneration. My quoted sample was the hut of the yellow man who sticks stubbornly with the wooden hut, unable to adopt the Vitruvian standard of stone building. Architectural history, inspired by anthropological models, outlines a process of evolution ending in a distinction and segregation between racial winners and losers.

Fig. 12 There was once a built version of global architecture, performed by Charles Garnier at the foot of the Eiffel Tower.[11] For the fourth Paris World's Fair in 1889, the architect of the Opéra's recent location designed forty-four model habitats from all parts of the world, inspired by the motto: "Dis-moi quelle maison tu habites, comment tu t'es logé et comment tu as organisé ta vie intime, je dirai quelles sont tes mœurs, quel est ton développement intellectuel, quel rang tu occupes dans la société humaine".[12] To the connoisseur of architecture, the entire genetic code of humankind was decipherable in the styles of building. A xylograph, showing us the difference between the humble troglodyte shelter in the foreground and the Eiffel Tower rising majestically towards the clouds, tells us more than every learned anthropological argument about the superiority of Western progress.

Fig. 13 That the primitive huts proved to be the most cherished place for open-air picnics nevertheless illustrates the dialectics of industrial civilization. The urban Parisians loved to gather between the Germanic pole construction and the circular straw huts of the Gauls. Was it revenge in the spirit of the nationalist Boulangist party? The loss of Alsace-Lorraine after the Franco-Prussian War in 1871 was symbolically recompensed

here: By a hearty *déjeuner sur l'herbe* one could indulge in an illusion of greatness, having recaptured, again, the terrain between Rhine and Vosges from the Teutons.

By the title of the architectural exhibition, *Histoire de l'habitation humaine*, Garnier refers bluntly to Viollet-le-Duc's novel without acknowledging the source of inspiration. The reason for the evident omission was conceitedness. The four-teen-years-younger Garnier had once worked as a draughtsman in Viollet-le-Duc's office – for seventy-five centimes per hour. Later they became rivals in the competition for the Opéra project, obtained finally by Garnier.[13]

Fig. 14

In one crucial point, Garnier did not follow the narrative of Viollet-le-Duc: there is no Aryan habitat in the succession of architectural heritage as shown at the *Exposition Universelle* in 1889.[14] This fact was even admonished on the occasion of an expert conference in July 1889.[15] The show of habitat models might not have considered condignly the influential theories of Arthur de Gobineau, spiritual father of the Aryans, who sired four comprehensive volumes, titled *Essai sur l'inégalité des races humaines* (1853–55). Gobineau's ideas would not gain momentum until later, achieving their violent break-through with segregation in the southern United States and apartheid in South Africa to Nazi extermination strategies. With scientific arguments, Gobineau fleshed out the race policy that would inform each of these currents.

The distinction between stubborn racism and average Eurocentrism was fluctuating. Garnier's *Histoire de l'habitation humaine* tends to the latter. His exhibition represented the ordinary nineteenth-century evolutionism that considered the white race to be the leading one, the nations of the Occident having created the highest grade of civilization. Only Occidental architecture has a history of its own, represented in the exhibition by a Romanesque, a Gothic, and a Renaissance model.

As already mentioned, Semper's theory is different from these average evolutionary concepts. His originality consists less in the textile paradigm as such, than in the

_Figure 14.
Histoire de l'habitation humaine: Constructions édifiées par M. Charles Garnier, illustration from "L'Exposition de Paris de 1889", 1, no. 7, supplement, [15 March] 1889 (Wyss, *Bilder von der Globalisierung*, 2010, pp. 140–41).

187

Fig. 15

way he adopts and transforms at once the Vitruvian topos of architecture's origin. We have to clarify first the commonly overrated influence of Darwin on his contemporary intellectual field. The epistemic paradigm of Darwinism is an ex post projection of today's history of science. Gobineau was, like the conservative *juste-milieu*, a fervent anti-Darwinian anyway, because the evolutionary concept of every creature's perfectibility did not match with racist ideology. Semper, on the other side, was no accurate Darwinian simply because he had not studied him properly. When explaining the concept of *Vergleichende Baulehre* (comparative building theory) in a letter to the editor Eduard Vieweg some fifteen years before Darwin's *Origin of Species* got published, and again in one of his London lectures, he referred to Alexander von Humboldt and Georges Cuvier, two representatives of comparative morphology, two generations elder than Darwin. The biological notion of *Urformen* (primordial forms) of building were, as Debra Schafter analyses it, inspired by Cuvier,[16] whose comparative exhibitions of skeletons at the Jardin des Plantes Semper had studied during his early Paris stay as a student in the 1820s.

Comparative anatomy was practised not only in Paris. A German authority was the physician and painter Carl Gustav Carus, whom Semper had known during his Dresden period.[17] Carus's approach relies on the natural scientific writings by Johann Wolfgang Goethe, the thinker of the *Urphänomen* (primordial phenomenon). The epistemic difference in the notions of comparatism and evolution consists in the turn from a classification of morphological bodily shapes to an analysis of inner functional structures, the former represented by Étienne Geoffroy Saint-Hilaire, the latter by Cuvier. Semper's theory, though imbedded into an idealistic proto-Darwinian comparatism, performs a compromise between both positions.

His move from a morphology of shapes to functional structure becomes evident in the way Semper transforms the three Vitruvian topoi of architectural archetypes –

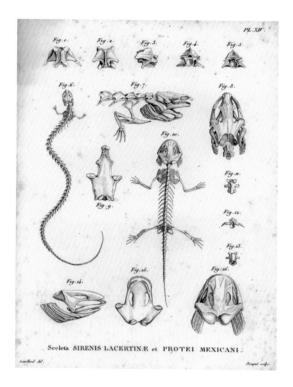

Sceleta SIRENIS LACERTINÆ et PROTEI MEXICANI.

188

the tent, the hut, and the cave – into *Die vier Elemente der Baukunst* (*The Four Elements of Architecture*), which constitute the *Urzustände* (primordial conditions) of human society. The nucleus of human dwelling is the hearth, which has to be defended against the hostile effects of climate: by walls, roofs, and foundations. The publication of *Die vier Elemente der Baukunst* coincided with the opening of the London world's fair in 1851. Here, Semper found his theory attested by the products of primitive handcraft from the colonies and emerging nations. He was in charge of curating the exhibition sections of Canada and the Cape of Good Hope, Turkey and Egypt, Sweden and Norway, and Denmark.[18]

_ Figure 15.
Osteologie der Sirene und des Axolotl, plate from Alexander von Humboldt and Aimé Bonpland, *Beobachtungen aus der Zoologie und Vergleichenden Anatomie, gesammelt auf einer Reise nach den Tropen-Ländern des neuen Kontinents, in den Jahren 1799, 1800, 1801, 1802, 1803 und 1804*, 1806, anatomical representation according to Cuvier's studies (Courtesy of Humboldt Universität Berlin).

Die vier Elemente der Baukunst establishes the crucial assumption that every crafted shape is formed by the means and techniques of production. Building forms are originated by functional motives.[19] The four *Urmotive* (primordial motives) of building – hearth, enclosure, roof, and mound – correspond to four primary crafts, or four elements of architecture: ceramics, textiles, carpentry, masonry. By this functional theory, architecture as the leading discipline in the Vitruvian tradition came to be deconstructed into four elementary crafts.[20]

The textile paradigm was not only solidly introduced in architectural theory; it also matched with the tastes of nineteenth-century consumers. At world's fairs, colonies and emerging nations preferentially presented and sold ethnically specific tapestry for the private bourgeois interior. In fact, the fabrication of textile represents the leitmotiv of industry, as it belongs to the first mass products of modern industrialization.

Fig. 1

In his magnum opus *Spätrömische Kunst-Industrie* (1901), Alois Riegl took up the notion of industry in Semper's sense as a universal characteristic of craft work.[21] The Viennese art historian may have continued to have reservations against the "Semperians", but his historico-philosophical approach was pretty similar to Semper's latent Hegelianism.[22] *Spätrömische Kunst-Industrie* and *Der Stil in den technischen und tektonischen Künsten* show the intention for material comprehensiveness, an attempt which produces an incongruence between theoretical assumptions and heuristically compiled source matter. The elegant and rather reductionist theories try hard to match with the abundance of collected objects whose provenience testifies to a transcultural confluence of human creation.[23]

Figs. 16, 17

Whereas the nineteenth-century mainstream views of world architectural history presented by Viollet-le-Duc and Garnier mirror the colonialist mentality, legitimized by anthropological theories, Semper and Riegl apply a strictly formal comparatism of style, beyond assuming radically cultural or even racial hierarchies.[24] The central idea in Riegl's *Spätrömische Kunst-Industrie* is the assumption that there are no decay times in history. Every "Kunstwollen" (artistic intention) is able to express itself accurately – a concept which matches with the enlightened idea of perfectibility and Darwin's evolutionism. Every historical manifestation of style is a product of transformation, so there is no decline or even degeneration in art and architecture.

The early, primordial forms find their correspondence to the late forms of modernity. Semper had traced this idea already two generations earlier. His criticism of odd industrial mass production has no cultural pessimist aftertaste. His theoretical effort was just meant to clarify the confusion of modern industrial mass production by reflecting on the true origin of craft work. He was not against machine-made design. But the machine had to be tuned according to the functional rationality of operations, qualified to be of archetypal and universal validity. Similarly, he was not against non-European cultures, but they had to be attuned to Western cultural standards. In the end, there was no return to the primordial state of craft work. In this sense, Semper was a true Hegelian. His concept of style followed the concept of perfection.

189

_ Figure 16.
Griechische und assyrische Helmzierden: Assyrische Mitra mit Federkrone. Griechische Akroterien, page from G. Semper, *Der Stil*, vol. 1, 1860 (Private ownership).

_ Figure 17.
Durchbrochene Bronzen, plate from Alois Riegl, *Die spätrömische Kunst-Industrie*, 1901 (Courtesy of Universitätsbibliothek Heidelberg).

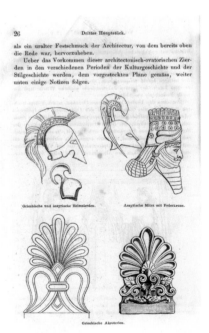

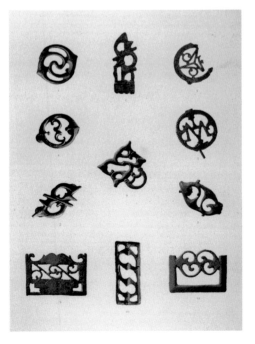

_1. E.E. Viollet-le-Duc, *Histoire de l'habitation humaine depuis les temps préhistoriques jusqu'à nos jours*, Hetzel, Paris 1875, p. 7. For the English translation, see E.E. Viollet-le-Duc, *The Habitations of Man in All Ages*, trans. B. Bucknall, Sampson Low, Marston, Searle, and Rivington, London 1876, p. 7: "'Why thus alter the Creator's work?' 'Who knows', answers Epergos: 'let us return here in a hundred thousand days, and we shall see whether these creatures have forgotten my instructions and live as they were living yesterday. If so, then I am wrong in meddling with their affairs and I have not found what I have been seeking; but if they have profited by my suggestions, – if the huts we see then are better made than these, I have been successful, for in that case these creatures are not mere animals'".

_2. E.E. Viollet-le-Duc, *Histoire*, see note 1, p. 4. E.E. Viollet-le-Duc, *Habitations*, see note 1, p. 4: "Are they Men?"

_3. E.E. Viollet-le-Duc, *Histoire*, see note 1, p. 17. E.E. Viollet-le-Duc, *Habitations*, see note 1, p. 17: "'No useless tears!' said the Arya. 'Let us set to work before the sun disappears behind the mountain. Come with us, mother, and tell this stranger what thou wantest in addition to that which we had before, since he shows a desire to help us'".

_4. E.E. Viollet-le-Duc, *Histoire*, see note 1, p. 35. E.E. Viollet-le-Duc, *Habitations*, see note 1, p. 39: "'We have admired thy habitation and thy gardens; but when one possesses such an abode, one is little disposed to leave it. Dost thou ever go out?'"

_5. E.E. Viollet-le-Duc, *Histoire*, see note 1, p. 36. E.E. Viollet-le-Duc, *Habitations*, see note 1, p. 40: "'So', said Doxius, when he and his companion had quitted the house, 'thou hast gained nothing for thy pains here; and now thou art gone, things will remain as we found them'. 'I have not lost any time', replied Epergos; 'I have left here words of truth. If the fat Fau does not profit by them himself, art thou sure that his wife, children, and servants will forget them?'"

_6. In one of his London lectures, Semper states that the Chinese "became stagnant" at a given moment in history; in the same lecture, he linked Chinese architecture with the Caribbean hut that he saw in model form at the 1851 Great Exhibition in London: "The Chinese Architecture, is, with the exception of this Caraib Hutt, the most elementary of all". See Gottfried Semper, *General Remarks on the Different Styles in Art*, draft of a lecture given in London on 23 December 1853, gta Archives/ETH Zurich, 20-MS-124, fols. 7v, 16v, edited in G. Semper, *London Writings 1850–1855*, edited by M. Gnehm, S. Hildebrand, and D. Weidmann, gta Verlag, Zurich 2021. Semper's final verdict appears in *Der Stil*, where he says that "an ancient building principle has been kept alive, as it were, in China down to the present day", adding: "if it is permissible to endow something inorganic with metaphorical life". See G. Semper, *Der Stil*

in den technischen und tektonischen Künsten, oder Praktische Aesthetik: Ein Handbuch für Techniker, Künstler und Kunstfreunde*, vol. 1, Verlag für Kunst und Wissenschaft, Frankfurt am Main 1860, vol. 2, Bruckmann, Munich 1863, vol. 1, p. 242; translation modified from G. Semper, *Style in the Technical and Tectonic Arts; or, Practical Aesthetics*, introduction by H.F. Mallgrave, trans. H.F. Mallgrave and M. Robinson, Getty Research Institute, Los Angeles 2004, p. 256. For Quatremère de Quincy, see S. Lavin, *Quatremère de Quincy and the Invention of a Modern Language of Architecture*, MIT Press, Cambridge, MA 1992, p. 109.

_7. Marcus Vitruvius Pollio, *On Architecture*, trans. F. Granger, vol. 1, Harvard University Press, Cambridge, MA 1931, II.1. See also Vitruv, *Baukunst*, trans. A. Rode (1796), edited by B. Wyss, with an introduction by G. German and annotations by A. Gieré, Artemis, Zurich 1987, vol. 1, p. 295.

_8. D. Schafter, *The Order of Ornament, the Structure of Style: Theoretical Foundations of Modern Art and Architecture*, Cambridge University Press, Cambridge, MA 2003, p. 37.

_9. G. Semper, *Der Stil*, see note 6, vol. 2, p. 276. See also the translation in G. Semper, *Style*, see note 6, pp. 665–66.

_10. Vitruvius, *On Architecture*, see note 7, II.1.5–6, p. 83.

_11. B. Wyss, *Bilder von der Globalisierung: Die Weltausstellung von Paris 1889*, Suhrkamp-Insel, Berlin 2010, pp. 138–69.

_12. A. Ammann, *Guide historique à travers l'Exposition des habitations humaines reconstituées par Charles Garnier*, Hachette, Paris 1889, p. 6, quoted in S. Roux, *La Maison dans l'histoire*, Michel, Paris 1976, p. 7. See also M. Wörner, *Vergnügung und Belehrung: Volkskultur auf den Weltausstellungen 1851–1900*, Münster, Waxmann 1999, p. 68.

_13. A. Labat, *Charles Garnier et l'Exposition de 1889: L'Histoire de l'habitation*, in C. Mathieu (ed.), *1889: La Tour Eiffel et l'Exposition universelle*, Réunion des musées nationaux, Paris 1989, pp. 130–61 (here p. 145).

_14. *Ibid.*

_15. Cf. B. Wyss, *Bilder*, see note 11, p. 146.

_16. D. Schafter, *Order of Ornament*, see note 8, pp. 35, 209.

_17. H.F. Mallgrave, *Gottfried Semper: Architect of the Nineteenth Century*, Yale University Press, New Haven 1996, pp. 71, 159.

_18. W. Herrmann, *Gottfried Semper im Exil: Paris, London 1849–1855. Zur Entstehung des "Stil" 1840–1877*, Birkhäuser, Basel 1978, pp. 52–53, and the chapter by Claudio Leoni in the present volume.

_19. H. Laudel, *Die Urtypen: Urelemente – Urtechniken*, in H. Laudel, *Gottfried Semper: Architektur und Stil*, Verlag der Kunst, Dresden 1991, pp. 77–101; D. Schafter, *Order of Ornament*, see note 8, pp. 32–44; H.F. Mallgrave, *Introduction*, in G. Semper, *Style*, see note 6, pp. 1–67 (here p. 44).

_20. See also G. Semper, *Wissenschaft, Industrie und Kunst: Vorschläge zur Anregung nationalen Kunstgefühles: Bei dem Schlusse der Londoner Industrie-Ausstellung*, Vieweg, Braunschweig 1852; translated as *Science, Industry, and Art: Proposals for the Development of a National Taste in Art at the Closing of the London Industrial Exhibition (1852)*, in G. Semper, *The Four Elements of Architecture and Other Writings*, trans. H.F. Mallgrave and W. Herrmann, Cambridge University Press, Cambridge, MA 1989, pp. 130–67.

_21. A. Riegl, *Spätrömische Kunst-Industrie*, Kaiserlich-Königliche Hof- und Staatsdruckerei, Vienna 1901; translated as *Late Roman Art Industry*, trans. R. Winkes, Bretschneider, Rome 1985.

_22. See D. Schafter, *Order of Ornament*, see note 8, pp. 44–59.

_23. Mallgrave writes on Semper's *Der Stil*: "The book (like its galleys) sometimes takes on the character of a palimpsest with its layering of views and interpretations, often appealing to different disciplines". H.F. Mallgrave, *Introduction*, see note 19, p. 21.

_24. Semper's sophisticated colonial attitude towards contemporary non-European cultures like that of China or, for that matter, India would ask for further discussion.

191

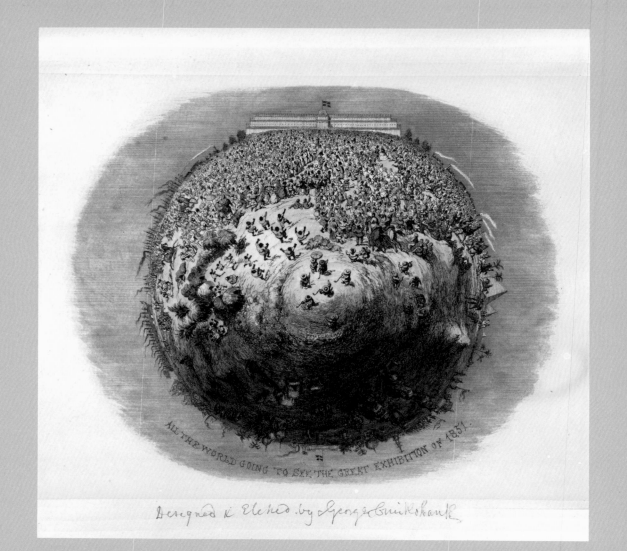

ALL THE WORLD GOING TO SEE THE GREAT EXHIBITION OF 1851.

Designed & Etched by George Cruikshank

Alina Payne

Gottfried Semper and the Global Turn

It is a well-established fact that Gottfried Semper used other disciplines to develop his vision of architecture in *Der Stil* (1860–63) and earlier writings. Indeed, much attention has been paid to his sources and their transformation at his hands.[1] However, rather than look at these sources as they affected his thought, in this chapter I would like to explore what it meant epistemologically that so many sources were brought together under the one 'roof' of his treatise and, furthermore, whether and what the reciprocal effect of such translational activity on the other disciplines might have been, if any at all. What I would like to posit therefore is that Semper's work provides us with a unique opportunity to recover the traces of a process whereby a number of epistemic impulses were received, transformed, and passed on, at a particular moment – the 1850s, on either side of the Great Exhibition in London – that marked what one might call 'the globalization of knowledge'. Secondly, what interests me here is a further and contemporary phenomenon of globalization of which, I contend, Semper may be seen likewise as an index and trace: the advent of the first global art history and the sites of its 'birth' in the World Exhibitions and the museum of the mid-nineteenth century. 'Global knowledge' and 'global art history' may trigger resistance qua terms, contaminated as 'global' is nowadays with the language of political and economic exploitation and contestation. Yet 'global' stands here for 'worldwide' and therefore is consonant with a profoundly positive term in the 1850s – an actors' term – that signified the world and its recent connectivity in the wake of improved

Fig. 1   means of transport and communication.[2] To be sure, it all happened on the crest of the wave of colonialism and its industrial, social, economic, and cultural underpinnings – one facilitating the other(s) in a chicken and egg(s) relationship. Perhaps then, for this chapter, the term 'interconnectedness of art and knowledge' might have been preferable. But 'global' retains the flawed meanings and hopes – both equally present – that the first realization of an interconnected world available to be known in its entirety (not as marvellous encounters but as real-time events connected reliably by devices) gave its actors.

Semper and the globalization of knowledge

When Vitruvius wrote *De architectura* in the first century CE, he claimed architecture as a meta-science and argued that architects needed to know mathematics, history, philosophy, medicine (*climata*), law, and astronomy, as well as drafting and the various crafts.[3] And such remained the claims of architecture – to draw on many disparate areas of knowledge – from Leon Battista Alberti to Palladio, from Perrault to Quatremère de Quincy. Thus, the fact that Gottfried Semper should look beyond the professional boundaries of architecture to other disciplines need not have come as a surprise. Yet, his referents were no longer those of Vitruvius and his early modern predecessors but had shifted significantly and embraced newly rising domains of inquiry. Thus, over the years Semper turned to archaeology (especially to the debate on polychromy), anthropology (to Gustav Klemm, among others), botany and biology (Carl Linnaeus and Goethe), art history (he read von Rumohr), natural history and palaeontology (Georges Cuvier, Alexandre Brongniart, and Charles Darwin), philology (Gottfried Herder), and early psychology.[4] Yet whereas in Vitruvius's time architecture as a learned discipline was the new arrival vis-à-vis philosophy, astronomy, rhetoric, and the like, in the mid-nineteenth century Semper's choices of cognate disciplines were not yet established as such. Indeed, when in the 1830s he began his writing career, they were not what they would be in the 1850s and even less what they would become by the 1880s.

Let us look at anthropology. To be sure, Wilhelm and Alexander von Humboldt mark the beginning of modern anthropology. But this embryonic field went through various formulations and searches for identity before it became an established academic discipline, with a methodology all its own and a set of problems, definitions, and vocabulary that distinguished it from other social sciences. To take

Fig. 2

Fig. 3

194

Australien.

_ Figure 2.
Frontispiece of G.F. Klemm, *Allgemeine Cultur-Geschichte der Menschheit*, 1843 (Courtesy of the Harvard Libraries).

_ Figure 3.
Trilobites, plate from
A. Brongniart, *Histoire
naturelle des crustacés
fossils,* 1822 (Courtesy of
the Harvard Libraries).

_ Figure 4.
Prozesse: Geflecht
(Processes: Latticework),
page from G. Semper, *Der
Stil,* vol. 1, 2nd edition, 1878
(Courtesy of the Harvard
Libraries).

Fig. 4

only one example, in Austria a formal professional *Verein* (association) of anthropologists under Carl Rokitansky (who was an anatomist) was formed only in 1870; the first anthropology museum in Vienna was established in 1876 (as part of the Natural History museum, since in Austria it evolved out of natural history, as the natural history of man); and finally, the first university chair in anthropology was established only in 1913.[5]

The same is true of the other disciplines Semper drew on. And it is precisely because they were not established and their methodologies were still in flux at the time of his writing that he could absorb them into his own somewhat bizarre architectural history-cum-architectural treatise, in which he scarcely dealt with architecture at all. Indeed, he created an alternative history of architecture and a very revolutionary one at that, as he upended many cherished myths (and, for example, argued for textiles and thatching as the origin of monumental architecture, the *Urform* of the wall, deriving from *Bekleidung* [dressing] and the deep-seated need to cover the body). Instead, Semper proposed a metabolism theory in which materials and instruments, hand movements and body parts blended with religious myths and carried the memories of earlier materials into later ones as ornament and ultimately into monumental art, from textiles through clay, wood, and metals to stone.[6]

Everything in any part of the knowledge spectrum was grist to his mill, and he achieved a glorious synthesis of most of the then-emerging academic disciplines that he had avidly followed. I will not go into detail with respect to each discipline, but as a group, embedded and reshuffled inside his treatise, they turned it into an up-to-the-minute compendium of scientific knowledge of which architecture was the climax, even if paradoxically

195

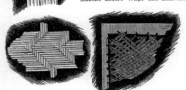

it was not very much discussed as such. As a result, Semper's treatise became a grand box of ideas, rather in the way that the Great Exhibition was a grand box containing the world: a 'global' treatise that matched and entered into dialogue with a 'global' exhibition.

But what is equally important to stress here is the consequence of Semper's interweaving of disciplines: having drawn from many disciplinary academic pools, he also returned his powerful insights *back* into the disciplinary melting pot from which he had drawn his own inspiration. Thus, not only did he create a synthesis of knowledge for use in architecture; he in turn also affected the individual areas of knowledge that he drew into his orbit as well. And since – whatever else he had posited – ornament and style were two fundamental categories that he showcased, these too traversed into the cognate disciplines he had involved in his thinking.

Of course, and not surprisingly, most of Semper's impact was therefore on disciplines in which style and ornament *could* be useful, or rather, on those disciplines that could appropriate both style and ornament as key instruments. These were predominantly the display-and-object-focused disciplines – that is, those disciplines with a museum dimension. And they were surprisingly many: anthropology, art history, archaeology, and folk studies (of high visibility in the era of nationalism). In many ways they were related, although their objects of study were quite different – and the reason they seem related to us now is precisely because they share methodologies. In short, having put ornament on the map as a fundamental diagnostic site for culture, and style as the means of reading it, Semper offered significant bridges to any discipline focused on understanding, reconstructing, and exhibiting culture.

Anthropology

Once again, anthropology is a good example. Speaking its language, Semper was easily reabsorbed and reprocessed, and, indeed, most of the early anthropologists had read Semper and had taken his theories to heart. Thus, it became the norm for anthropologists such as Hjalmar Stolpe (who inaugurated the practice within his discipline) to use ornament as a means to identify style and to establish the provenance of objects on this basis. In his 1892 essay on *Entwicklungserscheinungen in der Ornamentik der Naturvölker* (which, incidentally, was read and footnoted by Alois Riegl in his *Stilfragen*, thus returning the argument back to an art historian), Stolpe argued that the comparative study of ornament ("das vergleichende Studium der Ornamentik") was the most valuable aid in developing a classification system of objects for both museum display and research purposes.[7] Likewise, Henry Colley March, an early British anthropologist and polymath, in his article *The Meaning of Ornament, or Its Archaeology and Its Psychology* of 1889, also sounded very Semperian: "As soon as man began to make things, to fasten a handle to a stone implement, to construct a wattled roof, to weave a mat, skeuomorphs [structure-form] became an inseparable part of his existence, grew, as it were, with the growth of his brain, and ultimately occasioned a mental craving or expectancy".[8]

Writing only three years later, Henry Balfour, curator of the ethnographic museum at Oxford, stressed the importance of the decorative arts for the development of Oxford's museum, which was essentially the collection of General Pitt Rivers. The latter's work in the 1870s provided stimulus and interest in the "absolute origins" of man, and Balfour described it in these terms in his *Evolution of Decorative Art* of 1893: "The illustration of the gradual growth of Decorative Art from simple beginnings was a part of his scheme for establishing series of objects with a view to tracing the stages in the evolution of all the material arts of mankind".[9] Indeed, in many ways Pitt Rivers's method and findings were of one piece with Semper's: his series, intended to show the origin, growth "step by step", and variations of certain patterns, identified "degradation" of designs, successive copying, and derivations such as on gourds and pottery "from the strings by which once vessels were carried". And in a prophetic conclusion that anticipates Riegl's exactly contemporary *Stilfragen* (1893) with his concentration on the arabesque and palmette as key ornaments in ancient and Middle Eastern art, Balfour added, "whole chapters might easily be written upon the history and variations of single designs or patterns".[10]

In the wake of Semper's interest in tattoos and the general admiration for Maori decorations (another anthropology-related interest of his), German-trained anthropologist Franz Boas went even further and used decorative typology to examine body painting among North American Indians.[11] Finally, Alfred C. Haddon, in his *Decorative Art of British New Guinea: A Study in Papuan Ethnography* (1894) and the better known *Evolution in Art: As Illustrated by the Life-Histories of Design* (1895), argued that "Professor G. Semper was the first to show that the basket-maker, the weaver, and the potter originated those combinations of line and colour which the ornamentalist turned to his own use when he had to decorate walls, cornices, and ceilings".[12] A biologist, professor of zoology at Dublin, and anthropologist,

197

_ Figure 5.
Motu Tattoo, illustration from A. Haddon, *Evolution in Art*, 1902 (Courtesy of the Harvard Libraries).

Haddon focused on the decorative transformation and transference of artificial objects such as fastenings, textiles, and pottery (which he termed "skeuomorphs") and on the decorative transformation of natural objects (which he termed "zoomorphs", "phyllomorphs", "anthropomorphs", etc., depending on their origins in the natural world). He was interested in classification and hence in style, but also (mainly) in meaning. "It will often be found that the more pure or the more homogeneous a people are, the more uniformity will be found in their art work, and that florescence of decorative art is a frequent result of race mixture", he concluded.[13]

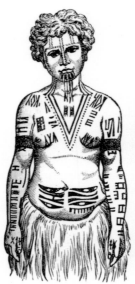

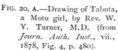
FIG. 20, A.—Drawing of Tabuta, a Motu girl, by Rev. W. V. Turner, M.D. (from *Journ. Anth. Inst.*, vii., 1878, Fig. 4, p. 480).

B —Back view of the same. (The hair of this girl is incorrectly drawn, it should be frizzly and not wavy.)

Art history and archaeology

Art history was another discipline in a 'receiving' mode that appropriated much from Semper, and by way of him from anthropology, in what thus became a three-way dialogue between these disciplines. In its early years, art history was not separate from architectural history (which was ostensibly Semper's subject).[14] Thus, Jacob Burckhardt wrote a history of architecture; so did Heinrich Wölfflin (whose *Renaissance und Barock* of 1888 is mostly on architecture and whose *Prolegomena zu einer Psychologie der Architektur* of 1886 is entirely on it); so did August Schmarsow; and so did Alois Riegl (his *Barockkunst in Rom*, conceived in 1901–2, is largely focused on architecture). Since Semper wrote as an architect/theorist and focused so much on style, which was normally the art historian's province, both the architect and the art historian responded. Archaeology also provided a bridge between them, thus creating an even more complex intersection of disciplines. The style category emerged as a profoundly useful classification system and united everything and everyone.

For archaeologists, style was fundamental as well, as they needed a quick method to sort out the enormous amounts of excavated materials brought up on vast excavation sites and shipped in quantities to the museums of the world. And the architect's and art historian's style offered a perfect 'sorting' instrument.[15] In addition, Semper's focus on the impact of materials and their handling on the production of ornament encouraged a 'materialist' reading from archaeologists such as Alexander Conze (director of the Berlin sculpture museum and of the German Archaeological Institute in Rome) – although this reduction of Semper's theory (which included a significant concern with symbol) was not overlooked by art historians, who sharply criticized it.[16]

Fig. 6

However, as I have shown, it is in art history that most of architecture's categories identified by Semper were telescoped, worked out, and then imported back into architecture.[17] Style, its history, and its evolution became staple topics both in teaching and publications; that is, both in the 'strong' academic discourse and through more popular treatments, such as Julius Langbehn's *Rembrandt als Erzieher* of 1890. Indeed, art history became a melting pot of, or a funnel for, available theories about living, culture and civilization, art, society, economics, race and nationhood, daily life, etc. And Semper provided much persuasive support for these inquiries, having himself achieved a synthesis of disciplines with a strong idea uniting them. As an art historian, his history was wrong, as Riegl demonstrated eventually in *Stilfragen* (stone ornaments predated textile ones in the Middle East, rather than the opposite, as Semper had argued). But it is important to stress that Riegl had to write a major, long book in order to refute Semper and that he felt it was important to do so (all the while criticizing the followers of Semper rather than Semper himself) – which in itself confirms just how popular and important Semper had become for the field at that time.[18]

Most important across all disciplines, but especially for art history, was the concept of culture, its origins, where it is expressed and how. And of particular interest for architects was also the question of how culture can be defined and affected by artistic (architectural) intervention. The issue had been central for Semper and constituted the kernel around which much of his theory had revolved ever since the

198

TAFEL I.

_ Figure 6.
Plate from A. Conze,
Melische Thongefässe, 1862
(Courtesy of the Harvard
Libraries).

Great Exhibition, when he deplored the sorry state of contemporary art as present-ed there and sought to identify a means of rectifying it.[19] In fact, in a revolutionary move, Semper had posited the decorative arts and the most basic objects of daily use as being the first to signal cultural shifts, as their ignition mechanism and as the origin of the language of the monumental arts, and it was to those 'minor' arts that he looked as the possible saviours of the contemporary morass. Ultimately, he proselytized for the architect's agency, rather than historical research for its own sake – he wanted to intervene in modern culture, especially in the production of objects, and create the conditions for its reinvigoration, starting from this ground zero. In the process, he gave the study of the decorative arts an added theoretical weight, and art historians responded both in their writings and in their museums.

Finally, in developing its own methods, art history emphasized and theorized the detail (central to Semper) through the development of connoisseurship. While there is no recorded link to architecture here, this methodological turn to give prime importance to the detail (as the site of artistic essence and hence authorship) had received much early visibility from Semper and had been broadly disseminated. His diagnostic elements in architecture that display evolution were the details and the small gestures – be they forms or ornamental patterns – and it is these that, in his view, stood in direct communication with the crafts and the artisan's hand. That "Gott ist im Detail" (God is in the detail) should become a commonplace of discourse not only for Aby Warburg but also for Mies van der Rohe conveys the centrality it acquired over the next decades for both fields. Although, in a brilliant essay, Carlo Ginzburg credited detective fiction (Conan Doyle), early psychiatry, and forensic medicine for this turn towards the detail, it was an architect, Semper, who was actually the first (by a generation) to identify the significance of the detail.[20] An obvious site of attention for architecture, it was only later transported to art history.

Empathy theory: Psychology, art history, and architecture

But more than style, ornament, and detail, one of the key imports from Semper into art history was his proto-empathy theory approach to the arts, which put the body as producer and recipient of art at its centre. And here the founders of the discipline – Heinrich Wölfflin, Alois Riegl, August Schmarsow, Aby Warburg – all drew from Semper because he was one of the first, if not the very first, to convert what was available in philosophy and proto-psychology into a full-blown theory. Indeed, the second printing of *Der Stil* in 1878–79, co-edited by Semper's art historian son Hans, and likewise the publication of his *Kleine Schriften* in 1884, had brought Semper back to the attention of the generation working in the late 1880s and 1890s on empathy theory and had given him a second life in their works.

For Wölfflin, for example, the line of thinking he inaugurates in the *Prolegomena zu einer Psychologie der Architektur* (1886, his doctoral dissertation) would have been unthinkable without Semper and without early psychology writings.[21] To be sure, Wölfflin does not credit Semper in his text with a determining role in shaping his thought, but he hardly credits any art historian or architectural historian, only a handful of psychologists.[22] Yet in *Renaissance und Barock* (of 1888, his *Habilitationsschrift*), he states:

> Nor, in my opinion, is a style a uniformly accurate mirror of its time throughout its evolution. … when the style, having become hardened and exhausted by uncomprehending misuse, turns more and more into a lifeless scheme. When this happens the temper of a people must be gauged not in the heavy and ponderous forms of architecture, but in the less monumental decorative arts; it is in them that formal sensibility finds an immediate and unchecked outlet, in them that the renewal takes place. A new style, in fact, is always born within the sphere of the decorative arts.[23]

And he proceeds to make the now famous argument on the Gothic shoe as the origin of the Gothic arch. This is a word-by-word repetition of a passage in the *Prolegomena zu einer Psychologie der Architektur*, although in 1888 the statement is footnoted to Semper (*Der Stil*, vol. 2, p. 5). Indeed, Semper's presence among Wölfflin's sources should not be surprising, since two of Wölfflin's teachers, the philosopher Wilhelm Dilthey and archaeologist/art historian Heinrich von Brunn, were admirers of Semper and used his work.[24]

I have already mentioned Alois Riegl, one of the founding fathers of the discipline of art history, and his engagement with Semper: refuting his historical findings did not mean that he did not use him, and he had many positive things to say about *Der Stil*. The main thrust of *Stilfragen* was to correct Semper's claim that textile forms predated stone ones, but as for the importance of the decorative arts as cultural DNA, this also became a major theme for Riegl, who argued that there lay the clearest signs of "Kunstwollen" (will to art) in any culture. And the two categories he introduces – "taktisch/haptisch" and "optisch" – to evaluate the evolution of art are deeply engaged with Semper's proto-empathy aesthetics.[25]

Another figure influenced by Semper in the domain of empathy theory was Theodor Lipps. He was no art historian but a philosopher who taught aesthetics and psychology at the university in Munich (and was a very popular lecturer, just like Wölfflin). He had a significant impact on the development of empathy theory, which was profoundly Semperian in his hands. Like Wölfflin, he also included no footnotes and no acknowledgements in his writings, but when Lipps describes "das technische Kunstwerk" (the technical artwork), the term includes architecture alongside decorative and industrial arts, furniture (seating), pots, and carpets – and it sounds as if it were a straight quote from Semper.[26] More important still, many of his examples were taken from architecture (the column, the capital), and he, too, turned to materiality as key category of artistic making.[27]

For sui generis art historian Aby Warburg (who used empathy theory to propose "Pathosformeln", recurrent deep-seated images that cut across cultures historically), Semper was also one of his principal sources. As Gertrude Bing, his lifelong assistant, put it, Semper was "a towering figure in the art theory of the late nine-

Fig. 7

201

_ Figure 7.
Page from T. Lipps, *Raumästhetik und geometrisch-optische Täuschungen*, 1893–97 (Courtesy of the Harvard Libraries).

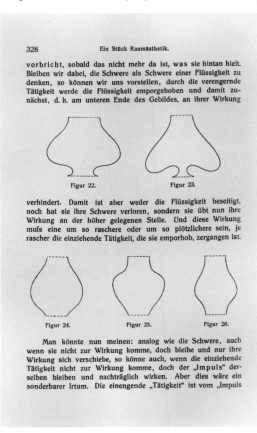

teenth century", and together with Adolf von Hildebrand they both affected Warburg deeply.[28] Most revealing is the fact that for Warburg "no sphere of existence must be considered too lowly, too obscure or too ephemeral to provide evidence".[29] This was precisely Semper's approach, as he had blurred the edges between high and minor arts, effectively raising the significance of the latter above that of the monumental ones. Indeed, Kurt Forster has noted that both Warburg and Riegl, at about the same time, "shared a special feeling for the apparently inconsequential and marginal", Riegl working on nomads and rug making and the migration of individual motifs (see, for example, his analysis of the Ionic capital volute), while Warburg looked at waxworks and votive sculptures in the Renaissance, rituals among North American Indians, anthropology (Franz Boas), etc.[30] Without Semper's lead, this orientation would have been inconceivable.

Fig. 8

202

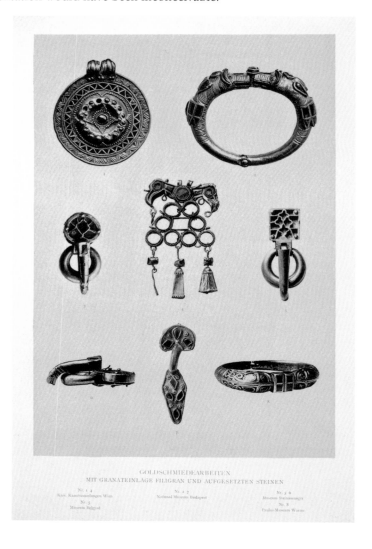

_ Figure 8.
Goldschmiedearbeiten (Goldwork), plate from A. Riegl, *Spätrömische Kunstindustrie nach den Funden in Österreich-Ungarn*, 1901–23 (Courtesy of the Harvard Libraries).

A noted architectural historian, Cornelius Gurlitt, also turned to Semper: in his numerous writings, he was very pro-Baroque, a staple topic for empathy theorists (he had written the first history of Baroque architecture) and very pro-Semper; and he was himself very active in the decorative arts movement, especially in Dresden, where he taught for many years and had a whole generation of architects as his students (notably including Hermann Muthesius, Hugo Häring, members of Die Brücke, and others). Moreover, in his book on the nineteenth century, he argued forcibly for the greater importance of Semper's time in Britain and his leadership role in the conception of the South Kensington Museum (today the Victoria and Albert Museum), claiming that he had not been sufficiently credited in Britain for his innovations.[31]

Finally, Ernst Kapp, a scholar at the intersection between fields – part philosopher of technology, part member of the empathy theory sodality, part architecture/art theorist – was likewise indebted to Semper's brand of architectural anthropology and empathy theory.[32] Speaking to and drawing from several fields, like Semper, and bringing them into an unexpected conversation, Kapp argued that unconscious "Organprojection" (organ projection) was a fundamental feature of instruments and also of higher-level modern inventions such as the telegraph, which resulted from the projection of the human nervous system.[33] Furthermore, he defined "Bekleidung" (dressing) as "eine portative Wohnung" (a portable habitation) and argued for the etymological connection between "Gewand" (garment) and "Wand" (wall) – the same argument Semper had made when he derived architecture from textiles.[34]

Figs. 9, 10

203

_ Figure 9.
Die amerikanische Axt und der menschliche Arm (The American axe and the human arm), illustration from E. Kapp, *Grundlinien einer Philosophie der Technik*, 1877 (Courtesy of the Harvard Libraries).

_ Figure 10.
Tiefseekabel von 1865 (Deep-sea cable from 1865), illustration from E. Kapp, *Grundlinien einer Philosophie der Technik*, 1877 (Courtesy of the Harvard Libraries).

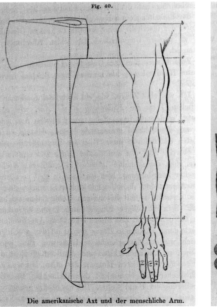

Die amerikanische Axt und der menschliche Arm.

Tiefsee-Kabel vom Jahre 1865.

Global art and comparative aesthetics (*vergleichende Ästhetik*)

Following this review of Semper's mediation between scientific fields and participation in the globalization of knowledge, there are two further important points to raise here. In the first place, it is essential to state that the Great Exhibition of 1851 had been the agent facilitating this melting pot of disciplines – from anthropology to economics – as no other event, library, or publication could have done. Whatever may have already been present in the culture to invite dialogue – and I do believe that no event occurs ex nihilo, but is prepared by countless previous gestures – the Great Exhibition mobilized and gave powerful impetus to this collision of discourses precisely because it had a visual – and therefore physical, that is, tangible – form and hence impact. People could see and touch 'alien' objects in a way that they had not been able to before and that no single journey or book permitted them to do. Assyrian and Chinese artefacts rubbed shoulders with steam engines and machine-produced wares, as well as with Maori and Canadian Indian canoes. This global aspect could not be missed, and moreover the entire publicity for the event underscored this dimension. Inevitably, it caused methodological dislocations, and Semper responded to these in such a way that his ideas before 1851 and after 1851, although seemingly similar, are on two sides of a deep chasm.

Fig. 11

_ Figure 11.
Perspective of the Crystal Palace at London's Great Exhibition, plate from *Dickinsons' Comprehensive Pictures of The Great Exhibition of 1851*, 1854 (Courtesy of the Harvard Libraries).

Indeed, beyond the intersection of disciplines it invited, the realization of a global and connected art (and its history) was the other major contribution of the Great Exhibition to Semper's work. This then is my second main argument here – that what had entered discourse decisively at this moment was the possibility of what we now call global art. At the conceptual level, the Great Exhibition caused a *mise-en-abyme* of all that was known before. This enormous *Handelsraum* (mercantile space) charged and dramatized everything by unexpected adjacencies, contrasts, and connections. Semper described it as Babel. One could also describe it as a Humboldtian playground of cultural simultaneities and comparisons. For Renaissance scholars, this resembles an Industrial Revolution version of the sixteenth-century *paragone* (comparison) between the arts at a grandiose level – materials, techniques, nationality, ethnicity, scale were on display, clashing and bouncing off each other.[35] Comparison was the very mode of the Great Exhibition.

In this global context, Semper proposed what amounts to a *vergleichende Ästhetik* (comparative aesthetics) as an analytical tool, and this became another major contribution he made to scholarship of many stripes.[36] The Great Exhibition invited, indeed presupposed, the museum and its aestheticizing mode: it was a visual display of things compared to each other. And comparative aesthetics comes straight out of it. Certainly, this method was already present in Semper's work in Paris, and his treatise *Die vier Elemente der Baukunst* (*The Four Elements of Architecture*; written 1850, published 1851) bears the subtitle *Ein Beitrag zur vergleichenden Baukunde* (*A Contribution to the Comparative Study of Architecture*). This approach went back further, to the anthropological atlas, which had gained its traction precisely from such comparisons between peoples and cultures.[37] But with the multitude of historical times and geographic variation showcased by the exhibition, this tendency in his thought was much enhanced and dramatically justified. Fabrication moving decisively into the foreground at the London exhibition – after all, its principal aim was to showcase Manufacture – also confirmed Semper's interest in making as his red thread.[38] But appearance, hence style, remained the backbone of his system of classification, and it gave his comparative aesthetics a focus that could be used to compare and find commonalities between the heterogeneous objects gathered in London's Crystal Palace above and beyond their cultural diversities. In short, the global aspect of the exhibition facilitated the development of his comparative aesthetics and sharpened it into a sophisticated tool.

This event, then, that collected the world inside one glass box on a lawn in London also encouraged two essentially contradictory impulses: one global, the other local. One cut across nations without differentiating between them and had a universalist cast; the other recognized the specificity of each culture. Both were present as lessons to take home from the Great Exhibition: on the one hand, the study of man in general terms that encouraged finding and sometimes forcing commonalities across space and time and deeply marking the field of anthropology and related disciplines to this day (the internationalist stream); on the other, the study of manifold but specific cultures within their own local peculiarities, which remained embedded in ethnographic work focused on the folk art of the European nations primarily but evolved to include Asia (Japan, China, Central Asia, etc.) as well as Africa. The two impulses did not intersect much, and their respective museums did not either (and this continues to this day – folk museums are separate from anthropology museums).

Semper was much more taken with what the global view had to offer; for him, the world became his oyster. Indians and Inuit, Assyrians and Trinidadians, Chinese and Maoris, Celts and North Africans shared one (glass) roof with the Europeans and their wares. Faced with such variety, he did not attempt any nation-by-nation analysis of form-making, in the manner of Owen Jones's *Grammar of Ornament* (1856), but tried to tease out an evolutionary sequence of stages in the development of monumental form, cutting across nations and the globe. In the process, he dignified not only the wares of daily life, the so-called *Kunsthandwerk*, putting it alongside the high arts, but also raised the issue of looking broadly geographically. One could say he was the first global art historian. Warburg certainly owed a great deal to the anthropologists – Boas, Tylor, etc. – but his impulse, as an art historian, to visit the Pueblo Indians as well as his turn towards a psychology of cultures may still be traced back to Semper. Indeed, as we have seen, Semper operated upon anthropology and may have penetrated Warburg's thinking both directly and indirectly through the next generation of anthropologists (e.g. through Tylor's *Primitive Culture* of 1871) and through August Schmarsow, with whom Warburg studied in Florence.[39]

Fig. 12

206

_ Figure 12.
Savage Tribes N° 3,
Ornamentation of objects,
plate from O. Jones, *The Grammar of Ornament*, 1856
(Courtesy of the Harvard Libraries).

As I argued earlier, Semper was acting powerfully upon art history as a discipline, and it is therefore important to recall just how different his comparative universalist approach was from what Jacob Burckhardt, for example, was doing at exactly the same time – both in his 1855 *Der Cicerone* and his 1867 *Geschichte der Baukunst* (later called *Geschichte der Renaissance*).[40] Both works drill deep into a single culture (Italian) and a focused historical period (the Renaissance) and explore its art, customs, politics, personalities, archives, and so on. In fact, the comparison of Semper with Burckhardt is very pertinent here, for they were completely contemporary in their publication dates and were also colleagues at the Eidgenössisches Polytechnikum (Swiss Federal Polytechnic, today the Eidgenössische Technische Hochschule/ETH) in Zurich, while they were in every other way so diametrically opposed in approach.[41] To be sure, art history went the way of Burckhardt, not Semper, and Alois Riegl's *Stilfragen* was written precisely to put to rest any historical claims that Semper may have had for his 'global' arguments (such as the derivation of stone ornament from textiles).[42] But even if art history did not embrace a global perspective at the time, some of it lingered – most notably in Josef Stryzgowski's work – and permitted the current return to this methodology to find reference points in the discipline's past nevertheless.[43]

It should be noted that Semper's brand of *vergleichende Ästhetik* was particularly important for the developing museum display, especially in collections of anonymous objects (rather than those of major artists) – meaning anthropology museums and archaeology collections.[44] The power of this model was so strong that it took a public debate for a movement in a different direction to be initiated. In 1887, German anthropologist Franz Boas fought against the classification and display, in the museum setting, of objects according to their physical resemblance, irrespective of their cultural origins and argued instead that they should be placed in the setting of their own culture, to allow their real meaning to be understood. It was he who pioneered the "vitrines" as a display strategy – as a re-enactment of a moment in time that displays objects in use. This approach was perceived as novel and radical at the time and caused a well-publicized debate between Boas and Otis T. Mason, curator at the U.S. National Museum in New York.[45] Perhaps it is not surprising that Boas, educated in the German environment in which the history of culture was a prominent concern across disciplines, should have pioneered it for anthropology. His vitrines – so illustrative and visually appealing – spoke equally to the scientific concerns of the field and to the exhibition-as-show (or as panorama) mentality that was generated by the universal exhibitions and pervaded the world of scholarly museums. Indeed, Boas conceived his vitrines as panoramas in which sculpture and painting blended into each other to create lifelikeness, figures and objects emerging from a chiaroscuro background that facilitated and enhanced the illusion of life. But if his display ran counter to Semper's proto-structuralist model, it did nevertheless retain his focus on man as a maker of tools, objects, artefacts, and so on.[46]

Fig. 13

Which brings me back to where I started. The impact of Semper on the disciplines, especially of art history, also passed through the reconceptualization of the museum – and perhaps most deeply so. What Semper had done was to reinterpret the Great Exhibition, as a mentality-changing event, into a methodology for analysis – of art,

207

_ Figure 13.
Killer-whale mask worn
by Kwakiutl man, photo
by Franz Boas (Courtesy
of the American
Museum of Natural
History).

architecture, crafts, and the relation of man to the products of mind and hands, of labour and memory. He laid the foundations of a first global art history, as well as providing a site for the globalization of knowledge – meaning not only that he engaged with territorial geography but also with disciplinary territories, with a broad geography of disciplines. A powerful synthesis of available knowledge, Semper's work offered endless points of contact with other fields – returning the insights of art-making to the growing number of disciplines focused on man. Equally important is the fact that Semper's lens for analysis was twofold: on the one hand, the maker; on the other aesthetics as an analytical underpinning. Imperceptibly entwined, these both carried over the connection to other disciplines too.

Perhaps it might be useful to think alongside philosopher Gianni Vattimo, who has argued that art (and artists) rather than science (and scientists) may have generated the concept of progress.[47] Although in this case Vattimo is thinking of Giorgio Vasari and his history of Renaissance art based on progress, Semper may be another, later example of leadership coming from the visual arts in the domain of the history of knowledge. With Semper, architecture effected a synthesis and led the way – a final, grand gesture before its demise as the Vitruvian meta-science.

_1. By now the literature on Semper is vast. In addition to the chapters in this volume, for general bibliographies and discussions of Semper's sources see H.F. Mallgrave, *Gottfried Semper: Architect of the Nineteenth Century*, Yale University Press, New Haven 1996; W. Nerdinger and W. Oechslin (eds.), *Gottfried Semper 1803–1879: Architektur und Wissenschaft*, Prestel and gta Verlag, Munich and Zurich 2003.

_2. The term 'global' emerged in the 1670s to denote 'spherical'; the meaning 'universal, worldwide, pertaining to the whole globe of the earth' is first found in French in the 1890s (Online Etymology Dictionary, www.etymonline.com).

_3. Marcus Vitruvius Pollio, *On Architecture*, trans. F. Granger, vol. 1, Harvard University Press, Cambridge, MA 1983, I.1.10, p. 9.

_4. See H.F. Mallgrave, *Gottfried Semper*, see note 1; and for a more specific focus on this issue, A. Payne, *From Ornament to Object: Genealogies of Architectural Modernism*, Yale University Press, New Haven 2012, Chapters 1 and 2.

_5. See A. Payne, *From Ornament to Object*, see note 4, p. 99.

_6. *Ibid.*, Chapter 1.

_7. H. Stolpe, *Entwicklungserscheinungen in der Ornamentik der Naturvölker*, "Mittheilungen der Anthropologischen Gesellschaft in Wien", XXII, 1892, pp. 19–62 (here p. 20).

_8. H. Colley March, *The Meaning of Ornament; Or Its Archaeology and Its Psychology*, "Transactions of the Cheshire and Lancashire Anthropological Society", 7, 1889, pp. 160–92 (here p. 180).

_9. H. Balfour, *The Evolution of Decorative Art: An Essay upon Its Origin and Development as Illustrated by the Art of Modern Races of Mankind*, Rivington, Percival, London 1893, p. vi.

_10. *Ibid.*, p. vii.

_11. F. Boas, *The Decorative Art of the Indians of the North Pacific Coast*, "Bulletin of the American Museum of Natural History", IX, 1897, pp. 123–76.

_12. A.C. Haddon, *Evolution in Art: As Illustrated by the Life-Histories of Design* (1895), Scott, London 1902, p. 75. See also his *Decorative Art of British New Guinea: A Study in Papuan Ethnography*, Royal Irish Academy, Dublin 1894.

_13. A.C. Haddon, *Evolution*, see note 12, p. 10. Quoted from his own earlier article in "The Illustrated Archaeologist", I, 1893, p. 108.

_14. For the issues behind this separation of cognate fields, see A. Payne, *Architectural History and the History of Art: A Suspended Dialogue*, "JSAH Special Millennium Issue", 59/60, September/December 1999, pp. 292–99.

_15. S. Marchand, *Down from Olympus: Archaeology and Philhellenism in Germany, 1750–1970*, Princeton University Press, Princeton 1996.

_16. Conze and his school of materialists are the real target of Riegl's criticism. See A. Riegl, *Stilfragen: Grundlegungen zu einer Geschichte der Ornamentik* 1893, 2nd ed., Schmidt, Berlin 1923.

_17. A. Payne, *From Ornament to Object*, see note 4, Chapter 3.

_18. A. Riegl, *Stilfragen*, see note 16.

_19. See G. Semper, *Science, Industry, and Art: Proposals for the Development of a National Taste in Art at the Closing of the London Industrial Exhibition (1852)*, in G. Semper, *The Four Elements of Architecture and Other Writings*, trans. H.F. Mallgrave and W. Herrmann, Cambridge University Press, Cambridge, MA 1989, pp. 130–67.

_20. C. Ginzburg, *Clues: Roots of an Evidential Paradigm*, in C. Ginzburg, *Clues, Myths and the Historical Method*, trans. J. and A.C. Tedeschi, Johns Hopkins University Press, Baltimore 1992 (1st Italian ed. 1986). The sequence of publications all later than Semper's *Der Stil* confirms Semper's key role. Morelli published his *Die Werke der italienischen Meister* in 1880; Conan Doyle's Sherlock Holmes appeared first in 1886 (Doyle was born in 1859, a year before the first volume of Semper's *Der Stil* saw the light of print); and Freud's work is also of a generation later than Semper's (he obtained his doctorate in 1886, received his *Habilitation* degree in 1885 and set up his practice in 1886).

_21. H. Wölfflin, *Prolegomena zu einer Psychologie der Architektur* (1886), in H. Wölfflin, *Kleine Schriften*, ed. by Joseph Gantner, Schwabe, Basel 1946, pp. 13–47.

_22. See, for example, his mention of J. Volkelt, *Der Symbol-Begriff in der neuesten Ästhetik*, Dufft, Jena 1876, p. 11 (ed. 1999).

_23. "Den Pulsschlag des *Volksgemüts* muss man dann anderswo beobachten: nicht in den grossen, schwerbeweglichen Formen der Baukunst, sondern *in den kleineren dekorativen Künsten*. Hier befriedigt sich das Formgefühl ungehemmt und unmittelbar und von hier wird man dann auch die Spuren einer Erneuerung des Stils vermutlich immer zuerst entdecken". H. Wölfflin, *Renaissance und Barock: Eine Untersuchung über Wesen und Entstehung des Barockstils in Italien* (1888), 2nd ed., Bruckmann, Munich 1907, p. 58. For the English translation, see H. Wölfflin, *Renaissance and Baroque*, trans. K. Simon, Cornell University Press, Ithaca, NY 1975, p. 79.

_24. See the dedication of his *Habilitation* thesis, *Renaissance und Barock*, to both von Brunn and Burckhardt. Wölfflin was a student of Dilthey's and was close to Burckhardt throughout his life. Wölfflin's mention of Semper regarding the Gothic in the *Prolegomena* is to an analogy with scholasticism only, not to the passage he now cites in detail in *Renaissance und Barock*.

_25. On these concepts and Wölfflin's critique, see A. Payne, *From Ornament to Object*, see note 4, p. 149; A. Payne, *Beyond Kunstwollen: Alois Riegl and the Theoretization of the Baroque*, in A. Riegl, *The Origin of Baroque Art in Rome*, Getty Institute, Los Angeles 2010, pp. 1–33.

_26. "Unter technischen Kunstwerken verstehe

209

ich Erzeugnisse der gewerblichen oder industriellen Künste oder des Kunsthandwerkes. D. h. … künstlerische Bauwerke, Sitzmöbel, Gitter, Gefässe, Teppiche". T. Lipps, *Ästhetik: Psychologie des Schönen und der Kunst*, 2 vols., Voss, Hamburg 1903–6, vol. 2: *Die ästhetische Betrachtung und die bildende Kunst*, p. 483.

_27. "Der 'Sprechende' aber ist im technischen Kunstwerk letzten Endes jederzeit das Material". *Ibid.*, vol. 2, p. 520.

_28. G. Bing, *A.M. Warburg*, "Journal of the Warburg and Courtauld Institutes", 28, 1965, pp. 299–313 (here p. 307).

_29. *Ibid.*, p. 305.

_30. See K.W. Forster's introduction in A. Warburg, *The Renewal of Pagan Antiquity: Contributions to the Cultural History of the European Renaissance*, Getty Research Institute, Santa Monica 1999, pp. 52–53.

_31. C. Gurlitt, *Die deutsche Kunst des XIX. Jahrhunderts, ihre Ziele und Thaten*, 2nd ed., Bondi, Berlin 1900, p. 73.

_32. E. Kapp, *Grundlinien einer Philosophie der Technik: Zur Entstehungsgeschichte der Cultur aus neuen Gesichtspunkten*, Westermann, Braunschweig 1877. For an in-depth evaluation of Kapp and his intersection with architecture culture, see A. Payne, *From Ornament to Object*, see note 4, pp. 79–82.

_33. A. Payne, *From Ornament to Object*, see note 4, pp. 139–42.

_34. *Ibid.*, p. 267. For Semper's argument, see, for example, G. Semper, *The Four Elements of Architecture: A Contribution to the Comparative Study of Architecture (1851)*, in G. Semper, *The Four Elements of Architecture*, see note 19, pp. 74–129 (here pp. 103–4).

_35. The comparison between the arts, in particular between sculpture and painting, became a critical debate in the Renaissance and has its locus classicus in the collected letters of several major artists canvassed by Benedetto Varchi to express an opinion on the subject and the ensuing (bitter) debate. The artists included Michelangelo, Bronzino, Vasari, and others. See B. Varchi, *Discorso su la maggioranza delle arti*, Florence 1545.

_36. Semper titles his treatise "praktische Ästhetik", yet he also discusses the "vergleichende Stillehre", which he equates with his "praktische Ästhetik", bringing it full circle to a "vergleichende Ästhetik". He also turns to "vergleichende Sprachforschung" with approval – language is indeed a frequent analogue for him – indicating that the comparative method is central to his thinking. G. Semper, *Der Stil in den technischen und tektonischen Künsten, oder Praktische Ästhetik: Ein Handbuch für Techniker, Künstler und Kunstfreunde*, vol. 1, Verlag für Kunst und Wissenschaft, Frankfurt am Main 1860, p. 2.

_37. Semper consulted Gustav Klemm, but the tradition carried on and was already quite strong in the area of dress/costume. See, for example, J.

Falke, *Die deutschen Trachten- und Modenwelt: Ein Beitrag zur deutschen Culturgeschichte*, Meyer, Leipzig 1858; J.A. von Eye and J. Falke, *Kunst und Leben der Vorzeit vom Beginn des Mittelalters bis zu Anfang des 19. Jahrhunderts*, Bauer and Raspe, Nuremberg 1868.

_38. Henry Cole, one of the promoters of the 1851 Great Exhibition, emphasizes the term as the guiding principle of the exhibitions. H. Cole, *Paris Exhibition of 1855*, in H. Cole, *Fifty Years of Public Work*, Bell, London 1884, vol. 2, pp. 257–68 (here p. 258).

_39. Georges Didi-Huberman points to Edward B. Tylor's *Primitive Culture* of 1871 as a major influence on Warburg, especially on his concept of *Nachleben*. Like Semper's survival of motifs, Tylor argued that "[l]a ténacité des survivances, leurs 'puissance' même … vient au jour dans la ténuité de choses minuscules, superflues, dérisoires ou anormales. C'est dans le symptôme récurrent et dans le jeu, c'est dans la pathologie de la langue et dans l'inconscient des formes que gît la survivance en tant que telle". G. Didi-Huberman, *L'image survivante: Histoire de l'art et temps des fantômes selon Aby Warburg*, Minuit, Paris 2002, p. 57. Schmarsow also owed much to Semper but acknowledged him only to criticize his concept of architecture – in his inaugural lecture given in Leipzig in 1893. A. Schmarsow, *Das Wesen der architektonischen Schöpfung: Antrittsvorlesung, gehalten in der Aula der K. Universität Leipzig am 8. November 1893*, Hiersemann, Leipzig 1894. See A. Payne, *From Ornament to Object*, see note 4, p. 140.

_40. J. Burckhardt, *Der Cicerone: Eine Anleitung zum Genuss der Kunstwerke Italiens*, Schweighauser, Basel 1855; J. Burckhardt, *Geschichte der Renaissance in Italien*, Ebner & Seubert, Stuttgart 1868.

_41. Semper nevertheless wished to highlight common interests with Burckhardt, who by then had moved to Basel: "Es fehlt noch an einer umfassenden Geschichte der Kleinkünste Italiens, trotz ihrer Wichtigkeit und ihres mächtigen Einflusses auf den Gang der höheren Kunstgeschichte. Um so erwartungsvoller sehen wir dem Erscheinen der Geschichte der Renaissance in Italien von Prof. Jacob Burckhardt in Basel entgegen, einer Arbeit, deren Bedeutung sich schon aus des Autors Cicerone verkündet". G. Semper, *Der Stil in den technischen und tektonischen Künsten, oder Praktische Ästhetik: Ein Handbuch für Techniker, Künstler und Kunstfreunde*, vol. 2, Bruckmann, Munich 1863, p. 336. For a recent discussion of their relationship, see W. Oechslin, *Gottfried Semper und Jacob Burckhardt: Der unterschiedliche Blick auf die Renaissance*, "Zeitschrift für Kunstgeschichte", 72, 1, 2009, pp. 99–110.

_42. A. Riegl, *Problems of Style: Foundations for a History of Ornament*, trans. Evelyn Kain, Princeton University Press, Princeton 1992, p. 304. Riegl did not reject Semper entirely and indeed used him in support of his notion of "Kunstwollen". Yet he stated that Semper had "exaggerated the status of textile arts over other media, something that we can no longer prudently accept". *Ibid.*, p. 40.

_43. On Josef Stryzgowski, see C. Wood (ed.), *The Vienna School Reader: Politics and Art Historical Method in the 1930s*, Zone, New York 2000; S. Marchand, *German Orientalism in the Age of Empire: Religion, Race, and Scholarship*, Cambridge University Press, Cambridge, MA 2010.

_44 Archaeology museums tended to exhibit the major works of art rather than objects of daily use, which were used for research and dating and were kept in the collections but not exhibited as such. I am grateful to Suzanne Marchand for discussing this aspect of museology with me. It should be noted that with the major find of Roman objects in Austria, which were famously catalogued and discussed by Alois Riegl in his *Spätrömische Kunstindustrie* (1901), simple objects began to receive validation as worthy of exhibiting (belt buckles, harness hardware, pots, etc.). Earlier, Alexandre Brongniart (director for many years of the Sèvres manufactory and one of the authors read with interest by Semper) had created a museum at Sèvres in which he showed materials, tools, and products brought from all over the world (Chinese, Japanese, African, from Iznik and the Indian Ocean, etc). This example, known to Semper during his years in Paris, may have found an echo in his own conception of the museum. I am grateful to Susanne Marchand again for sharing her research on the porcelain industry with me. See T. Préaud, *Brongniart and the Art of Ceramics*, in D.E. Ostergard (ed.), *The Sèvres Porcelain Manufactory: Alexandre Brongniart and the Triumph of Art and Industry, 1800–1847*, Bard Graduate Center, New York 1997, Chapter 5.

_45. On the controversy, see M. Bunzl, *Franz Boas and the Humboldtian Tradition: From* Volksgeist *and* Nationalcharakter *to an Anthropological Concept of Culture*, in G.W. Stocking Jr., *Volksgeist as Method and Ethic: Essays on Boasian Ethnography and the German Anthropological Tradition*, University of Wisconsin Press, Madison 1996, pp. 17–78.

_46. See A. Payne, *From Ornament to Object*, see note 4, p. 101.

_47. G. Vattimo, *The End of Modernity: Nihilism and Hermeneutics in Postmodern Culture*, Johns Hopkins University Press, Baltimore 1988.

211

Index

214

Mendrisio Academy Press
largo Bernasconi 2
6850 Mendrisio, Switzerland
www.arc.usi.ch/en/map

gta Verlag, ETH Zurich
Institute for the History and Theory of Architecture
Department of Architecture
8093 Zurich, Switzerland
www.verlag.gta.arch.ethz.ch

Printed by Ostschweiz Druck, Wittenbach
in October 2021